State and Nation in the United Kingdom

State and Nation in the United Kingdom

The Fractured Union

MICHAEL KEATING

OXFORD
UNIVERSITY PRESS

OXFORD
UNIVERSITY PRESS

Great Clarendon Street, Oxford, OX2 6DP,
United Kingdom

Oxford University Press is a department of the University of Oxford.
It furthers the University's objective of excellence in research, scholarship,
and education by publishing worldwide. Oxford is a registered trade mark of
Oxford University Press in the UK and in certain other countries

First Edition published in 2021

Impression: 1

Published in the United States of America by Oxford University Press
198 Madison Avenue, New York, NY 10016, United States of America

British Library Cataloguing in Publication Data
Data available

Library of Congress Control Number: 2021932111

ISBN 978–0–19–884137–1

DOI: 10.1093/oso/9780198841371.001.0001

Printed and bound in the UK by
TJ Books Limited

Preface

Over the years, I have written a lot on nationalisms within these islands and beyond (Keating 1988, 2000; Keating and Bleiman 1979) as well as about Scottish independence (Keating 2009; Keating and McEwen 2017). This book is different. Taking as given the earlier work on nationalism and Home Rule movements, it focuses on union in the United Kingdom. This is less a change of topic than a shift in perspective. Unionism and nationalism exist, to a large degree, only in relation to each other. Neither is easy to pin down. While nationalists and unionists may claim to rely on different normative principles, they are engaged in the same task, setting the bounds of the polity and of legitimate authority. With the spectacular exception of the southern part or Ireland in 1922, unionism has been the more successful, but nationalism has received more scholarly attention. The core argument of this book is that the United Kingdom must be understood as a union rather than a unitary state. The principle of union, properly understood, precludes a single, consistent narrative about the constituent people (*demos*), its historic trajectory and purpose (*telos*) and its special values (*ethos*). Unions are sites of contested sovereignty and borders. Union*ism* has consequently taken different forms, has often been unstated or 'banal' and has had to articulate itself explicitly only at critical moments. At other times, it is better understood as political practice or statecraft.

Since the late twentieth century, challenges to the Union have become more frequent and powerful, in Northern Ireland, Scotland and, to a lesser extent, Wales. Even England's place in the Union has come into question. The devolution settlement at the Millennium was an effort to restabilize the Union in a new equilibrium, transferring power from the centre to the smaller nations. This is not a federal system but an asymmetrical and differentiated response to distinct demands across the component parts of the Union. Resting on a combination of quasi-federal and unitarist principles, it introduced radical change at the periphery but altered almost nothing at the centre. It did not resolve the nationalities question as that has been an issue, on and off, since the late nineteenth century, but did provide structures within which it could be accommodated. Nationalist pressures have not, as widely expected, attenuated since devolution and the issue remains very much alive. This is not because of divergence in economic or social structures or in political values across the Union. It is not even that differences in national identity have increased, but rather that they have taken on new political meaning. In an era of spatial rescaling and challenges to the nation-state, politics have increasingly (but by no means exclusively) revolved around the national question and the basis of political community. For its part, unionism has struggled to adapt to devolution, has moved into a defensive mode and sought itself to become a nationalism rather than a mode of government. The departure of the UK from the European Union, which provided a vital external support system for the UK as a union and the devolution settlement has increased strains. The pattern of the 2016 referendum vote has exacerbated tensions. Scotland and nationalist Northern Ireland voted to remain while England and Wales voted to leave, and Brexit can, in some respects, be seen as an expression of a certain English nationalism.

The United Kingdom can be understood only in its historical context but the chapters that follow are thematic rather than chronological. While there is a rich literature on the individual unions and unionisms, the aim of the work is comparative. The idea of the United Kingdom as a union has long been a commonplace but rather little attention has been given to exactly what that means. The first chapter seeks to understand union as a concept and practice and demonstrate its continuing utility in a changing world. The second chapter historicizes the United Kingdom as a union and the centrifugal and centripetal forces that have waxed and waned over the centuries. Chapter 3 examines the devolution settlements at the Millennium and how they fit into understandings of the UK constitution. Chapter 4 explores a central and contested issue in the settlement, the matter of sovereignty. It argues against a narrow and legalistic conception of sovereignty in favour of a broader epistemic understanding of the constitution, challenging the orthodox view associated with A. V. Dicey. The big gap in the settlement is at the centre, where there is little by way of a federal spirit. This is closely connected to the question of England. These two issues are addressed in Chapter 5. Chapter 6 puts the union settlement in the wider European context and argues that, if we understand the UK as a union rather than a unitary nation-state then, far from it being incompatible with the European Union, it was rather a good fit and that Brexit undermines the settlement. In Chapter 7, I explore the nature of unionism, seeing it as a complex and polyvalent set of beliefs and practices that can never be reduced to a simple core. Neo-unionism as it has developed since the devolution settlement, appears to be making this error. As it is increasingly challenged, unionism has relied heavily on the instrumental economic and social arguments. Chapters 8 and 9 examine these ideas, arguing that the high point of economic and social union was in the heyday of the developmental state after the Second World War. While the UK remains an integrated economic area and important social welfare responsibilities lie with the centre, some of the claims to territorial cohesion and equity are questionable. Public attitudes to the Union vary across the nations, are complex, and shift over time. Chapter 10 shows that they are not amenable to either a simple nationalist or simple unionist interpretation. This is a work of analysis and not prescription. The final chapter does not provide the 'answer' to the national question in the United Kingdom but some thoughts on understanding the Union and its prospects.

When I signed the contract for this book, there was a reasonable expectation that, by the time it was completed, the main issues around Brexit would have been resolved. In the event, by the original deadline, Brexit had not even happened. By the revised deadline, many of the constitutional issues are still not resolved and perhaps never will be. There is no end to the saga of relationships among the peoples of 'these islands' but there are, perhaps, moments to pause and reflect.

I have had a great deal of help in completing this work. It was funded by the Economic and Social Science Research Council large grant (ES/P009441/1) for the project I led on *Between Two Unions: The Constitutional Future of the Islands after Brexit.* Before that, I had an ESRC Senior Fellowship (ES/N004302) in the UK in a Changing Europe programme to examine the effects of Brexit on devolution, and directed an ESRC project on the Scottish independence referendum (ES/L003325/1). I have benefitted enormously from the ideas of my research partners in *Between Two Unions*: David Bell, Coree Brown Swan, Daniel Cetrà, Michael Kenny, Nicola McEwen, Mary Murphy and Daniel Wincott, and their teams in Cork, Cardiff, Stirling and Cambridge: Greg Davies, Jonathan Evershed, John Houston, Giada Lagana, Willem Sas and Jack Sheldon. David McCrone, John McGarry, Jennifer Todd and Neil Walker read and commented on draft chapters. At the Centre on Constitutional Change, Nick Bibby, Ellen Cummings and Claire de Mowbray provided inestimable support. During the project, we had the immense advantage of regular discussions with officials of the UK, Scottish and Welsh governments, the Northern Ireland Executive and the Irish Government, and with parliamentarians in the Scottish Parliament, National Assembly for Wales/Senedd, House of Commons, House of Lords and European Parliament. At the risk of missing someone out, I should also acknowledge how much I have learned from exchanges during these projects with Leyton

Andrews, Angus Armstrong, Neal Ascherson, Arthur Aughey, Graham Avery, Harald Baldersheim, Lynn Bennie, Paul Beaumont, Alice Brown, Michael Brown, Rainer Bauböck, Ciaran Byrne, Paul Cairney, Elisenda Casañas Adam, John Coakley, John Curtice, Andrew Davies, John Denham, Sionaidh Douglas Scott, Anwen Elias, Marianne Elliot, Richard English, Federico Fabbrini, Yale Ferguson, Colin Fleming, John-Erik Fossum, Robert Frost, Michael Fry, Gregor Gall, Jim Gallagher, John Garry, Tom Garvin, Paul Gillespie, Brian Girvin, Mark Hannify, Niamh Hardiman, Malcolm Harvey, Gerry Hassan, Katy Hayward, Robert Hazel, David Heald, Ailsa Henderson, Eve Hepburn, David Hope, Kirsty Hughes, Jo Hunt, Francis Jabobs, Alvin Jackson, Colin Kidd, Brigid Laffan, Tobias Lock, Martin Loughlin, Robin McAlpine, Chris McCrudden, Peter McGregor, Aileen McHarg, Iain MacLean, Anand Menon, Rachel Minto, James Mitchell, Margaret Moore, Kalypso Nicolaïdes, John O'Brennan, Daithí Ó Ceallaig, Brendan O'Leary, Lindsay Paterson, Richard Parry, Henry Patterson, David Phinnemore, Matthew Quinn, Rick Rawlings, Richard Rose, Michael Rosie, Elin Royles, Joe Ruane, Kirstein Rummery, Meg Russell, Philip Rycroft, Drew Scott, Roger Anwen Scully, Eric Shaw, Keith Shaw, Kim Swales, David Torrance, Stephen Tierney, Adam Tomkins, Richard Wyn Jones. The wisdom of the late Michael Burgess, Craig McAngus, David Donald, Colin Imrie, Elizabeth Meehan, Jacques Leruez and Bob Young will be sorely missed. Viktoria Eriksson helped with analysis of survey data. Thanks, also, to Dominic Byatt, Olivia Wells and Oxford University Press for their customary professionalism.

The hardest part of writing a book is often choosing the title. A snappy title can be simplistic and misleading. A descriptive one can be boring. A medical website (https://www.healthline.com/health/fracture) gives the following definition of fracture:

> A fracture is a broken bone. It can range from a thin crack to a complete break. Bone can fracture crosswise, lengthwise, in several places, or into many pieces. Most fractures happen when a bone is impacted by more force or pressure than it can support.

The metaphor seems apt. The United Kingdom has not, at the time of writing, suffered a complete break, but the Union is subject to increasing stress.

Michael Keating

Aberdeen and Edinburgh
July 2020

Contents

List of Figures and Tables

Figures

Tables

1

Nation States and Political Unions

States and Unions

The United Kingdom has been described as an 'intellectual puzzle' (Rose 1982). For a generation of political scientists, it was widely taken as a paragon of a homogeneous, unitary state (Blondel 1974; Finer 1974). Other observers have seen the United Kingdom as a phase in the building of (and retreat from) a larger empire. Hechter (1975), in a much-disputed analysis (Bryant 2006), presented it as a case of 'internal colonialism'. For Nairn (1977), 'Ukania' was a dysfunctional post-imperial polity, destined to go the way of the Austro-Hungarian Empire. Rokkan and Urwin's (1983: 187) characterized the United Kingdom as a 'union-state', which Mitchell (2010) expanded into 'state of unions'.

Studies of the European Union have similarly employed different analytical frames. Some see the EU as essentially a league of independent nation-states, cooperating in their mutual self-interest. Others identify an emerging federal order, with a diffusion of power to two levels (Burgess 2009). Colomer (2006) and Zielonka (2006) have used the analogy with empire as a form of differentiated polity. For Jacques Delors (1985), it was a 'unidentified political object'.

Much of the literature on both the UK and the EU has drawn on historical and conceptual analogies with European states, whether this be the nation-state, the unitary state, the federal state or alliances of states. The argument of this book is that both are better understood as political unions. They are, moreover, connected, as the UK devolution settlement at the end of the twentieth century was embedded in membership of the European Union and modern 'post-sovereign' understandings of political order. The project of withdrawal from the EU, on the other hand, was predicated on a return to a unitary nation-state that had never fully existed and from which the devolution settlements had further deviated. This is not an argument for British exceptionalism. Rather, the United Kingdom may be experiencing, in concentrated form, the challenges to the established state order that are being played out across Europe and beyond.

State and Nation in the United Kingdom: The Fractured Union. Michael Keating, Oxford University Press (2021).
 DOI: 10.1093/oso/9780198841371.003.0001

A political union has been defined as 'a joining of two or more nations or other political entities under one government; an alliance between states, a federal union' (*Oxford Living Dictionary*). In this sense, most European states are unions, formed by the merger of pre-existing units. The majority of these, however, are constituted as nation-states with fixed territorial boundaries, within which are enclosed distinct national societies; national economies; policy-making systems; and systems of representation. This does not preclude decentralization or even a federal division of powers on a consistent basis across the territory. A union is something else, but difficult to define. The key element is differentiation and the retention of pre-union forms. Bryce (1901) recognized cases in which territories with their own constitutions are allowed to keep elements of these after incorporation into a larger state. For Rokkan and Urwin (1983 181), similarly, the key is the survival of 'pre-union rights and infrastructures'. Herrero de Miñon (1998) emphasizes historic rights of territories as a counterpart to claims of complete sovereignty on the part of states. Unions, however, are not merely a relic of the past or evidence of an incomplete process of integration. Nor are they necessarily 'frozen' in time. Union, and the historic rights underpinning it, should, rather, be seen as a living principle (Herrro de Miñon and Luch 2001; Herrero de Miñon and Lluch 1988). They can be created and they can disappear. Unions might be defined as something less than unified states and more than international alliances but that would imply that those two forms are somehow more natural. In a more positive sense, unions are characterized by certain features. One is the concept of contract, in which adherence to union is, ultimately, voluntary, however difficult it might be to break it.[1] Unions are also characterized by divided sovereignty, as the constituent units never entirely surrender their original authority even if they choose not to secede.

Rokkan and Urwin whose definition has become almost canonical, actually refer to one specific form of union in which the state exercises direct political control over most of its territory but recognizes contractual limitations in other parts. This bears some resemblance to Jellinek's (1981) earlier concept of 'state fragment', in which parts of a state retain some, but not all, properties of older polities.[2] This is particularly relevant for the United Kingdom and for states like Spain and Canada where citizens in some territories feel they live in a nation-state while others prefer formulas such as the

[1] This issue was settled in the United States in the Civil War, after which it ceased to be a union in this sense.

[2] Jellinek himself, curiously, did not include the United Kingdom in his list, seemingly blinded by the common idea that it was a unitary nation-state.

Spanish 'nation of nations' or the Canadian theory of 'two nations', now expanded to three with recognition of the indigenous peoples.

This book will make use of three key dimensions of unity which in nation-states are assumed but which in unions are, to various degrees, contested: *telos, demos* and *ethos*. *Telos* refers to shared historical meanings and destiny, as well as shared understandings of the purpose of the polity. Such an idea underpins most national projects but a union may be supported by different sections of the polity for different reasons. *Demos* refers to the people, which in the nation-state is seen as unitary and as the source of legitimate authority but in the union can be plural. *Ethos* refers to shared meanings and values, which may be peculiar to the polity or be universal.

Two other elements are critical. *Sovereignty*, the foundation of legitimate authority, is typically unitary and often invested in the nation itself. A union may work with divided sovereignty. Finally, nation-states will have fixed borders, which contain the gamut of social and political systems and turn inwards. While nation-states are all-encompassing units with potentially unlimited scope, unions may be functionally specific and looser. Economic union might not correspond to the unit for social union and solidarity or to political union. Yet, connections may be forged among these domains so that a union is more than a set of utilitarian or functionally specific arrangements. These are deeply political matters, as we see from the debates about the proper scope and nature of the European Union.

These are, of course, ideal types, or frames for interpretation. There is no objective way of distinguishing a nation-state from a union, but they do provide different starting points for constitutional analysis and argumentation. How much consensus across the domains is necessary to sustain a union is an open question. What is clear is that they can rarely ever be resolved definitively or reduced to a single logic. This is not to say that it is all about politics and power. Rather, unions require their own form of constitutional reasoning going beyond legalistic reductionism. This is more difficult in some historical eras and some places than in others.

Differentiated Polities

History has known a variety of polities that do not fit into the modern nation-state form (Ferguson and Mansbach 1996). Large parts of Europe have been characterized by asymmetrical forms of government, territorial privileges, non-contiguous domains, enclaves and exclaves and combinations of religious and secular authority. This all allowed multiple allegiances and horizontal as well as deep vertical solidarities. Composite monarchies made up of disparate territories that kept their own institutions, were a common feature in pre-nineteenth century Europe (Elliot 1992). Artola (1999) refers to these simply as 'monarchies' to distinguish them from kingdoms, which had a single legal system and parliament. *Ancien regime* monarchies relied on traditional or personal allegiance to the regime or ruler and did not necessarily require mass allegiance to a motherland: the loyalty of key central and territorial elites would suffice. Spain was formed as a union of the kingdoms of Castile, Navarre and Aragon in the early sixteenth century, but until 1714 Aragon retained its own institutions, themselves federal in nature. Navarre was a distinct kingdom until the early nineteenth century. Within Castile, the Basque provinces retained their own foral rights until the mid-nineteenth century and some of these survive to the present. The Union of Kalmar united the Nordic countries from 1397 to 1523 and was succeeded by a union of Norway with Denmark until 1814 and then with Sweden until 1905. France under the *ancien régime* (before the Revolution) consisted of a patchwork of jurisdictions, privileges and institutions (Braudel 1986).

Monarchy facilitated the survival of composite states since, with the common factor represented by the figure of the monarch, it was not necessary to seek deeper institutional or sociological unity. Yet composite states did not have to be monarchical. The United Provinces of the Netherlands was formally a republic, albeit with monarchical features, and survived for two hundred years until the monarchy forged a unitary state in the post-Napoleonic era. The Polish-Lithuanian Commonwealth (with an elective monarch) was formally established in the late sixteenth century on the basis of an earlier union and lasted until the end of the eighteenth century (Frost 2013, 2015a). Switzerland survived for centuries as a republican confederation before turning into something like a modern federal system in the mid-nineteenth century.

Much of Europe, up to the twentieth century, was governed in the form of empire, which also did not demand cultural or linguistic homogeneity and in which territories could have a different relationship with the centre. The European landward empires—Habsburg, Ottoman, Romanov (Russian) and Hohenzollern (German)—gave way to nation-states only at the end of the First World War. The Habsburg Empire was organized around an imperial core, with a motley of territorial systems across its domains. The Ottoman Empire was focused on dynasty, and power was concentrated in the hands of the Muslim elite, but it never imposed religious or cultural uniformity or territorial unity (Barkey 2008). The Holy Roman Empire, before its abolition in the Napoleonic era, provided another form of order, cutting across other jurisdictions.

Beyond Europe were the overseas empires resulting from the global expansion into Africa, Asia, and the Americas. Arising from the domination and displacement of indigenous peoples, these can be distinguished from the European landward empires but the constitutional differences were not always clear cut. The colonial experience affected not just the colonized territories but also the imperial centres and their eventual emergence as nation-states. Settler societies beyond Europe developed their own national identities, often with an ambiguous and complex relationship with the centre, and imperial governments did not always draw a sharp line between the metropolis and the colonies. France regarded its overseas territories as part of the motherland, although without extending full rights to their inhabitants. Ireland hung uneasily between the status of colony and part of the metropolitan state.

The Spanish empire was a composite polity, including the Iberian territories, outposts across the Mediterranean and possessions in America and Asia (Artola 1999), and was often expressed as in the plural as *Las Españas*. Only with the loss of most of the American empire in the Napoleonic era was a Spanish national project constructed. The loss of the remaining colonies in the Caribbean and Asia in 1898 provoked a political trauma at home and competing 'regenerationist' projects for Spain, for Catalonia and for the Basque territories. The war in Algeria and its eventual loss were similarly traumatic for France as Algeria was seen as an integral part of the homeland. Indeed, it provoked some regionalist actors to argue for the 'decolonization' of the mainland (Lafont 1967).

In the interstices of the emerging early modern state system, there was space for other forms of polity, including the city-states of Germany, Flanders and Italy.

Modernization and the Demise of Union

It was widely believed at one time that this form of differentiated polity could not survive into the modern era. There was an element of methodological nationalism (Wimmer and Schiller 2002) at work as the social sciences emerged within the framework of the nationalizing state. Historians, working within national traditions, were prone to teleological accounts tracing the emergence and unification of the nation as though it were pre-ordained, for example writing of the 'unification' of Germany or Italy rather than their creation. Sociologists argued that an intrinsic aspect of the modernization process consisted of territorial integration and functional differentiation as older territorial particularisms disappeared (Durkheim 1964). Modern modes of production would dictate a uniform division of labour, while markets would integrate to break down local production systems. Cultural diffusion (Deutsch 1972) would even out norms and social practices until one nation-building project met another one. At this point, clear boundaries would be drawn between self-contained polities.

Normative theorizing, where it was not cosmopolitan, also had a bias to the nation-state. Popular sovereignty and democracy, the offspring of the American and French revolutions, required a *demos*. This *demos* was provided by the nation while the state furnished the cultural and institutional basis for equal citizenship and social solidarity. As John Stuart Mill (1972) put it, '[F]ree institutions are next to impossible in a country made up of different nationalities': minorities would need to be assimilated. Following the Second World War, social citizenship provided another motive for uniformity. Welfare states were organized on a national basis, the nation providing the principle of affective social solidarity, and the state the administrative machinery. Modern scholars like David Miller (1995) and Brian Barry (2000) have continued to invest these normative values in the unitary nation, which was thus credited with a superior *ethos*.

Composite states and empires faced practical problems of governing in the modern era. They had typically practised indirect rule, relying on territorial intermediaries to maintain order and extract resources. These, in turn, traded loyalty to the regime in exchange for recognition and reward. The modern administrative state in the nineteenth century needed directly to penetrate into peripheral territories, carrying the principles of rationality, order and uniformity. At the same time, traditional elites in the periphery were weakened by economic and social modernization and the rise of market capitalism, industrialization and urbanization. Social hierarchies were undermined and mobility increased. This was the context for the rise of the modern state. Some polities forged centralized states; others found new forms of territorial management; others again disintegrated into smaller units.

In some cases, the old patrimonial elites were replaced by new intermediary classes such as the *notables*, *notabili* or *caciques* of France, Italy, and Spain, drawn from the new middles classes (Keating 1988b). Rising Scottish elites were incorporated into the British Empire and state, although efforts to co-opt the Irish Catholic middle class ultimately foundered on the rock of sectarianism. The Ottoman Empire never managed either to control the notables or to establish a system of centralized finance and administration (Barkey 2008). The Habsburg Empire long managed a mixture of central control, multilingualism and playing off territorial, linguistic and social demands (Judson 2016). External forces were another centrifugal factor as territories within imperial polities were drawn differentially into transnational economic and geo-political networks. Strong states on their borders intervened in their affairs, either to prop up their regimes or weaken them, sometimes using national minorities as their instrument. In many cases, the critical factor was not the strength of peripheral secessionist forces but failure at the centre and the consequent growing national consciousness, with central territories such as Anatolia (Turkey), Russia or the German heartland of the Habsburg domains. The balance of internal and external forces, centrifugal and centripetal, created growing territorial tensions, which peaked in the years around the First World War, bringing the central empires to an end (Roshwale 2001).

It came to be believed subsequently that unions were inherently unstable, especially in the era of mass politics, as the relationship between their constituent parts could never be resolved and the existence of territorially rooted institutions created constant centrifugal dynamics. The principle of national self-determination, it was thought, would never be satisfied until complete sovereignty was attained.

The legacy of modernization theory was a view of differentiation as the detritus of the past, of the *ancien régime* (referring to both pre-revolutionary France and pre-Napoleonic Europe generally). Yet, since the late twentieth century, attitudes have begun to change. The mystique of the nation-state has been broken as state sovereignty is questioned from above by transnational integration and below by territorial rescaling. As so often happens, questioning of the present has spurred revisionist interpretations of the past. Ideas of union have come back into play and have been rescued from the charge of backwardness and anti-modernism. Historians have mostly abandoned teleological visions of the transformation from unions into nation-states (Frost 2015a, b; Elliot 2018; Keating 2001). Some unions lasted for centuries, longer than their successor states. There has been renewed interest in empire as a conceptual alternative to the nation-state, if the historic comparison is made with empires in Europe rather than the overseas empires that resulted from European seizures of territory in Africa and Asia. There is a more appreciation of the complexity of nationalism and its aims. While the nationalities question undoubtedly played a key role in the fall of the central empires, nineteenth-century nationalists were by no means all committed to the ideal of the independent nation-state. In the Habsburg domains, demands often focused on modernizing the Empire to recognize the equality of nations and give them a degree of self-government within a Danubian confederation; Austro-Marxists debated at length about ways to reconcile the nationalities without territorial fragmentation. The end of the empire was by no means inevitable before the First World War precipitated its collapse (Macartney 1969; Judson 2016). Nationalists in Germany and Italy debated the merits of the federal and the unitary state; federalists won the argument in the former and lost it in Italy (Ziblatt 2006). Early Catalanists described themselves as regionalists and aimed to transform Spain rather than break it up (Llobera 2003). While it is a mistake to romanticize pre-modern regimes or anachronistically prescribe them as the answer to twenty-first century problems, there is a renewed interest in imperial concepts for understanding the emergence of the European Union (Colomer 2006; Zielonka 2006). Looking at the *longue durée* and abandoning nationalist and statist teleologies allows us to reconsider the conventional distinctions among states, empires and other polities, and the idea that empire must give way to nation (Kumar 2010; Berger and Miller 2015; Storm 2018).

Thinking about liberalism has moved on from the Millian idea of a unitary people within a large state, to embracing pluralism and the rights of communities as well as those of individuals (Kymlicka 1995, 2007). Empires and composite monarchies of the past may not have been democratic but they often recognized cultural pluralism; the uniform nation-state does the reverse. The challenge now is to embrace national diversity without losing democracy.

This goes along with wider challenges to the concept of the unitary nation-state. For social scientists, the state no longer represents the 'cage' (Mann 1993) for all functions and social relations. In a process of spatial rescaling, the domains of culture, society, politics, economics and welfare, previously contained within contiguous national boundaries, have migrated to new levels, above, below and across the state system (Keating 2013). The nation-state has lost its assumed normative primacy in the face of new and renewed challenges from national and territorial movements within it. European integration has created a supranational level of authority, which encroaches heavily on national monopolies in defining markets, regulation and, to some degree, welfare. Methodological nationalism has come under attack (Wimmer and Schiller 2002). Faced with these challenges, the nation-state has for the first time since its emergence had to find normative arguments for its existence and primacy. In response to these fragmenting tendencies, there has been a search for new forms of political order and integration. Here the principle of union has returned but is realized in multiple forms.

The Union Principle

Political unions may derive from earlier dynastic alliances but in the modern world they are more than that and, in an age of democratic mass politics, they must demonstrate their utility and legitimacy. Here we return to the elements identified earlier: *telos*, *demos*, *ethos* and sovereignty.

Telos has two faces. One is a tale of the past as purposive development. The other concerns the instrumental value of union in the present and future. Unions have often started for the purpose of security, moving from an alliance of states towards strong provisions for mutual defence and a common military hierarchy (Forsyth 1981). 'Publius' (1787), in the *Federalist Papers*, stressed the needs of security, the need for a common approach to avoid divisions and a chain of command. An early motive for European integration was security and peace following the wars of the twentieth century.

Another purpose is economic integration. Pre-modern polities were often characterized by multiple internal tariffs, restrictions and local monopolies. The French Revolution swept these away abruptly, a model followed by the new Italian state in the 1860s. Integration was slower in Spain, where the Basque provinces retained customs duties with the rest of Spain but free trade with the rest of the world until the 1820s. Within the Hapsburg Empire, tariffs were removed between Austria and Hungary only in 1851. In other cases, economic integration preceded political unity. The German customs union or *Zollverein* dates from 1834. A Latin Monetary Union lasted from the 1860s to the 1920s, underpinned by the gold standard.

Economic integration at the transnational level has taken the form of international treaties, but these have become denser and more encompassing over time. Old-style trade agreements mainly concerned tariffs on goods. In the modern regulatory state, however, non-tariff barriers in the form of product standards also need to be addressed. Services are the largest part of present-day European economies and are not typically subject to tariffs but do face regulatory obstacles. Mobility of workers is linked to trade in services. So, a 'single market' as in the European Union requires common product standards, free access to services and free movement of people. This in turn has raised further questions about the conditions for fair competition among producers from different territories, hence rules about competition, public procurement, state aid and environmental and labour protection. So economic union may require common policy-making institutions, going beyond the idea of free trade. Such bodies may be purely intergovernmental or may be independent of the constituent units, drawing their legitimacy from their functional efficacy or from a deeper idea of political community.

Social welfare has been an important task of the modern state and has in turn provided a *telos* to legitimize it. It rests upon an *ethos* of social solidarity and on a *demos* that provides the sense of shared community. The welfare state has been a centralizing factor in modern polities, as social citizenship comes with expectations of equal treatment and states strive for uniform welfare coverage. In mono-national states, the nation provides the affective solidarity that makes redistribution tolerable, while the welfare state itself may help to create and solidify that national identity and incorporate all social classes into the national project. National welfare coverage may also serve as a form of territorial mutual insurance, as asymmetrical economic shocks may hit different parts of the polity at different times. Redistributive payments may also be a form of compensation for parts of the whole that lose out, relatively or absolutely, from economic modernization. For all these reasons, theorists of fiscal federalism have argued that redistributive competences should be held at the highest level, while other kinds of policies can be held in the constituent units. In the face of secessionist pressures, unionists in the United Kingdom, Spain, Belgium and Italy have insisted that the larger unit is needed in order to sustain welfare and social solidarity.

In the modern state, peoplehood, or *demos* and nationality, have been linked to the concept of citizenship to the point that the terms are sometimes treated as synonymous. In a historical perspective, however, citizenship regimes have been very complex and, in the multiscalar modern world, they are increasingly so (Diener 2017). Unions typically embrace common citizenship, which may be combined with citizenship of the constituent units. These may be identical, as in the United States, or one may be derived from the other, as in the European Union. Citizenship itself is a complex concept. It may be reduced to the right to hold a passport for the purposes of travel but usually comes with a bundle of rights and obligations and extended, as social citizenship, to provision for welfare (Marshall 1992).

Political citizenship refers to the right to participate in public affairs, notably by voting and standing for office. Bauböck (2017) distinguishes this from citizenship in the broader sense by calling it 'demos'. In principle, citizens could vote directly for legislators at the level of the union or alternatively, the constituent units could be represented. In practice, most unions combine individual with territorial representation in various ways. Second legislative chambers are one way of doing this, often by giving more weight to smaller units, so that the system is not majoritarian at the level of the union. So, there is 'compounded representation' (Brzinski, Lancaster and Tuschoff 1999), in which both territories and individuals are represented. Union citizenship may give the right to all to participate in the affairs of any constituent unit, or this might be subject to residence requirements or stronger restrictions. European citizens can participate in European and local, not state-level, elections, in any EU member state. Many would go beyond formal rights to vote and argue that there needs to be a common communicative space in which the citizens can intervene. This is at the basis of many of the debates about the European Union and its 'democratic deficit'. The argument is that, lacking a *demos* in the deeper sense, as self-recognizing people, it cannot attain the democratic consent necessary to legitimate a modern polity. The idea is not new but harks back to the concerns of Mill (1972).

Democracy also implies representation and the articulation of interests. There are states in which the territorial party systems are completely separate, as in Belgium. In the United States, an apparently uniform party system incorporates a high degree of differentiation. Canadian federal parties mostly operate across the entire territory but are separate from their provincial counterparts. The United Kingdom and Spain contain a mixture of state-wide and territorial parties. Where territorial parties participate in state-wide government, either through coalition of parliamentary support, as happens in Spain, that may be an integrative factor. In the United Kingdom, state governments have occasionally relied on support from territorial parties (in 1910–16, 1976–9 and 2017–19), but at other times have rejected the idea of allying with peripheral nationalism. In the European Parliament, there is a conscious effort to sustain an EU-wide sphere of party competition by obliging the parties to sit in cross-national groups based on common ideological affiliation, although this has had limited effects in promoting a transnational sphere of political debate and exchange.

Unions typically go beyond mere international alliances in their commitment to a common *ethos*, or set of values. Historical nationalisms have often been rooted in particularist values, claimed as unique to the entity concerned, but others have drawn on universal human rights, as in France or the United States. The same is true of unions. The Convention on the Future of Europe (2001–3) witnessed a debate over European values, between those who stressed the Christian heritage and others who promoted a secular or a multicultural vision. The need for universal rights above those available in the component parts, has featured in debates in the United States, Canada and the United Kingdom, where they are presented as the necessary counterpart to differentiation of policies and the resulting inequalities. One set of rights are traditional civil and political rights, including freedom from discrimination and access to justice. In Europe, many such rights have been incorporated into the European Convention for the Protection of Human Rights and Fundamental Freedoms (under the Council of Europe). There is a growing debate about the recognition of social rights, partly met by the European Union's Charter of Fundamental Rights.

Yet, teleological or instrumental accounts of the formation and persistence of polities (whether states or unions) are always incomplete and inadequate on their own. A polity may have been formed at one time for a particular purpose but survive after that is no longer relevant. The key principle since the nineteenth century has been that of nationality, as the foundation of *demos*. Renan (1882) famously declared that a nation is not a *Zollverein* (customs union) but a living principle, which implies something more than utilitarian cooperation. Yet, nationality is a contested term which defies definition; replacing it with 'people' or some other label does not help much. It is not an objective matter, based on scientific principles. Nor is it purely objective, as for me to be a national, other people must feel the same way. It is, rather, an inter-subjective concept, referring to relationships among people and groups. It must also be understood as a claim, in a twofold sense. One is an ontological claim, that the nation exists as a social reality. The other is a teleological and normative claim that it is destined for, and has a right to, self-determination. Walker (2019) makes a similar distinction between reflexive and teleological nationalism. While the nation-state formula is based on the idea of a single nation constituting the *demos*, a union may contain multiple groups or *demoi*. Whether these call themselves nations or not is perhaps a secondary issue from a normative perspective and can even be a distraction (Marko 2020). In the modern era, however, the term 'nation' has been used to legitimate claims to self-determination.

The central argument then becomes whether polities require a single *demos* and how this relates to nationality. J. S. Mill provides the classic argument for homogeneity. Another school of thought holds that polities may rest less upon affective or cultural ties than on shared institutions and civic values or *ethos* which do not need to be specific to that polity, as long as the union is presented as a place for their realization. Modern republicans demand a stricter code of citizenship, involving active participation and commitment, which some see as also requiring a commitment to common values, although these values may include recognition of difference and pluralism (Honohan 2017). Jürgen Habermas (1998), referring to both a post-ethnic Germany and to the European Union, has argued for a 'constitutional patriotism' based on loyalty to institutions and the democratic constitutional order; others have criticized this as too 'thin'. Weinstock (2017) argues that the requirements of liberalism and even republicanism can be met without imposing cultural homogeneity: a shared identity may be less important than a shared *ethos* of governing.

Against the classic arguments for nation-states, there is now a substantial body of literature arguing that multiple national claims can be accommodated within unions (Gagnon and Tully 2000; Requejo 1999; Keating 2001). New conceptions of democracy pay attention to the rights of self-governing communities and pluralism. Liberal democracy has in many cases embraced national pluralism (Kymlicka 1995, 2007), although other liberals demur (Barry 2000). There are 'compound democracies', in which representation and accountability work at multiple levels (Fabbrini 2007). More generally, the concept of 'democracy' allows the existence of plural *demoi*, not as self-contained and self-validating entities, but as components of union (Nicolaïdis 2012, 2013). In this vision, the emphasis is on horizontal relations, openness and mutual recognition. This is not a mere second-best to the integrated state, but a normatively desirable recognition of pluralism.

Such approaches to democracy are increasingly relevant in a changing world reality In the ideal-type nation-state, *telos*, *demos* and *ethos* are linked and mutually reinforcing. Confined within national boundaries, social groups are encouraged to engage in positive-sum social compromises in partnership with the state (Bartolini 2005). Social welfare works as the counterpart to market integration, compensating losers and assuring loyalty, while also providing public goods and social investment without which the market cannot thrive. A shared community (*demos*) and values (ethos) further underpin social stability and exchange. Competitive politics allows for the alternation of power without disrupting the basis of political order.

The process of spatial rescaling may delink these elements. If market regulation is moving to higher levels, allowing capital to move freely, while social compensation remains at the lower level and workers cannot move so easily, then social compromises may break down. There is a risk of territorial competition to attract mobile investment and, consequently, a race to the bottom in the form of reduced taxes, public expenditure and social welfare. On the other hand, rescaling does provoke political reactions, including demands for the establishment of new political arenas in which the competing or complementary requirements of economic competitiveness and social cohesion can be reconciled. Thus, fragmentation may have its counterpart in new forms of union. The optimistic predictions of neo-functionalist theory of European integration, that there would be a spillover from one sphere to another, leading to political union, however, have not been realized. The linkage between functional rescaling and integration and social welfare is highly contested, as is the connection between these and political union. Economistic explanations of rescaling such as Alesina and Spoloare's (2003) arguments about the 'size of nations', are equally misleading. Rescaling is a highly contested process, altering the balance of power and producing winners and losers (Keating 2013). This is not new. The consolidation and enclosure of national spaces in the nineteenth century provoked territorial tensions between protectionist forces seeking to monopolize local markets and other territories that were linked into international trading systems beyond the state level (Keating 1988b). In the modern state, such tensions are increased by the demands of social welfare.

Rescaling is also political in that boundaries and scale shape the inclusion and exclusion from political communities, the balance of power and the distribution of benefits. Unions are typically embedded in historical narratives about the coming together of discrete territories in a pact that allows them to maintain their existing institutions and practices. Yet, the rescaling thesis is rooted in a constructivist perspective in which territories are continually being constructed and reconstructed, along all their dimensions. These may or may not correspond to historical or pre-union entities. Demands for recognition and self-government look back in history but also rely on arguments about the present will of the inhabitants. History, however, is contested, and the idea of the 'will' of a group of individuals is a hard one to test. The nation-state formula seeks to close these arguments with the powerful argument of national sovereignty as the ultimate source of legitimate authority, but they have already escaped that frame. The idea of sovereignty itself is called into question.

Sovereignty and Post-Sovereignty

Sovereignty, in the modern era, refers to the constituent power, the source and foundation of all other forms of legitimate authority. It is another elusive concept because, if a body is sovereign, that fact cannot be derived from anything else. Hence, sovereignty is often merely asserted, but is asserted precisely when it is not working to define the political world, and neglected when it is not contested. Jean Bodin's (1992) formulation in the sixteenth century was a response to civil division in France. Thomas Hobbes and John Locke were preoccupied with the breakdown of order in the seventeenth century. A. V. Dicey elaborated his version (not always consistently) as he sought arguments against Irish Home Rule.

The classic view of sovereignty, associated with Bodin (1992) is that there has to be an ultimate foundation of legitimate authority, from which all law is derived. With the demise of divine right, it was vested in the state. Later, following the democratic revolution, it has commonly rested with the people (*demos*). Yet in a composite political order or union there is no single *demos*. Vesting sovereignty instead in the constituent units may just reduce the union to an international organization or alliance when something deeper is required. Even the federal constitution of the United States vests sovereignty in 'we the people'. In normal times, most of this does not matter but at times of crisis, clarity is called for, just when agreement is most difficult to reach.

In recent years, new 'post-sovereign' understandings of political order have emerged, arguing not that sovereignty has disappeared but that it can be divided and shared (MacCormick 1999; Keating 2001). It is not always feasible or necessary to drill down to the foundations of authority in search of essential agreement. Rather, different views and traditions can co-exist in practice; shared institutions do not always need shared foundations. These ideas are not entirely new but look back to traditions of pactism and contractual order historically embedded in the experience of unions, and forward to a world in which the mystique of the unitary nation-state has been challenged. They have taken the debate on European integration away from the old debate between intergovernmentalists, insisting on the primacy of the nation-state, and federalists or neo-functionalists looking to its demise. They have also informed debates both on the state and on Europe within places that have historic traditions of contested sovereignty, such as Scotland, Catalonia or the Basque Country (Keating 2001). For some thinkers, post-sovereignty is a second-best option, given the difficulty of resolving conflicting sovereignty claims. For others, it is a principle in itself, linked to a constitutional pluralism in which different normative orders and claims can coexist. The fact that sovereignty is no longer master narrative or meta framework from which everything else flows does not mean that sovereignty claims are irrelevant or lack normative force Walker (2003). Indeed, in a world where the practical limitations of sovereignty are ever more evident, sovereignty claims seem to be proliferating. Constitutionalism is not about resolving these claims but about establishing institutions and practices in which they can co-exist.

By the end of the twentieth century, there was evidence of broad acceptance of the idea that sovereignty was not (if it ever had been) an absolute or a zero-sum game. The European Union had not superseded the idea of national sovereignty but that was never its intention. It had, however, pooled sovereignty to the degree necessary for security, economic integration and the defence of a shared, if differentiated, social model.

National independence movements in Europe had largely accepted the European project with its post-sovereigntist implications, viewing the emerging European political space as an arena for the projection of their ambitions rather than as a threat (Keating 2001). The Spanish Constitution of 1978 with its ambiguous wording about the indissoluble unity of the Spanish people and the 'regions and nationalities' which comprise it, provided enough room for moderate Catalan and Basque nationalists to carve out a distinct role in Spain's 'state of the autonomies'. The United Kingdom had embraced limited self-government for Scotland and Wales and an ambitiously post-sovereign dispensation for Northern Ireland. Belgium had evolved into a complex federation. None of these entailed a deep consensus on issues of nationality and sovereignty. Indeed, they papered over some profound differences on *demos*, *telos* and sovereignty while providing workable compromises.

A few years later, however, the sovereignty question was back. Some of this was due to disappointment with the European project and the failure of ideas of a Europe of the Peoples or Europe of the Regions. Other factors were domestic. After the Spanish Constitutional Court had unpicked key parts of their new statute of autonomy (agreed with the Spanish Parliament), Catalan nationalists turned to independence.[3] Plaid Cymru opted for independence for Wales. The New Flemish Alliance (N-VA) became the largest party in Flanders, committed, at least in principle, to independence. There may have been specific reasons in each case, but the return to classic notions of independence is striking. One reason may be the ontological conundrum. Where the concept and meaning of nationality and community are contested, one way of establishing the existence of the people in question is by gaining independence in a legal sense.

On the other hand, if and when independence is spelt out in practice, nationalist movements have turned back to post-sovereignty and ideas of

[3] This was not the only reason. Fiscal issues and the repercussions of the Global Financial Crisis played their part.

union. The Catalan independence prospectus is heavily dependent on Europe.[4] The Basque National Party distanced itself from its Catalan counterpart, arguing for a 'right to decide' that would be used to negotiate a new accommodation with Spain. Plaid Cymru is ambivalent about independence and the N-VA sees it as a long-term goal, with confederalism as the immediate aim. Even the SNP's independence prospectus in 2014 relied on ideas of union, proposing that Scotland stay in five unions (European; monarchical; defence; monetary; and social) and leave only one (the 'political union') (Keating and McEwen 2017).

Constitutional Formulas

Union is not a specific institutional mechanism or a legal concept but rather a principle which may underpin various constitutional forms. It has affinities with federalism as a system of government in which powers are constitutionally divided between a central (federal) level and the component territorial units. Yet not all federations are unions and not all unions are federal (Frost 2015b). Bryce (1901) recognized that most unions are federal but noted that the United Kingdom was not; nor, in his view, could it be. The United States and Germany have long stood for distinct modes of federalism, coordinate and cooperative respectively, but neither is a union in our sense. American scholars long tended to generalize from their own experience to argue that federations could only work if they were symmetrical and based on the existence of single nation, without critical differences of nationality or culture (Tarlton 1965). Germany has a long federal tradition and the federal republic was created in 1949 from the unification of separate Länder. Yet these units were in many cases created on arbitrary boundaries after the Second World War, lacking popular identity and tradition and in a context of strong shared identity and commitment. In both federations, the union is for ever and there is no right of secession.

Rokkan and Urwin (1983) distinguish among mechanical and organic federalism, where the former corresponds to the German or American type and is mainly concerned with limiting central power, while the latter builds upon historic or identity communities and aims to recognize diversity. More recent accounts of federalism also present it as a way of managing states where there

[4] Which included the erroneous belief that the European Union would support it because of its Europeanist vocation.

is national diversity or multiple peoples (Burgess 2006, 2012; Gagnon and Seymour 2012; Requejo 1999; Noël 2013; Hueglin 2013). In these accounts, federalism is less a strict constitutional form and more a set of principles based on the division and balance of power, observance of subsidiarity and respect for difference.

Just not all federations are unions, so not all unions are strictly federal, although that term has often been stretched. While there has long been support for federalism in Spain, it is resisted both by Spanish nationalists who see it as undermining the unity of the state, and by Catalan and Basque particularists, who see it as too uniform and as a way to dilute their specificity by extending it to regions without historic personalities. Nor is the United Kingdom a federation, although arguably it is developing along federalizing lines (Tierney 2018). British Eurosceptics have always argued that federalism is a centralizing principle, often associating it with the term 'super state'. Greek and Turkish Cypriots have agreed on a federal form of government but give it very different meanings. As we will see, the term has been used in the internal UK debate in very different ways.

A looser form of association is confederalism, usually seen as an association of separate states without a common central government. Forsyth (1981) calls these 'federal unions', as opposed to federal states. Again, the term can be confusing as in Canada, confederation has referred to the process of creating the federation. The New Flemish Alliance (N-VA, 2019) sees a confederal Belgium as a stepping stone to independence. The term has also been used in the United Kingdom to support a very loose form of federation but often without a precise institutional blueprint.

The Stability of Unions

It has been a criticism of unions that they are inherently unstable under modern conditions of democratic and responsible government, and prone to centrifugal forces. It may just be possible to cede recognition to the component territories, without conceding power, as was the case in the United Kingdom before 1999,[5] or to concede self-government to all territories without recognizing the national status inherent rights of some of them, as in Canada or Spain. What is not viable, it is argued, is to concede both at the same time: if recognition of

[5] Northern Ireland between 1921 and 1972 had a form of autonomy which unionists had accepted as a second best to rule from London for the whole of Ireland.

nationality is combined with self-government, the component units will assume sovereign rights, leading ineluctably to secession. Decentralization itself will set in train a further centrifugal institutional dynamic as leaders of devolved units will always demand more powers. Asymmetrical unions in which the larger part of the citizenry has only one set of national references, to the state, while the minorities have either separate reference points or multiple ones, are inherently weak.

Yet balancing these are centripetal forces, which may include instrumental considerations connected to security, economic efficiency and risk-sharing. These may be buttressed by a sense of affective loyalty or just a passive acceptance of the polity as an enduring reality. In asymmetrical unions, the larger part may provide an anchor, subsuming its own identity into the whole or at least paying a price for union in return for larger benefits. O'Leary (2004) has argued that multinational unions can survive as long as there is a dominant *Staatsvolk*. Ascherson (2020) argues that the United Kingdom can work only under the condition of English dominance. The threat to unions has, indeed, often come not from complaints from the smaller components but from a growing reluctance of the larger one so to subsume its identity into the whole to accommodate the smaller ones. Unions are also conditioned by their external environment, which may provide a support framework or else pull the components apart, selectively incorporating them into other economic, cultural or political networks to such a degree as to undermine their internal cohesion.

The balance of factors may change according to time and circumstance so that unions designed for one purpose may survive to serve others. Strands of union may be mutually supportive or work at cross purposes. They may even unite people pursuing rather different long-term goals but willing to compromise in the interim. In this way, they may last a very long time but there is always the possibility of disintegration. Maintaining unions is thus a specific form of statecraft, sensitive to variety and the contested and negotiated nature of claims to authority. These cannot be reduced to a single principle, or hierarchy of principles, to provide undisputed legitimacy. The relationship among the constituent units is always open to argument, institutional dynamics and power.

Unions and nation-states are not part of a rigid taxonomy such that a given polity must be one or another. They are, rather, ideal types or interpretive keys for understanding individual cases. There are insights to be gained from seeing the United Kingdom from each perspective, and this has been at the heart of many arguments about political order. The European Union has similarly been interpreted as international organization, federation in the making or 'unidentified political object'. For our purpose, it can be seen as a union. From 1973 until 2020, the United Kingdom was a union within a union and Europeanization combined with renewed nationality movements to shape the rescaling of political authority, As the same time, the EU provided an external support framework for the devolution programme launched at the end of the twentieth century. By the time of the Brexit referendum in 2016, all the parties seeking to break away from the UK union wished to remain within a European framework. Indeed, the project for the withdrawal of the United Kingdom from the European Union shows how difficult it is to rebuild the old nation-state or, in that case (as we shall argue), build a nation-state from the beginning.

2

Union and its Challengers in the United Kingdom

Interpreting the United Kingdom

For a generation of political scientists, the United Kingdom was widely taken as the epitome of a homogeneous, unitary state following the modernist path of territorial integration and functional differentiation. Starting from a core in the south-east of England, the state and nation were extended into the surrounding territories to create a 'homogeneous' polity (Blondel 1974). Finer (1974: 137) claimed that 'Britain, too, has had its "nationalities" problem, its "language" problem, its "religious" problem. These are problems no more.' For most constitutional lawyers, the United Kingdom was a unitary state, based on an uninterrupted parliamentary tradition, with the peripheral territories tacked on over time. As Finer (1974: 134) put it, 'But for all this [the administrative arrangements for Scotland, Northern Ireland and Wales] the "Constitution"... is not British at all. It is *English*.' This built on the earlier ideas of the Whig historians (Butterfield (1968), with their teleological vision of the expansion and integration of England, imbued with a strong *ethos* of order, liberty and, eventually, democracy, and with the peripheral nations playing walk-on parts without interrupting the central narrative. Nationalists on the periphery tell a different tale. In Ireland, it is one of foreign invasion, annexation and oppression. In Scotland, the themes are trickery and bribery and selling out on the part of local elites. The incorporation of Wales is described as colonialism (Price 2019).

The return of nationalities conflicts in the 1970s provoked a re-appraisal. For some social scientists, the national revival was evidence of retarded modernization, even a 'revolt against modernity' (Lipset 1985). Others argued that the United Kingdom had never really been a nation-state but was held together by factors such as empire, monarchy and religion that had lost their force, leaving the constituent nations to re-emerge from the wreckage. These reactions, like their assimilationist predecessors, reflected the concerns of

State and Nation in the United Kingdom: The Fractured Union. Michael Keating, Oxford University Press (2021).
© Michael Keating. DOI: 10.1093/oso/9780198841371.003.0002

their own times, an urge to predict the future, an excessive systemization and the ambition to causal explanation.

A third phase of understanding was represented by a growing body of scholarship aimed at understanding the complex relationships among the peoples of 'these islands'. The 'islands' approach to history sought to break with the Anglocentric and Whig history as well as nation-based approaches to the individual components, to trace the complex relationships among peoples and institutions over time (Davies 1999; Pocock 1975; Smyth 2001). The United Kingdom is increasingly seen as a union. In the Republic of Ireland, a teleological nationalist historiography has been under attack by the revisionist school since the 1940s but particularly since the 'Troubles' from the 1960s. Social scientists, too, have abandoned older forms of determinism.

There is always a danger that the abandonment of old teleologies will lead to mere empiricism, a directionless narrative of events and pragmatic adjustments with no explanatory power. We can, however, discern a set of themes in British and islands history. One is the emergence of England as an early nation-state. The creation of the United Kingdom, is a very different matter, better understood in the language of union. Incomplete nation-building (by the standards of other European states) left intact important internal boundaries, while the external boundary of the state was never entirely closed or settled. The process involved both consent and coercion. Force was deployed where necessary (notably in Ireland), the state was marked by sectarianism, and demands for local autonomy were resisted for long periods of time. On the other hand, there was little forcible cultural assimilation and much of administration was left in the hands of local collaborators (Bulpitt 1983). The national diversity of the polity was rarely questioned, but there was a rigid insistence that the fundamental principle of authority was that of the centralized Monarch-in-Parliament.

The Old Regime

The historian J. R. Seeley (1883: 12) wrote in his *The Expansion of England*, 'We seem, as it were, to have conquered and peopled half the world in a fit of absence of mind.' The construction of the United Kingdom has similarly been seen as a set of pragmatic steps, without much resort to principle or overall design. This is probably true of almost all states but in the case of the United Kingdom there was no thoroughgoing national revolution to consolidate the state and bind the nation together as *demos*, *telos* and *ethos*. Thinking about the Union occurred only sporadically, and usually in periods of internal or external challenge.

England did establish a precocious form of unified state, based on the monarchy, which gradually embraced Parliament to constitute the political nation. Following the so-called Glorious Revolution of 1688–90, a strong monarchy and strong parliament came to rule together so that monarchical and parliamentary claims to sovereignty, instead of competing, were fused into the institution of Crown-in-Parliament. While this is seen in England as the basis of liberalism and constitutional government, it left no place for alternative conceptions of sovereignty or federalist ideas.

The creation of the United Kingdom is a different matter. Ideas about the island of Britain or Great Britain[1] have been around since ancient times, but this did not of necessity lead to political union. Anthony Smith (1998) argues that the United Kingdom was formed from an English 'ethnic core'. In fact, the penetration of the English state into the neighbouring territories began in earnest under the French-speaking Norman and Angevin dynasties as a completion of their invasion of England itself. A military conquest of Ireland in the twelfth century was effectively undone as the invaders merged into the local population except in the Pale around Dublin. The Tudor dynasty brought Ireland back under Crown control and erected it into a 'kingdom' in 1542. Wales, where the medieval English Crown had been concerned with securing stability on the frontier, was legally annexed to England under the Tudors (Johnes 2019).[2] The Normans arrived in Scotland by invitation of the Scottish Crown and helped build an early independent state. Attempts on the part of English monarchs to subdue the country militarily, pursued into the sixteenth century, never achieved lasting success as Scotland maintained its independence by playing off England and France until, as a result of dynastic marriage, its king ascended to the throne of England.[3] The dynastic wars of the seventeenth century saw Protestantism triumphant in all four nations but, while this was tailored to the local population in England and in Scotland, the bulk of the Irish people remained faithful to Catholicism.

Thereafter both Scotland and Ireland remained in monarchical union with England but on different terms. The Scottish Parliament retained full legislative competence, although in practice it was subordinate to government

[1] The Great is not, as sometimes thought, a piece of imperial bombast but to distinguish it from Brittany.

[2] There was no treaty or Act of Union, but the relevant laws have since 1948 been known by the short title 'The Laws in Wales Acts'.

[3] Although there was short-lived conquest by Oliver Cromwell in the seventeenth century.

domination and manipulation. Day-to-day administration was undertaken by local governments and boards run by local elites. Ireland took on the characteristics of an autonomous colony, retaining a degree of self-government but in the hands of the Protestant minority which constituted the 'political nation'. Under the Tudor 'Poyning's Law' its Parliament was subordinate to the English Privy Council. Catholics were not given the vote until 1792 and then still denied the right to sit in Parliament. A Lord Lieutenant sent from England was responsible for administration in Dublin Castle, working with the local elites.

In spite of this both parliaments enjoyed something of a revival in the last decades of their lives (Jackson 2012). The Scottish Parliament passed some improving legislation and even provided for an independent foreign policy, thus provoking England. In the latter part of the eighteenth century, the Irish Parliament modified or repealed Poyning's Law in 1782–3. This created the myth of 'Grattan's Parliament' as a point of reference for a self-governing Ireland although historians have cast some doubt on attempts to present this as a proto-nationalism (Kanter 2009; Mansergh 2005).

Towards Union

From the seventeenth century, there were numerous schemes to incorporate Scotland and Ireland with England-and-Wales in a single state, but union was never a guiding *telos* or prime aim of statecraft (Jackson 2012). It was pursued intermittently, usually at times of crisis, and took a minimal form, leaving in place much of the old governing infrastructure. The motivation was military and dynastic security, trade and economic considerations rather than nation-building. The Unions of 1707 and 1801 followed neither the unitary state nor the federal model but rather a *sui generis* arrangement in each case. Although federal ideas were canvassed during the Scottish Union, the requisite doctrines existed only in inchoate form (Kendle 1997; Fry 2006; Whatley 2006; Devine, 2008b). Bulpitt (1983) suggests that the unions came too late to absorb the peripheries but too early for coherent doctrines of either federalism or a unitary state.

Union took the shape of legislation ratified by each of the parliaments, preceded, in the Scottish case, by a treaty. In 1707, an 'incorporating union' abolished the Parliaments of both England and Scotland and replaced them with a new Parliament of Great Britain. From the outset, the new Parliament acted as a continuation of the English body, adopting all its prerogatives, procedures and precedents. Some guarantees for Scotland were written into the Acts, including security for the Established Church and local government. A provision declared that:

> Laws in use within the Kingdom of Scotland do after the Union and notwithstanding thereof remain in the same force as before (except such as are contrary to or inconsistent with this Treaty) but alterable by the Parliament of Great Britain with this difference betwixt the Laws concerning publick right Policy and Civil Government and those which concern private right that the Laws which concern publick right Policy and Civil Government may be made the same throughout the whole United Kingdom But that no alteration be made in Laws which concern private right Except for evident Utility of the Subjects within Scotland'. (Act of Union 1707, Article 18)[4]

No mechanism, however, was provided in case these guarantees were breached, as they were soon after the Union with the restoration of lay patronage in the Church of Scotland (McLean 2010).

The 1801 Union of Ireland with Great Britain was also an incorporating one, but with weaker securities than Scotland appeared to have gained. All Irish laws were to remain the same but subject to alterations which 'circumstances may appear to the Parliament of the United Kingdom to require' (Article 8). Such securities as Ireland did gain were aimed at the Anglo-Irish Protestant Ascendancy community, further alienating the mass of the population (Jackson 2012). Yet a section of Protestantism still opposed the Union as a threat to its privileges (Connolly 2014). As in Scotland, the Union was declared to be permanent.

Post-union politics in both Scotland and Ireland were marked by limited government and central intervention. Scotland was initially governed by a Secretary of State but the office was suppressed after the 1745 Jacobite rebellion. Until the 1830s, it was run by a 'Manager', a local notable able to work at both levels, delivering votes to the government of the day in return for a free hand over patronage (Fry 1987). From 1885, a Secretary (of State) for Scotland, chosen from among the MPs of the governing party, assumed responsibility for administration, working with local collaborators (Paterson 1994). In Ireland, the colonial mode of government from Dublin Castle

[4] Articles can be viewed at https://www.parliament.uk/globalassets/documents/heritage/articlesofunion.pdf

continued, tempered by reliance on local elites.[5] Lords lieutenant and chief secretaries were sent over from England (O'Leary 2019a, b) and no Irish Catholic held either post during the entire period of union (Jackson 2012), although there was some co-option of the Catholic middle classes with the election of county councils from the 1880s. It was not until 1817 that the Irish and British exchequers were amalgamated, and only in 1824 was free trade achieved (Kanter 2009).

In none of the unions was there a thoroughgoing programme of cultural integration to create a unitary *demos* as in other European states. No single education department was ever established for the United Kingdom. Scotland's system remained proudly independent. In Ireland, national schools were intended to improve educational standards in a secular context while spreading the use of English. In practice, they came under Catholic influence and the use of Irish was increasingly tolerated from the late nineteenth century. In Wales, the notorious Blue Books of 1847, produced by a commission of inquiry into the state of education, made some gratuitously offensive remarks about Welsh, but the language continued in everyday use and the number of Welsh speakers continued to expand with the population (Johnes 2019). Scottish Gaelic was confined to a diminishing zone in the Highlands and Islands but did survive.[6] The decline of vernacular languages, however, continued in the face of urbanization and social change, as well as the attractions of English for social mobility.

Colley (1999) identified religion as a key element in holding together the Union across Great Britain. As a factor for cohesion across the Union, however, it was much less clear. The guarantees to the Church of Scotland assured the maintenance of an institutional basis for national identity as well as religious doctrine steeped in contractual loyalty and suspicion of state control. The Irish Union merged the established churches of Ireland and England, but the former commanded the allegiance only of a minority. In contrast to their strategy in Quebec (Stevenson 2006), the British failed to co-opt the Catholic Church into the Union, despite it being a potentially conservative and stabilizing force (Girvin 2002). Some efforts were made to reduce the influence of ultramontane Catholicism, including a grant to the seminary at Maynooth,

[5] There is a debate on whether Ireland was a colony (Howe 2000). My argument is that, while it was not like the colonies in Asia or Africa, there were colonial elements in the relationship.

[6] The Scots language, on the other hand, lacking support from either church or state, lost prestige after the successive monarchical and parliamentary unions and, like other European patois, retreated to being the language of 'poets and peasants'. Only in 1983 did a Scots translation of the Bible appear.

and the idea of state payment for the clergy was floated (Bew 2007) but the Church itself was unwilling to accept further incorporation into the state (O'Leary 2019a). Union was not accompanied by Catholic emancipation, as had been promised. Even the Protestants of Ireland were divided between the Established Church and the dissenting religions. Indeed, union was born as a polity with a distinctly sectarian *ethos*. Catholics in all four nations were denied full political rights until emancipation in 1829. Non-conformists suffered disabilities until the repeal of the Test Acts in 1828 (but were still barred from Oxford and Cambridge, the only universities in England and Wales). By the mid-nineteenth century, the Established Church commanded only minority support in Wales. Payment of Church tithes by non-Anglicans remained a grievance through the nineteenth century. The United Kingdom was thus not, in the strict sense, a 'Westphalian' state (Osiander 2001) in which religion and polity coincided.

Nor was it a state with a defined external boundary since, as it became a union, the United Kingdom simultaneously expanded into an empire and it was not always clear where the metropolitan state ended and the empire began, especially in relation to Ireland (Mansergh 2005). The empire provided an outlet for ambitious young men from Scotland, Wales and Ireland; this is the class whose frustration over the prospects of social mobility at home has been identified as a source of early nationalism in other European countries. Ireland contributed disproportionately to the Indian Civil Service and imperial military until the early twentieth century; this included Protestants but also Catholics (Kenny 2004; Townend 2016). Scotland contributed disproportionately to the imperial military, civil service and medical presence (Devine 2004; Fry 2002).[7] Wales was also deeply involved in Empire, including trade, missions and colonization (Johnes 2019). The relationship between empire and developing national consciousness across the nations, however, was different. Scotland was presented as one of the mother-countries of the Empire—one of the few institutions always described as British and never as English. So, in Craig's (2018) formulation, what in other European countries was a defensive nationalism gave way to a 'projective nationalism' as the diaspora established Scottish institutions and communities overseas. As Irish nationalism rose in the late nineteenth century, on the other hand, it became increasingly anti-imperialist, especially at the radical end. The Irish diaspora

[7] Kumar (2003) writes that in 1830, 43 per cent of the Crown forces were Irish and 13.5 per cent were Scots.

also became a source of political and financial support for republicanism. Anti-imperialism also affected sections of radical liberalism in Wales and Scotland in the late nineteenth century. There was some outrage at the treatment of colonized peoples, but few people drew an analogy with the peripheral nations of the United Kingdom. Anti-imperialists, rather, expressed a fellow-feeling with the Boers, a small European people taking on the might of Empire in the name of Home Rule. Empire also provided an economic framework for union, itself anchored in a global free-trading regime. This obviated the need for a programme of national economic protectionism or mercantilism, as characterized other emerging European nation states.

Perhaps the most striking feature of union is something that did not happen. None of the three unions made any difference at all to the government of England. This allowed the theory and practices of the unitary state to remain untouched at Westminster, with the peripheral nations enjoying various dispensations within it. English public and political opinion continued to speak of England, Great Britain and the United Kingdom as though they were the same thing. There was no forum for the expression of a distinct English voice within the state, but English representatives were so numerically dominant that it made no difference.

Legacy of Unions

Successive unions did not leave a consistent state doctrine for the United Kingdom comparable to those of other European states. Issues of central importance remained unstated, leaving them to be contested in the future. While the franchise was gradually extended to the whole adult population, it was never accompanied by the principle of popular sovereignty. There was thus no need to define the *demos*. Instead, the state was personified in the monarchy. Royalty itself was careful to present a composite image, mixing elements of the four nations and three kingdoms[8] in its various regalia. Following the conquest under Edward I, the monarch's eldest male child has rejoiced in the title Prince of Wales. After long neglect, the monarchy took a renewed interest in Scotland from 1834 with George IV's (much mocked) visit, garbed in Highland dress, choreographed by Sir Walter Scott. Queen Victoria established a summer residence at Balmoral and the royal family,

[8] Wales, not being a kingdom, does not feature in the royal coat of arms.

when in residence, attend Church of Scotland services. The monarchy's status in Catholic Ireland was much lower, although royal visits in the nineteenth century did attract some popular support. The military, too, was able to reflect the plurinational composition of the Union, with regiments drawn from, and proudly wearing the insignia of, the four nations.

Citizenship law emerged later on and was entangled with the concept of British subjects, which included people of the Empire. No charter of rights and duties of the citizens was ever produced, a matter that started to preoccupy some political activists in the late twentieth century. The celebrated Bills of Right introduced in England and Scotland after the 'Glorious Revolution' were sectarian and divisive, while in Ireland the Revolution paved the way for the notorious penal laws. Relaxation of these provisions was gradual and piecemeal and not linked to union. The United Kingdom had no 'constitutional moment' to define itself as a polity and never adopted a written constitution. Even those parts that were written down took the form of ordinary law, which Parliament could repeal.

There is limited point in scrutinizing the history of the unions to discern the 'original intent' or *telos* as a guide to interpretation of modern questions. In so far as there was intent, it is likely to have little to do with conditions in later periods. Yet the unions have left important legacies in the form of implicit claims and underdeveloped ideas that contain the germ of later developments. So, it can be argued that, so far as the unions stemmed from agreements, the latter could be repealed, although no mechanism was provided. Although the legislation for Irish union was careful to write about 'that part of the United Kingdom known as (England, Ireland or Scotland)', union did not extinguish those nations as administratively and politically relevant units in the way that revolutionary France or Spain of the *Nueva Planta* did. It was possible to argue that, as the old Scottish Parliament had never established absolute sovereignty, it could not have brought that attribute to the new Parliament of Great Britain and then the United Kingdom. A plausible case could be made that provisions in both Scottish and Irish Unions were permanent and thus must be considered fundamental law, even if neither Parliament nor the courts recognized such a category.

These questions have mostly remained dormant but have emerged at times of constitutional contestation. Such crises occurred in the late nineteenth and early twentieth centuries and again a hundred years later as successive phases of political modernization and changes in the United Kingdom's position in the world forced the constitutional question onto the political agenda.

Modernization and the Nationalist Challenge

Union preserved much of the cultural and administrative infrastructure of the constituent units but this is not to suggest that they were frozen, ready to re-emerge when external circumstances changed. It is widely accepted now that nations and nationalisms are the product of modernity (Gellner 1983; Smith 1998; Breuilly 1982); the insistence by nationalist intellectuals on their pre-modern lineage is actually part of that very process. This is not to say that nations are fabricated from nothing. Modernization is itself a historical phenomenon played out in specific times and places. So English, Irish, Scottish and Welsh nationalists can identify key moments back to the Middle Ages but they emerged as political movements from the nineteenth century and the entry of the masses into politics. As elsewhere in Europe, there were 'national revivals' as territorial societies faced new challenges from economic, social and political change (Keating 1998, 1998, 2013).

Industrialization shifted the economic geography of the United Kingdom, being strongest in the north of England, central Scotland, south Wales and the north-east of Ireland, whose business classes became stalwarts of free trade and empire. Class relations were transformed by the rise of the industrial proletariat and of the managerial and professional middle classes, which themselves were shaped by territorial conditions across the United Kingdom. Rural unrest linked to agrarian modernization and international trade impelled calls for land reform in Ireland, Scotland and Wales. Religious revivals occurred in all four nations. The Catholic Church established a social hegemony in Ireland, while distancing itself from the state. A Nonconformist revolution in Wales saw most of the population detach itself from the established Church of England and, at the same time, from the landowning class, who looked and sounded more English (Morgan 1981). In Scotland there were moves for Church disestablishment to restore its independence from the state. A breakaway (the Disruption) in 1846 took away a third of the Church of Scotland's membership, after which it could no longer claim to represent the entire nation within the union state. There were cultural and literary revivals in Ireland, Wales and both Highland and Lowland Scotland, although their relationship to politics was never straightforward. As elsewhere in Europe (Hroch 1985), national cultural revivalists sought the authentic primordial culture in the peripheral regions of the nation, while others sought to address the issues of modern industrial society and class relations.

The rise of mass politics followed the successive extensions of the vote and, especially the Reform Act of 1884, which also introduced a uniform franchise across the United Kingdom (Blewett 1965).[9] Rather than spurring a homogenization of voting patterns, this introduced a territorial cleavage that lasted until the First World War, and re-emerged in the later part of the twentieth century (Field 1997). Liberalism, especially after the breakaway of the Liberal Unionists in 1886, was informed by Radical ideas including church disestablishment and Home Rule. Advanced Liberals and the emerging labour movement in Scotland were immersed in myths of Scotland as a progressive nation, going back through the Scottish Enlightenment (a term invented in the late nineteenth century) to the Reformation. A section of their kin in the north of Ireland shared in these myths, which co-existed with a sense of ethno-religious particularism and destiny. Welshness also came to be seen as essentially progressive during the struggles for reform and church disestablishment (Morgan 1981). Scotland and Wales entered into a period of Liberal hegemony, which persisted almost unbroken until the rise of the Labour Party. Conservatism was correspondingly weak and, in Scotland, subordinated to Liberal Unionism, later taking the form of the Scottish Unionist Party with an electoral base different from English Conservatism. In the General Election of 1906 not a single Conservative was elected in Wales and only ten Unionists in Scotland (out of 70). In Ireland, reform coincided with nationalist agitation and resulted in politics fracturing on the nationalist–unionist cleavage, with unionism strongest in the north.

The expanding role of the state from the 1870s called into question the mechanisms for governing the nations. Middle-class elements in Scotland voiced increasing concern about the inefficiency of the ramshackle system of boards by which the country was governed and by the 1880s had persuaded both political parties to support the appointment of a Secretary for Scotland, and by the end of the century a convention had emerged that this should be an MP elected in Scotland for the governing party.

Modern nationalism was crystalized in the component parts of the United Kingdom in a series of political crises around self-government, or 'Home Rule' from the 1870s until the end of the First World War, in the context of social and political reform. The essence was the claim for self-government or autonomous legislative assemblies, first in Ireland and then in Scotland and Wales. These were not (except among Irish republicans) demands for separation, but pleas for recognition within the United Kingdom and the Empire, in some ways analogous to the movements for responsible government in the settler colonies.

[9] Sixty per cent of the adult male population were enfranchised but women were still barred.

Home Rule demands in Ireland brought together a broad coalition of political reformers and land campaigners. At the same time, a radical separatist tendency developed under the Irish Republican Brotherhood, more open to the idea of physical force. Early expressions of political nationalism in Ireland, around the rebellion of 1798, were secular, aiming to unite the diverse elements of the nation, but in the course of the nineteenth century it mapped onto other divisions, becoming strongly Catholic in its support base, albeit with a small but socially significant Protestant element in its leadership. The refusal of British Parliaments to concede Home Rule polarized the issue over thirty years until the republican and physical force elements of Irish nationalism triumphed following the Rising of 1916.

Scottish Home Rule agitation started in the 1880s, partly inspired by the Irish example, but firmly anchored on the political left. Working through the radical wing of the Liberal Party, Home Rulers sought a Parliament for Scotland within the United Kingdom and Empire and, eventually adopted the formula of Home Rule All Round, a federal-type solution for the United Kingdom. In contrast with Ireland, there was almost no support for independence and indeed the issue was not even broached until the 1920s. Since then, there has been a division between supporters of Home Rule (or devolution as it became known) and independence, but the line has been a very fluid one. Scottish Home Rule bills continued to gain the support of Labour MPs up to the 1920s and the policy was abandoned formally only between 1958 and 1974 (Keating and Bleiman 1979). Agitation in Wales was weaker and focused on recognition of Wales as a component nation in the Union (like Scotland and Wales) but evolved into demands for self-government as part of Home Rule All Round (Griffith 2006). Its main legacy was to be the idea of Wales as a political community distinct from England.

Early oppositions to the Scottish and Irish Unions were focused on Repeal, implying a dissolution of the parliamentary union and reversion to monarchical union. It was linked to the demand for responsible government in place of the management and jobbery that had characterized post-union regimes. Home Rule, as it emerged from the 1870s, was based on more explicitly federal principles. Isaac Butt's (1870) 'Home Government' proposals envisaged parliaments in England (including Wales), Scotland and Ireland, subordinate to Westminster. The Irish Party argued on similar lines from the time of Charles Stewart Parnell until 1918. A Scottish Home Rule Association was active after 1886 and again after the First World War, supported by advanced Liberals and Labour politicians with a similar agenda (Keating and Bleiman 1979). Home Rule proposals for Wales were on similar lines.

It was the Irish question, and particularly William Ewart Gladstone's conversion to Home Rule in 1886, that drove the constitutional debate. There were three Irish Home Rule bills between 1886 and 1912, sponsored by Liberal governments and a fourth one by the Coalition Government in 1920. Fifteen Scottish Home Rule bills were introduced between 1885 and 1924, with four of them gaining a second reading. All except one were supported by a majority of Scottish MPs (Kane 2015). There were numerous Home Rule motions, two federalizing bills and one Home Rule bill for Scotland and Wales (Mitchell 1996). None received government support, although Liberal and Labour ministers were usually sympathetic in principle. The Scottish bills were not presented as stand-alone measures but were largely inspired by the Irish example, and several of them pointed to a future system of Home Rule All Round. Around the turn of the nineteenth century, Home Rule notions met ideas of Imperial Federation promoted by imperialists as a way of keeping the Empire together while allowing self-government. In many versions, England, Ireland, Scotland and (possibly) Wales would have their own parliaments, along with the self-governing Dominions, under an Imperial Parliament at Westminster. Imperial federation did not gain much support in the Dominions themselves, where it was seen as a centralizing measure, which could increase their taxes, and had died out by the First World War.

A Speaker's Conference at the conclusion of the First World War toyed with federal ideas, but was overtaken by the Irish crisis following the radicalization of Irish nationalism and the eclipse of the old Home Rule party by the militant Sinn Féin. The settlement of the Irish question after two years of violent conflict saw the south of Ireland given Dominion status, although it had asked for an independent republic. The North was given Home Rule, which it had long opposed. Neither was to contribute much further to thinking about the United Kingdom as a whole. There was a radicalization of Scottish demands and the last Scottish self-government bills (in 1926, 1927 and 1928) provided for Dominion status but their failure provoked a parting of the ways between Labour and Liberal Home Rulers, inspired by federalist ideas, and nationalists pushing for more. In 1928 the National Party of Scotland was founded, later folded into the Scottish National Party.

It can be difficult in historic perspective to understand the vehemence of opposition to Home Rule, which stands in contrast to a supposed British propensity to pragmatism and compromise. Yet the failure of Home Rule did leave an important legacy, which was a more fully articulated idea of union*ism*, as opposed to the mere fact of union. This is more fully discussed in Chapter 7, but its essence was the impossibility of distinct national legislatures within a state based upon parliamentary sovereignty. With its failure, territorial management moved into a new phase, combining national integration with measures of differentiated treatment in a formula that was to prove successful until the late twentieth century.

Territorial Management in the Twentieth Century

The late nineteenth and early twentieth centuries had seen a series of constitutional challenges in the United Kingdom. The religious settlements in all four nations had been contested and the Anglican Church disestablished in Ireland (1871) and Wales (1920). The franchise was extended in phases by class and gender to reach full adult suffrage in 1928. There was a confrontation over the House of Lords, reaching a peak around 1910 when the upper house defied the Liberal Government's electoral mandate. The territorial constitution was challenged by new movement on the periphery. Few of these issues were definitively settled. The churches in England and Scotland remained established. Universal suffrage was not combined with reform of the electoral system to make it more representative. The veto powers of the House of Lords were limited and further curbed in 1949, but the composition of the chamber was not reformed until the end of the twentieth century, and even then some hereditary peers and bishops remained alongside those nominated for life; no peers were elected. The constitution remained uncodified.

The First World War drove constitutional issues off the political agenda and appeared to bring closure to territorial politics in the United Kingdom, stabilizing the Union. The larger part of Ireland was hived off in what became a separate state, taking Irish matters and Irish MPs out of the House of Commons. Northern Ireland, the place that had most resisted it, gained a Home Rule Parliament and Government. Its presence in Westminster was minimal and questions on Northern Irish affairs were not permitted in the House of Commons. The partitioning of the island, however, had left a historic and unresolved question (Moore 2019). Scottish Home Rule agitation died down as the Labour Party made its electoral breakthrough in 1922 and turned its attention to Westminster (Keating and Bleiman 1979); Wales followed the same path (Tanner 2006). The centre–periphery cleavage in electoral support waned (Field 1997). From the 1930s Labour focused on the potential of the British state to bring resources to the periphery and to plan on a large scale. For constitutional reformers, this was a missed opportunity, a failure to modernize in time. For others, it represented a resumption of the British tradition of pragmatism and gradualism against revolutionary ideas.

The twentieth century witnessed a project to create a British nation, complete with *demos, telos* and *ethos*. With the end of Empire, the United Kingdom emerged as a unit that was both territorially bounded and internally integrated. As references to Empire disappeared, the terms 'Britain' and 'British' gained currency. The Second World War cemented a wider British patriotism, and politicians and public servants learned not to use 'England' to refer to the whole. Competing for the electoral middle ground, both Conservatives and Labour Party emphasized a British patriotism. Edgerton (2018) sees the post-war years as the moment of the birth of a modern British nation as a distinct community, separate from Empire, and embarked on a common project. Economic and social modernization provided the *telos*. Both Conservative and Labour governments in ensuing decades focused on constructing (for the first time) a British national economy (Edgerton 2018). The welfare state both tapped into and reinforced a strong common social citizenship. Reflecting the shared *ethos*, the term 'national' was used freely to describe UK-wide institutions, including the health service and state-owned industries. The experience of the first majority Labour Government (1945–51) reinforced the commitment to centralization and managerial control (Jones and Keating 1985), not really questioned until the 1980s. As Douglas Jay (1976), often seen as the incarnation of the centralizing, planning spirit of post-war Labour governments put it in the devolution debates of the1970s, 'I invite those who have the future of Wales and Scotland at heart to realise how disastrous it could be if the economic and industrial link were severed between those countries and the heart of British industry and British Government.' There appeared to be no reason to believe that this project was in any way contrived or doomed to fail (Keating 2009).[10]

Yet if teleological unionism had triumphed, ontological nationalism persisted. The United Kingdom remained a composite state where competing national projects had not been resolved and which were to come back a hundred years later. The national revivals of the late nineteenth century in Scotland and Wales had established them as distinct nations within the Union at a time when they might have been integrated into a more homogeneous polity. So, alongside the integrative dynamics of the national developmental welfare state, there was a continuing policy of territorial management. The

[10] The economic and social dimensions of union are more fully discussed in Chapters 7 and 8.

Scottish Office took over most domestic administration in Scotland, with the exception of taxation and social security. Recognition of Wales followed (Rawlings 2003), starting from a weaker institutional base, but whose legacy can be seen in Cathays Park in Cardiff, whose buildings were set out to look like a national capital. A range of Welsh 'national' institutions emerged in civil society, matching those in Scotland and Ireland. From mid-twentieth century, ministers were appointed to look after Wales, culminating in the establishment of a Welsh Office in 1965. The territorial offices represented both the nations at the centre and the centre in the nations, lobbying for their territories while adapting the colour, if not the substance, of UK policy to their respective constituencies. Scottish MPs at Westminster played a distinctive role as territorial intermediaries, alongside and not in contradiction to their role as party representatives (Keating 1975). Northern Ireland was another matter, governed by local elites (financially sustained by Westminster) without the consent of the minority Catholic population and largely ignored by the centre.

Territorial demands were subsumed into the national developmental strategy in what became known as 'spatial Keynesianism' (discussed in Chapter 8). Industrial decline in Scotland, Wales and northern England led the Conservatives to add a regional dimension to their new-found economic interventionism in the early 1960s, and this was elaborated and expanded by Labour governments up to 1979. While initially this tied in the peripheral parts more strongly to the Union, in the longer run it reinforced their identity as economic units and the relevance of territory to public policy. So, what at the time was widely seen as state-wide uniformity in fact encompassed a new form of territorial brokerage and accommodation of the nations within the Union.

3
The Millennium Settlement

The Return of the National Question

The apotheosis of British unionism was from the 1930s to the 1960s, when the 'nationalities question' appeared as a thing of the past. Scotland and Wales were firmly anchored into British politics, while Northern Ireland was effectively insulated from the political mainstream in spite of flagrant violations of 'British' norms. Yet, from the 1970s, the issue came back on the political agenda across Great Britain and Ireland, albeit in different forms. Most scholars were taken aback at this apparent reversal of the modernist teleology. Some denied that it was real. Others claimed that the Union had been mere superstructure, bolstered by empire, and that once this skein was broken, it was natural there would be a reversion to pre-union identities. Both accounts ignore the way in which the nations of the United Kingdom were, if not invented, then profoundly shaped by the experience and structures of union.[1]

It is not that the nations were diverging in their economic and social structures. On the contrary, these were actually converging under common modernizing influences (for Scotland, see McCrone 2017). Nor was the return to the national question the product of relative deprivation at the periphery. Regional policies had helped Scotland, Wales and Northern Ireland catch up economically, a process that continued until the mid-1990s (see Chapter 8). In Scotland, rising support for self-government has historically been associated with relatively good times while depressions have heightened dependence on the centre (Keating 2009). Nationalism may, indeed, reflect a 'revolution of rising expectations' or dashed hopes rather than penury.

Nor were the nations diverging in *ethos* or values. It was not true that, as Weight (2002: 587) puts it: 'Nationalism also regained its appeal because the Scots and the Welsh rejected Thatcherism while most of England embraced it.' Scotland was not so different from England on these matters, and particularly resembled the north of England (Rosie and Bond 2007). Indeed, England

[1] See Judson (2016) for a similar argument about the Habsburg Empire Fusi (2000) on Spain.

State and Nation in the United Kingdom: The Fractured Union. Michael Keating, Oxford University Press (2021).
 DOI: 10.1093/oso/9780198841371.003.0003

was never converted wholly to the 'Thatcherite' agenda either (Crewe 1989), while the whole of the UK moved somewhat to the right under the New Labour Government after 1997 (Curtice and Ormston 2011). The same applies to social values. In Northern Ireland and Scotland, long considered to be more socially conservative, attitudes on the sensitive issues of abortion and gay rights have liberalized along with those in Great Britain (NatCen 2017; Gray et al. 2018; Knudsen 2016; McAlister et al. 2014). Attitudes to immigration remained similar, although hostility to immigration is correlated with *English* identity (Curtice and Montagu 2018).

The rise of nationalism cannot even be attributed, at least in a straightforward way, to the decline of British, and the rise of distinct national, identities. The national identities have always been there but, the majority of Irish Catholics excepted, have been compatible with wider British loyalties (Chapter 10). Rather these identities became more salient and politically relevant, providing new bases for political community or *demos*.

Far from representing a regression to pre-modern times, the territorial constitutional conflicts that resumed in the 1970s signified a reaction to the crisis of the national development state of the post-war years and the emergence of different paths to the latest phase of modernization. This was part of a broader European process of reconfiguration and rescaling of the modern interventionist welfare state and revival in modern form of older territorial identities (Keating 2013). Regionalism and peripheral nationalism, previously dismissed as backward-looking and conservative, were adopted by progressives, constitutional reformers and the left. In the United Kingdom, the frame of reference for political and social issues was being rebuilt around the constituent nations. The pattern of party competition in Scotland and Wales, which tilts to the centre-left, has further structured and channelled attitudes (Brown et al. 1999).

The UK developmental state experienced a crisis from the 1970s, with a turn away from the governing formula of the post-war years, which had combined full employment with welfare expansion and a commitment to territorial balance. The Thatcher Government from 1979 marked a further shift both in rhetoric and substantive policy. It is not that the welfare state was abolished but it ceased to expand its scope, while Conservative governments largely abandoned ideas of social citizenship in favour of the notion of welfare as residual provision for the deserving poor. Diversionary regional policy was run down in favour of the concept of regional competitiveness in which regions would find their own place in the international division of labour (Chapter 8). Yet there was a paradox in statecraft from the 1980s. On the one hand, most state industries and utilities were privatized and the welfare state denigrated. On the other hand, a strident British nationalism was deployed against the 'enemies' without and within (Thatcher 1984). This was a nationalism without a state foundation but with lingering imperial memes. A striking instance is the picture of Prime Minister Margaret Thatcher protesting against the removal of the Union flag from the aircraft of British Airways, a business she herself had privatized. In the face of these changes, the constituent parts of the United Kingdom could not just revert to the past because they themselves had been constructed as modern nations within the Union. Now they were being reconstructed in new conditions.

So, support for the welfare state in Scotland and Wales was expressed in a project of territorial defence. By the end of the century, the nationalist parties of the periphery were among the strongest defenders of the British post-war welfare settlement. There was a reaction to state-centralized policies for territorial management and regional development, which had raised the salience of territorial development without fully accomplishing economic integration. In Scotland and Wales, the British parties faced competition from territorial rivals challenging their claims to look after local interests; the first signs were by-election victories for the Scottish National Party and Plaid Cymru in the 1960s.

Modernization in Northern Ireland saw the rise of a new Catholic, university-educated middle class, influenced by universal ideas about human rights, which confronted the reality of a liberal British state unable or unwilling to enforce those rights. A movement demanding that the Union live up to its own *ethos*, however, quickly reverted to nationalism, questioning the Union itself and demanding unification of the island. As in the previous epoch, it divided into a moderate wing, open to compromise both with local unionism and Britain, and a radical republican element committed to violent struggle.

In Scotland, the main indicator of dissent was a rise in support for the Scottish National Party, prompting both the Labour and Conservative parties to look again at the idea of devolution. While SNP voting had initially been attributed to protest against the two-party system, it consolidated over time and eventually made inroads into the historically Labour-supporting working class in the industrial areas. Scottish identity, which had long been ubiquitous, came to take on a political meaning. The Welsh nationalist party, Plaid Cymru, gained some seats by concentrating its vote in the Welsh-speaking heartlands but was initially not a serious challenger to the British parties. Over time, however, it extended its support on the basis of a territorial nationalism which was only sporadically committed to independence but otherwise fell into the old Home Rule tradition. In spite of Labour's post-war commitment to centralization, that tradition was kept alive in sectors of the party in Scotland and Wales, allowing it to be recovered when needed (Jones and Keating 1985).

As in the late nineteenth century, the subsequent constitutional debate lasted for some three decades. Devolution legislation in the 1970s was frustrated by political opposition, only to gain acceptance at the end of the century in similar form to the original proposals. It was the Conservatives under Edward Heath who were the first to respond with the Declaration of Perth (1968) and proposals from a former prime minister, Alec Douglas Home (1970), which sought to square the circle of Westminster supremacy by proposing an elected assembly to take the second-reading debates on Scottish bills. It did not survive its first encounter with the Scottish Conservative rank and file at their 1970 conference. The Labour Government followed from 1969, setting up the Kilbrandon Commission[2] to examine devolution, which, after some party manoeuvring, led the returning Labour Government of 1974 to bring forward devolution proposals for Scotland and Wales.[3] A Scottish Assembly elected by first-past-the-post, would have legislative powers over a list of fields and an executive responsible to the assembly. A Welsh Assembly would have weaker powers than its Scottish counterparts and no legislative competence.

Separately, in 1973, an agreement was reached for Northern Ireland, involving the moderate nationalist and unionist parties. The Sunningdale Agreement provided the blueprint for all subsequent efforts in constitution-making for Northern Ireland, with an Assembly elected by proportional representation, a power-sharing Executive, all-Ireland institutions and a provision for Irish unification by referendum.

None of these efforts succeeded. Scottish devolution was sabotaged by opposition within the Labour Party, which had never been entirely convinced of the case. The critical moves were amendments requiring a referendum and support from at least 40 per cent of the entire electorate, and a campaign by hostile Labour MPs who presented devolution as a concession to separatists and as a way of dividing the working class. The Conservative Party, after its

[2] Kilbrandon was in fact the second chair of the commission.

[3] A first bill, covering both Scotland and Wales, was withdrawn after the Government had failed to secure a timetable motion, so opening it to filibuster.

flirtation with devolution under Heath, reverted to its historic unionism.[4] On both the Labour and Conservative sides, the anti-devolution arguments were the familiar ones about separatism and the impossibility of devolution in a unitary state. Devolution was endorsed in the Scottish referendum by 52 per cent, but a low turnout meant that the 40 per cent threshold was not met. In Wales, it was defeated by 80 per cent.

Sunningdale was an effort to unite the moderates in Northern Ireland and isolate the extremes. Supported by part of the Ulster Unionist Party and the moderate nationalist Social Democratic and Labour Party, it did not include Sinn Féin, the political wing of the Irish Republican Army (IRA). The Democratic Unionists were also opposed, as were loyalist militants, who were responsible for its demise through a political workers' strike. Sunningdale also had the effect of severing the formal alliance between Ulster Unionists and the British Conservative Party, which had existed since the 1880s so that the UK parties never again included Northern Irish MPs.[5]

Towards Devolution

Twenty-five years later, circumstances had changed. Support for devolution in Scotland was consolidated during almost two decades of Conservative Government, which represented the longest time that Scotland and Wales had been governed continuously by a party for which they had not voted. Home rulers and nationalists played on the image of Scotland as a social democratic space exposed to neo-liberalism from the south, consolidating support for devolution on the left. The Campaign for a Scottish Assembly (later Parliament), while not a prominent public presence, won over key sections of civil society. Under its inspiration a Scottish Constitutional Convention drew in civil society including churches, trades unions, small business interests and local government. It also brought in the Labour and Liberal Democrat parties, which themselves were looking at prospects for collaboration in the future; a key concession since 1979 was that the Parliament would be elected by proportional representation. After Labour's big election victory in 1997, it brought forward a scheme of devolution, which won the support of

[4] During the debate and referendum on the Scotland Bill, the Conservatives had promised unspecified better devolution proposals but dropped these when they came into government in 1979.

[5] A much later attempt (in 2010) to run joint candidatures between the Conservatives and Ulster Unionists failed when they did not win a single seat, helping to consolidate the hegemony of the DUP in the unionist community.

three-quarters of voters at a referendum, and a Scottish Parliament was elected in 1999.

There was no such broad consensus in Wales but a pro-devolution element within the Labour Party had succeeded in restoring the commitment to the party's programme and 1997 manifesto, albeit in a similar weak form as in 1978. In the referendum, it gained a slim mandate of just over 50 per cent of voters on a turnout of just over 50 per cent. A National Assembly for Wales, elected by proportional representation, was established in 1999.

A breakthrough in Northern Ireland came about at the same time but was the product of longer evolution as successive governments had sought to revive devolution since the failure of 1973–4. The key was drawing in the extremes of nationalism and republicanism into a settlement on very similar lines to that which they had rejected in 1973.[6] While the Scottish and Welsh settlements sought to bind those nations into the Union, the Northern Ireland provisions left the *telos* open. From the Anglo-Irish Agreement of 1985, the UK had recognized the Government of Ireland as a partner in the venture, in spite of unionist objections. In the Downing Street Declaration of 1993, it declared that it had no selfish strategic or economic interest in Northern Ireland. Both governments agreed that the future of Northern Ireland was for the people of Northern Ireland to decide by majority.

This 'Millennium settlement' was not a general territorial regime for the United Kingdom, with a single *telos*, but three dispensations, which responded to three different challenges. Scotland was given a Parliament with primary legislative powers over all matters that were not expressly reserved to Westminster (the reserved powers model). Wales initially got a National Assembly, with only administrative and secondary legislative powers over a prescribed range of matters (the defined powers model). In both Scotland and Wales, proportional representation was used, with a mixed system of constituency and regional members, the latter balanced to reflect the overall vote.

The Northern Ireland settlement (negotiated in the Good Friday or Belfast Agreement), addressed three dimensions of conflict: the relationship between the two communities in Northern Ireland; the relationship of Northern Ireland with Great Britain in the United Kingdom; and the relationship of Northern Ireland with the Republic.[7] The internal government of Northern Ireland is organized according to consociational principles (McGarry and

[6] Seamus Mallon of the moderate nationalist SDLP famously described it as 'Sunningdale for slow learners'.

[7] Rather confusingly, it was agreed that the Republic of Ireland would henceforth be known as 'Ireland'.

O'Leary 2006). The Assembly is elected by Single Transferable Vote, and members are invited (but not obliged) to designate themselves as nationalist or unionist. The Executive must include representatives of both, with a First Minister and Deputy First Minister of equal status, expected to be drawn from the respective communities. The reserved powers model is used so that the Assembly has legislative competence over matters not kept to Westminster.

Recognition of the all-Ireland aspirations of nationalists was provided by island-wide institutions, including a North–South Ministerial Council, with a remit to take forward cooperation in a range of policy issues. For members of the legislatures there is a North–South Inter-Parliamentary Association. To secure the east–west dimension, a British–Irish Council brings together representatives of both the Irish and Westminster governments, together with those of Northern Ireland, Scotland, Wales and, for good measure, the Channel Islands and the Isle of Man. There is a parallel Assembly of parliamentarians. A British–Irish Intergovernmental Conference, replacing the Anglo-Irish Conference founded under the 1985 Anglo-Irish Agreement, links the UK and Irish governments. While the UK explicitly accepted that Northern Ireland could unify with the south, the Republic of Ireland abandoned its assertion of sovereignty over the North, although not the aspiration to unity by consent.

Rather than seeking to forge a common identity, the settlement allowed citizens of Northern Ireland to adopt identities—including Irish, British and Northern Irish and combinations of them—at will. Northern Irish institutions, including the Assembly, the police and public services, were emptied of specific national connotations so as to serve the whole of a divided community. In this way, it was hoped that divisive identity issues could be parked, allowing a focus on economic and social issues and, in the longer term, the fading of ethno-national tensions.

Devolution Design

Home Rule as it was called in the nineteenth century, or devolution as it became in the twentieth, is a British invention, combining elements of the unitary and the federal state.[8] Its peculiar feature is to hand down power to the nations without infringing the sovereignty and supremacy of the

[8] It is not the only one in Europe, but both Spain's *Estado de las Autonomías* and the German Weimar Republic were embedded in written and codified constitutions.

Westminster Parliament. How this circle can be squared is the subject of the next chapter. All the schemes proposed the reservation of core state powers (what used to be called 'Imperial' matters), including the Crown and foreign and defence policy. All assumed the maintenance of economic union across the United Kingdom and reserved trade policy, with only the 1912 Irish bill allowing for customs controls. The early Home Rule provisions were premised on the Victorian state, and debates featured issues of temperance, land reform and Church disestablishment (Kane 2015). The assumptions had been that Home Rule governments would pay their own way. Although there were provisions in some of the early bills for adjusting the financial contributions according to taxable capacity or a 'just' allocation, these were never fully worked out.

By the twentieth century, emerging welfare issues started to cloud the old distinction between imperial and domestic matters. Already in the early 1900s, the issue of social welfare arose after pensions and national insurance were introduced by the Liberal Government from 1906 and came to be seen as key elements of social citizenship. They were to be reserved provisionally in early proposals for Ireland but devolved in Scotland. By the 1970s, the rise of the modern regulatory state raised broader issues of economic and social union, discussed in Chapters 8 and 9.

The legislation of 1998 drew the line at a different place from the old Home Rule schemes. Social welfare in the form of cash payments was reserved, in line with modern ideas about distributive functions operating at the higher level (see Chapter 9). The exception was in Northern Ireland, where the legislation essentially copied the earlier Stormont provision although, in practice, the UK Government had paid the deficit in welfare funds for Northern Ireland under Stormont.

In contrast to earlier schemes, the Millennium settlements devolved almost no taxes. The Scotland Act allowed the Scottish Parliament to raise or lower the basic rate of income tax by up to three pence in the pound, but this was never used. The initial draft of the Northern Ireland Act copied in old Stormont provisions allowing for tax powers but these were removed at the request of all parties. Instead, the Barnett formula, used before devolution to distribute money to the three territories was rolled forward. This provided for each to receive a population-based share of any increase or decrease in spending in England on equivalent services. These moneys were then put into a block grant, which the devolved bodies could spend freely. Barnett is based on practice rather than principle, and critics have argued for decades that it should be replaced by a system based on needs and resources. It suited the

UK Treasury, however, as an effective measure of controlling spending commitments and it was impossible to agree on an alternative.

Over the years, more taxation powers have been conceded, piecemeal and in different ways. Scotland gained tax powers in two stages and, with the Scotland Act (2016) controls income tax on earned income and some smaller taxes, and is assigned half of Value Added Tax. There are provisions for Wales to move to collect more of its own taxes and for Northern Ireland to set Corporation Tax. The implications of all this are discussed in Chapters 8 and 9.

By subtraction from the reserved powers, the devolved sphere includes education, health, social services, environment, local government, housing, agriculture and fisheries and, in Scotland and Northern Ireland, criminal law, justice and policing.

There have been few provisions for equal citizenship or human rights in the various devolution proposals. Reflecting the issues of the time, all the early bills included strong provisions prohibiting discrimination on grounds of religion and, in Ireland and Wales, prohibiting state establishment of religion. In the Millennium settlement, the matter of rights was entrusted to the European Convention for the Protection of Human Rights and Fundamental Freedoms, which is enforceable directly on devolved issues in the devolved territories. Courts can strike down legislation in these domains, but in England and on reserved matters can only invite Westminster to change an offending law.

The various bills have all provided for an expansion of judicial review of government but without encroaching on the omnicompetence of Westminster. In the Home Rule proposals, disputes on whether the devolved bodies were acting within their competences were to be referred to the Judicial Committee of the Privy Council. The Millennium legislation made the same provision, and in 2009 this task was transferred to the new Supreme Court of the United Kingdom. Devolved legislation can be referred to the Court by the UK or devolved law officers, or can be raised in the course of any ordinary court proceedings. The restriction, however, only operates in one direction. The UK Parliament can still legislate in areas of devolved competence and retains its old authority unchanged.

True to British constitutional tradition, some of the most difficult issues were not subject to institutional resolution but left to practice and convention. The main vehicle for squaring the circle of devolved powers and retained Westminster supremacy is the Legislative Consent (or Sewel)[9] Convention.

[9] After the minister who introduced it to the Scotland Act.

This provides that Westminster will not 'normally' legislate in devolved matters without the consent of the devolved legislature concerned. First formalized in a Memorandum of Understanding, this was put into statute in the Scotland Act (2016) and Wales Act (2017). By agreed extension, Westminster does not legislate to change the powers of the devolved bodies without their consent. The UK Government may devolve powers by statutory order, also subject to consent, and can take back powers, also subject to consent. None of these, however, are binding on Westminster. It can still legislate in devolved fields and, if the devolved legislature should resist, can make its own law a 'protected enactment', bringing it into the reserved field. Westminster's sovereignty and supremacy are thus unabridged, subject only to the power of consent convention, whose status is unclear (Chapter 4).

Nomenclature is important. While the historic Home Rule proposals had envisaged devolved parliaments and Northern Ireland had a Parliament under the Stormont regime, the 1978 Acts would have given 'assemblies', marking their non-sovereign status. Pressure from the devolution movement in the 1990s introduced the title of Scottish Parliament for the 1998 legislation. Wales had to wait until 2020 for the National Assembly of Wales to become the Welsh Parliament/Senedd. Neither Scotland nor Wales was initially given a government; instead, there were 'Executives'. In the event, both Welsh and Scottish Executives relabelled themselves as 'Government', a change later recognized in statute. Northern Ireland nomenclature is even more sensitive and Assembly and Executive were chosen by agreement with the parties, to distance the new institution from the legacy of Stormont and make it clear that nobody was arguing for the province to be sovereign.

Dynamic Effects

Devolution thus came about in the three territories with the common aim of securing a new equilibrium in the Union by lessening central control. It also represented a historic compromise between unionism and peripheral nationalism, but in different ways. The aim in Scotland and Wales was to secure a new consensus in the constitutional middle ground, where public opinion appeared to be concentrated. In Northern Ireland, it was to embrace opposite ends of a polarized spectrum without either having to abandon its longer-term ambitions (*telos*). The outcome was more complex.

Scottish nationalists, who had long divided between 'fundamentalists' and 'gradualists' or pragmatists (Mitchell et al. 2012; Lynch 2002) could now unite on the next stage in their constitutional journey towards independence. On the other side, Home Rulers opposed to independence could unite with unionists who were now reconciled to devolution, in a redefinition of unionism. Yet before long, a new middle ground emerged around the idea of 'devolution max', a more thoroughgoing form of Home Rule. When the SNP formed a government in 2007 and gained an absolute majority in the Scottish Parliament in 2011, the issue was joined and, with the agreement of the UK Conservative Government, a referendum was staged in 2014 on the 'clear question' of independence, excluding 'devolution-max' options. The campaign saw support for independence climb to 45 per cent and broke the old party system as Labour sunk in subsequent elections to third place and the SNP established an ascendancy. The constitutional issue thus became the principal cleavage in Scottish politics. Yet the middle ground had not collapsed. During the referendum campaign, the Yes side adopted what critics dubbed 'independence-lite', retaining close links with the UK. They even appropriated the vocabulary of union, arguing that Scotland was in six unions—political, monetary, monarchical, European, defence and social—and proposed to withdraw only from the first (Keating and McEwen 2017). The No side, for their part, suggested that they were open to some kind of devolution-max.

This was the standard unionist response to the nationalist challenge. After the SNP's election victory in 2007 they set up the (Calman) Commission on Scottish Devolution (2008), leading to the 2012 Scotland Act. Following the referendum, there was an all-party commission (the Smith Commission) whose recommendations on devolution of tax and welfare benefits were carried through in the 2016 Scotland Act. These may have slowed the movement of opinion towards independence but did not stop it (Chapter 10).

Welsh devolution also deepened, less because of separatist pressures than the institutional dynamics of the system itself. It rapidly gained acceptance (Chapter 10) but the initial system proved so dysfunctional that there was a strong incentive to move towards the Scottish model through a series of acts in 2006, 2014 and 2017, and a referendum in 2011. There was also some fiscal devolution, although Welsh politicians, conscious of the economic weakness, were wary. At the same time, the Labour Party in Wales started to develop ideas of cooperative federalism which, recognizing Wales' weakness and dependence on England, would enhance the role of the smaller nations in a renewed union (Jones 2014). The nationalists of Plaid Cymru, for their part, came out for independence, but this looked more like confederalism within Europe than the classical nation-state.

Northern Irish devolution has rarely been seen as part of a general reform, as opposed to it being used to support either positive or negative lessons for Scotland (Walker 2010). The 2009 settlement was intended to accommodate opposed teleological visions and was steeped in 'constructive ambiguity' (Powell 2008) but, for the first time, secured government legitimacy across the communities. Yet, while it committed nationalists, republicans and the Government of Ireland to respect the Union as long as the majority in Northern Ireland wanted to keep it, the main opposition came from the unionist side. Not until the St Andrews Agreement of 2006, did the Democratic Unionist Party (DUP) come fully on board, and popular rejection was larger among unionists, who appeared to experience an acute ontological insecurity for their future as a community. The post-agreement period also saw the moderate parties (Ulster Unionists and SDLP) overtaken by the more radical DUP and Sinn Féin. The stipulation for cooperation and concurrent majorities for important questions and the requirement for the purposes of government formation[10] ensure that community will remain the basis for political participation and power. Critics (Wilford and Wilson 2006), have argued that this is an intrinsic problem with consociationalism—that it polarizes the citizenry on ethnic grounds and encourages ethnic outbidding. Defenders of consociationalism (McGarry and O'Leary 2006, 2016; O'Leary 2019c) have disagreed, arguing that this is the only way to manage divided societies and that, rightly designed, it does not prevent other parties entering the political arena. Mistrust between the parties remained and crises were triggered by issues close to the identity concerns of the two communities, including language rights. Although few people in Northern Ireland have Irish as a first language, this became a touchstone issue for republicans; to assuage unionists, the dialects of the region were standardized and promoted as 'Ulster Scots'. Another sensitive issue is collective memories and dealing with the legacies of the Troubles. Power-sharing devolution in Northern Ireland was marked by regular interruptions, notably between 2002 and 2007 and 2017 and 2020.

The one part of the Union to be largely unaffected by devolution was England. The idea of Home Rule All Round was not pursued and, in contrast to the 1970s, there was little opposition to devolution from the regions of England. There was the occasional grumble about the perennial West Lothian Question, the anomaly that Scottish MPs can vote on purely English matters

[10] Members of the Northern Ireland Assembly are not obliged to designate themselves as unionist or nationalists but, if they do not do so, they are not taken into account on government formation.

(discussed in Chapter 5) and about the distribution of finance, but these did not represent opposition to self-government for the smaller nations. One section of the Labour Party pursued the option of devolution for the English regions (as they had in the 1970s) but, after this was rejected in a referendum in the North East in 2004, the idea was dropped. Local government in England was then detached from the wider issue of union.

A striking feature of the new territorial settlement was that, while there was radical change at the periphery, almost nothing changed at the centre. The new dispensation thus retained a historic element of UK statecraft and territorial management, dealing with the peripheral territories each in its own way. Politics in the smaller nations could be partially hived off, leaving the centre intact. There was no territorially based second chamber of Parliament, while the fairly clear division of competences meant that the need for joint policy-making was minimalized. A smooth transition in Scotland and Wales was helped by building on the existing institutions of administrative devolution. The civil service itself remained unified across Great Britain, although the historic Northern Ireland civil service remained distinct. On the other hand, the regular contacts that had existed before devolution gradually atrophied, and Whitehall departments showed a tendency to forget that the devolved administrations existed. This was exacerbated by the weakness of intergovernmental mechanisms such as are found in other devolved and federal systems. There was provision for Joint Ministerial Committees to discuss common matters and resolve disputes, but the absence of disputes in the early years meant that these fell into disuse and were only revived after the SNP came to power in Scotland. The only one that really worked was that on Europe, where it was necessary to agree a common line in advance of EU negotiations. This dimension is further discussed in Chapter 5.

Nor was party politics at the centre much affected by devolution. The Scottish and Welsh arms of the British parties failed to assert a distinct territorial interest at Westminster and, unlike in Spain, the distinct parties of the periphery were, with one exception,[11] left out of parliamentary alliances at Westminster. Over time, the British parties, especially the Conservatives, lost touch with politics in Scotland and their political instincts there were dulled.

[11] Between 2017 and 2019 a minority Conservative Government had a confidence and supply agreement with the Democratic Unionist Party of Northern Ireland.

The Open Constitution

Devolution, like Home Rule before it, is an ambiguous concept (Casanas Adam 2017; Tierney 2018). It both disperses power and retains authority at the centre. It represents a compromise among potentially incompatible choices or *telos*, and there are numerous abeyances and points of contestation. For, some, nothing essential has changed to the unitary state, founded on parliamentary sovereignty and supremacy, but decentralized to allow a degree of policy variation and local accountability. Others see in it the germs of a federal future on the lines of the old Home Rule All Round dream, or at least discern a federalizing trend which, while accepting that the UK is not a federation, sees it as based on federal principles. For others again, it represents a renegotiation of union for a post-sovereigntist era, with each nation belonging to the Union by consent and with the right to negotiate its own place with in it.

This ambivalence does not make the United Kingdom unique. While some constitutions may be based on shared *demos*, *telos* and *ethos*, others are there precisely to manage foundational differences. Such constitutions can be seen as 'incomplete contracts' (Montolio and Turati 2017), leaving key issues to be negotiated in time. The devolution settlement was consciously framed within the existing constitutional framework, which leaves a good deal to convention rather than written prescription. This, too, is not exceptional. Foley (2012) has argued that even written, codified constitutions rely heavily on silences, conventions and understandings.

For some critics, the lack of overall design, or agreed foundational principles is a weakness in the Millennium project, inviting conflict over the nature of the Union. The fraught issue of sovereignty, which had derailed previous Home Rule proposals, was dealt with in summary fashion, by declaring that nothing in the various acts affected the sovereignty of the UK Parliament and its ability to legislate in all spheres, a matter that is in fact contested. A convincing argument, however, can be made that, had an overall settlement been a necessary condition, then devolution might never have happened. In this view, the settlement is a necessary adjustment to the terms of union but not necessarily a definitive solution. The UK is not a state, unitary or federal, but a union, and as such does not necessarily need a hard core or sovereignty or purpose.

Successive UK governments by and large sought to take devolution issues off the political agenda and there was little concern in England about policy divergence at the periphery except when it looked as though the Scots or Welsh were getting social benefits of which the English were deprived. Even the West Lothian Question attracted only sporadic attention. Northern Ireland politics revolved around the difficulties in power-sharing rather than the constitutional status of the province, and neither the UK nor the Irish Government was interested in raising the latter issue. In Scotland, the first two parliaments (1999–2007) were controlled by a Labour–Liberal Democrat coalition aiming to stabilize the settlement and largely avoiding disputes with the contemporaneous Labour UK Government (1997–2010). The succeeding SNP Scottish governments were more assertive of Scotland's place but their principal concern was Scottish independence rather than reform and clarification of the UK constitution. In the meantime, they tended to prefer bilateral relationships with Westminster rather than federalizing reforms that could enhance their influence but bring them more within the embrace of Westminster. The exception is the Welsh Labour Government, which is perhaps the only unambiguously pro-devolution government in the United Kingdom and has sought to move towards a form of cooperative federalism in which Wales would be recognized as a full partner in union. Former First Minister Carwyn Jones (2014), regularly called for a new settlement as a union or partnership of four nations, defending the Union while criticizing the existing settlement. Scottish Labour, having taken the lead devolution in the 1990s, fell behind, seemingly fearing that any further decentralization would play into the nationalists' agenda.

While not part of a grand design, devolution did coincide with a series of constitutional reforms at the turn of the Millennium within a broader movement for modernization. In 2009 a Supreme Court took over the appellate jurisdiction of the House of Lords as well as the constitutional role of the Judicial Committee of the Privy Council in relation to devolution. The European Convention for the Protection of Human Rights was incorporated into UK law so that courts could apply it directly although, in relation to non-devolved matters, Parliament still has the last word. The momentum for constitutional reform, however, soon ran out and, except for some minor changes at the end of the Labour Government, little more was done. Electoral reform was debated both under the Labour Government and the Conservative–Liberal Democrat Coalition (2010–15) but the main parties refused to budge. Debates about the royal prerogative came to little:[12] while reformers talked about the need for a written constitution, the movement never gripped the

[12] Although this was to generate a major case in the Supreme Court in 2019.

popular imagination. Reform of the House of Lords stopped with the removal of hereditary members and even ninety of those were retained, chosen by their peers, alongside twenty-six bishops of the Church of England. Devolution thus recalls Tom Nairn's (1994) image of the UK constitution as the Advanced Passenger Train, a British invention of the 1970s intended to transform the railways, while running on existing track. The path of gradual evolution, however, was to be disrupted dramatically by the decision, following the referendum of 2016, that the United Kingdom should leave the European Union.

4

The Sovereignty Conundrum

Parliamentary Sovereignty

The devolution settlements cut the Gordian knot which had prevented devolution since Gladstone's time, the difficulty of national legislatures within a constitution based on parliamentary sovereignty. It simply asserted that the sovereignty of Westminster was unabridged. This followed the precedent of successive Home Rule and devolution bills back to the nineteenth century. While Gladstone's first Irish Home Rule Bill of 1886 had no such clause, Gladstone (1886) took care to distinguish it from Repeal and to assert continued Westminster sovereignty. All subsequent Home Rule and devolution bills for Ireland, Scotland and Wales[1] included assertions of the continued sovereignty and supremacy of Westminster, and sometimes explicitly stated that Westminster legislation would automatically override that of the devolved legislatures even in devolved fields:

> The power and authority of the Imperial Parliament shall in no wise be diminished or restrained by anything herein contained (Scotland, 1892); Nothing in this Act shall affect the powers of the Imperial Parliament with regard to Scotland (Scotland, 1899: subject always to the paramount control of the Imperial Parliament (Scotland, 1900, 1906 preamble); the supreme power and authority of the Parliament of the United Kingdom shall remain unaffected and undiminished over all persons (Scotland, 1914, 1919, 1922, 1924); the supreme power and authority of the Parliament of the United Kingdom shall remain unaffected and undiminished over all persons, matters, and things within His Majesty's Dominions (Ireland, 1912); Where any Act…deals with any matter with respect to which the Irish Parliament have power to make laws which is dealt with by any Act of the Parliament of the United Kingdom passed after the passing of this Act and extending to Ireland, the Act of the Irish Parliament shall be read subject to the Act of the

[1] With the exception of the Scotland Bill introduced in 1926. 1927 and 1928, which provided for Dominion status.

State and Nation in the United Kingdom: The Fractured Union. Michael Keating, Oxford University Press (2021).
 DOI: 10.1093/oso/9780198841371.003.0004

> Parliament of the United Kingdom, and so far as it is repugnant to that Act, but no further, shall be void (Ireland, 1922); This section does not affect the power of the Parliament of the United Kingdom to make laws for Scotland/ Wales/ Northern Ireland.
>
> (Scotland Act 1998/ Wales Act 1998/ Northern Ireland Act 1998).

This follows the orthodox, 'Westminster' or empirical account of authority, according to which the sovereignty of the Monarch-in-Parliament is the supreme *fact*, which brooks no argument or question. It is associated with A. V. Dicey, who drew on Blackstone and Coke (Wade 1959) to assert that '[t]he principle of parliamentary sovereignty means neither more nor less than this, namely that Parliament thus defined has, under the English constitution, the right to make or unmake any law whatever; and, further, that no person or body is recognised by the law of England as having a right to override or set aside the legislation of Parliament' (Dicey 1959: 39). There is no distinction of laws between those that are constitutional and those that merely state public policy or, as Dicey (1959) famously said, between the Dentists Act (1878) and the Act of Union with Scotland. Law, for Dicey, was that which judges will enforce (Walters 2012). Judges in turn do not enquire into how Parliament makes the laws but proceed according to the 'rule of recognition'. The argument has been played out in two contexts: over interpretations of the historic unions and whether they did secure pre-union rights against Parliament; and in the interpretation of modern developments, including devolution, human rights provisions and membership of the European Union.

The empirical claims to parliamentary sovereignty is a powerful doctrine but an intellectually superficial and precarious one as soon as it is challenged. Critics have long argued that it is a mere tautology and begs the question of where Parliament gets its authority from. Putting supremacy clauses into devolution legislation would surely be redundant, as parliamentary authority cannot be abridged in any case. Indeed, a supremacy clause was deleted during the passage of the 1978 Scotland Act by an alliance of SNP MPs who did not want Westminster to be sovereign, and unionists who regarded the clause as redundant and potentially dangerous in suggesting that supremacy was somehow dependent on that Act (Keating and Lindley 1981).

When parliamentary sovereignty is brought into question, its defenders may simply dig in and state that is an empirical fact; or they may fall back on deeper foundational arguments. This leads away from simple empirical claims to wider epistemic reasoning, drawing on a number of sources to encompass historical arguments about the origins of claims; logical reasoning about consistency and the coherence of the system; and normative argumentation. As soon as the argument moves onto this field, however, an opening is presented for alternative accounts, also based on epistemic reasoning, which question the simplicities of parliamentary sovereignty. Recent challenges, including devolution, human rights law and membership of the European Union, have given rise to numerous such arguments.

For parliamentary supremacists, the main historical source is the experience of the English Parliament, traced back to ancient times through the Tudor revolution to the struggles between Crown and Parliament in the seventeenth century. One objection to this is that those struggles were actually in the name of a broader conception of common law from which both parliamentary and monarchical authority were said to derive. For our purposes, the main objection has been that English experience alone cannot be decisive for the Parliament of the United Kingdom created by the unions of 1707 and 1801. Dicey's (1959) casual reference to the 'constitution of England' may have been a typical case of using England as a synecdoche for the United Kingdom, but was revealing. Critics have pointed out that the old Scottish Parliament was never fully sovereign. Notably, it had never established supremacy over the Established Church which, under the doctrine of the 'twa kingdomes' had emerged from the seventeenth-century struggles outwith the control of the state. Therefore, the Scottish Parliament could not have transferred complete sovereignty to the new Parliament of Great Britain. Dicey and Rait (1920: 239) countered that '[t]he legislative and ultimate executive power in Scotland was transferred from the Parliament of Scotland, which had never been either in theory or in fact a supreme or sovereign body, to the Parliament of Great Britain, which inherited both the tradition and, in legislation, the practice of supreme or sovereign authority'. Not everyone has been convinced, because the Acts of Union with both Scotland and Ireland contained provisions that were explicitly stated to last for all time, including those securing the respective national churches.[2] It is true that some provisions have been violated, as in the contested re-imposition of lay patronage in the Church of Scotland (McLean 2010) or the disestablishment of the Church of Ireland (O'Day 2001), but this meant the provisions could not be enforced, not that they were invalid (Tierney 2004). The assumption in Scotland seems to have been that Scots law would continue to be developed by judges in Scotland, although the negotiators may have been remiss in not specifying a

[2] The Church of Ireland was merged with that of England with permanent establishment.

mechanism to ensure that this happened (Ford 2007). The argument has rumbled on ever since.

In 1953 Lord Cooper delivered a famous *obiter dictum* in the case of *MacCormick v Lord Advocate* at the Court of Session to the effect that, as the old Scottish Parliament was not fully sovereign, it could not have passed this feature to the new Parliament of Great Britain.[3] While both Cooper and Lord Russell dismissed the plea of John MacCormick, they reserved their position on how they might act if a real breach of the Treaty of Union were brought before them. TB Smith (1961) in his Hamlyn lectures argued that the Acts of Union provided something of a written constitution for a new state and raised the possibility that the courts might uphold their provisions against Parliament, while noting that so far they had refrained from entering the field. He expressly noted that Parliament as a whole could not represent the 'subjects in Scotland' referred to in the Acts.

Similar arguments have resonated in Ireland. The pre-Union Irish Parliament in its later days (Grattan's Parliament) repudiated Westminster supremacy and passed an Act of 1783 declaring that 'the right claimed by the people of Ireland to be bound only by laws enacted by his Majesty and the Parliament of that kingdom, in all cases whatever shall be, and is hereby declared to be established and ascertained for ever, and shall at no time be questioned or questionable' (Mansergh 2005). The Irish Repeal movements built on Grattan's legacy, with the Irish Parliament exercising co-equal authority with Westminster on the basis of an original sovereignty that was never given away.

[3] MacCormick had challenged the right of the Queen to use the title Elizabeth II in Scotland. The Court dismissed the case on the grounds that the matter came under the royal prerogative. Lord President Cooper (1953) commented:

> The principle of the unlimited sovereignty of Parliament is a distinctively English principle which has no counterpart in Scottish constitutional law. It derives its origin from Coke and Blackstone, and was widely popularised during the nineteenth century by Bagehot and Dicey, the latter having stated the doctrine in its classic form in his Law of the Constitution. Considering that the Union legislation extinguished the Parliaments of Scotland and England and replaced them by a new Parliament, I have difficulty in seeing why it should have been supposed that the new Parliament of Great Britain must inherit all the peculiar characteristics of the English Parliament but none of the Scottish Parliament, as if all that happened in 1707 was that Scottish representatives were admitted to the Parliament of England. That is not what was done. Further, the Treaty and the associated legislation, by which the Parliament of Great Britain was brought into being as the successor of the separate Parliaments of Scotland and England, contain some clauses which expressly reserve to the Parliament of Great Britain powers of subsequent modification, and other clauses which either contain no such power or emphatically exclude subsequent alteration by declarations that the provision shall be fundamental and unalterable in all time coming, or declarations of a like effect. I have never been able to understand how it is possible to reconcile with elementary canons of construction the adoption by the English constitutional theorists of the same attitude to these markedly different types of provisions.

These historical arguments for entrenched rights could be conservative and might have prevented such measures as the abolition of hereditary jurisdictions in Scotland after 1757 or disestablishment of the Church of Ireland. That opened another line of argument for parliamentary supremacists, focused on the progressive ends that it might serve. Dicey's argument that England represented a higher level of civilization need not detain us long, although there is still within unionism an idea that Britishness is morally superior to the *ethos* and values of the smaller nations (Chapter 7). The more potent argument is that parliamentary sovereignty is really a proxy for the sovereignty and supremacy of the people. Dicey (1959: 83) did recognize that, given the restricted franchise, this was not quite accurate, asserting that '[s]peaking roughly, the permanent wishes of the representative portion of the Parliament can hardly in the long run differ from the wishes of the English people, or at any rate of the electors'. As the franchise expanded, however, it became more plausible to use parliamentary sovereignty as a equivalent to popular sovereignty (Gordon 2015). This also reconciled the political left with the established constitution and the British state because it both democratized authority and strengthened it as a tool for social change (Jones and Keating 1985). The Labour Party was also historically suspicious of reform projects that constrained political power, especially if it placed power in the hands of judges. While much of the centre-left moved away from this position in the 1990s, embracing ideas of constitutional reform usually associated with the Liberal tradition, a section of the left has always clung to the doctrine of parliamentary sovereignty as a powerful tool for social change and an expression of democratic control (Ekins and Gee, 2017).

Yet, while the democratic basis of Parliament might give it a legitimacy denied to private interests or to the hereditary jurisdictions in Scotland, the same reasoning cannot be applied to underpin supremacy over other elected bodies such as the devolved legislatures from 1999. The UK devolutionary settlements themselves grew out of a democratizing impulse, which challenged the concentration of power. They were ratified by referendum and include elections by proportional representation in contrast to Westminster, where it is normal for a parliamentary majority to be sustained by a plurality (or even a minority) of the popular vote. Their democratic credentials could thus be considered better than those of Westminster and they are certainly not *demos*-constraining. The difficulty, rather, is the presence of multiple *demoi*, and the definition of the people in which popular sovereignty rests.

If parliamentary sovereignty is really a proxy for popular sovereignty, then the ultimate test of authority would logically be the referendum. Dicey himself went down this road, although less as a matter of principle than in order to frustrate Irish Home Rule even though it had been approved by Parliament. Yet the referendum raises the issue of the *demos* in even starker form. Dicey was himself caught in this trap, although his habit of using England as a synonym both for Great Britain and for the United Kingdom does not clarify matters. In his earlier writings, he seems to identify the people with the whole electorate of Parliament. Yet when it came to resisting Home Rule, he suggested that it would need concurrent majorities in both Ireland and 'England' or 'Great Britain':

> For such a rearrangement Great Britain and Ireland must in fairness, no less than in logic, be treated as independent parties. Whether you make a Union or remodel a Union between two countries the satisfaction of both parties to the treaty is essential. Till England is satisfied the new constitution lacks moral satisfaction. (Dicey 1913; 120)

This takes us from unitarism back to the idea of contractual union. Dicey also resorted to arguments of *realpolitik* when insisting that England, as the largest and most powerful part of the Union, must always prevail and that the Irish are not fit for self-government.

This is no longer a purely abstract argument as, since the late twentieth century, the referendum has become part of the standard tool kit of constitutional reform (Tierney 2009) deployed in relation to the European Union (1975 and 2016), Scottish devolution (1979 and 1997), Scottish independence (2014), Welsh devolution (1979, 1997 and 2011), Northern Ireland (1972 and 1998) and electoral reform (2011). Yet, even though there is now legislation covering the conduct of referendums, there is no rule of recognition of the results. Some of them have mechanisms for translating the results into practice, giving them a mandatory appearance. Others are more clearly non-binding. Referendums have had varied electorates, sometimes covering the whole United Kingdom and at other times its constituent parts, recognizing the existence of different constitutional constituencies or *demoi*. The European Union referendum of 2016, in which two of the constituent parts of the UK voted to leave and two to remain provoked fierce arguments over the relevant *demos*.

Conceding Sovereignty

In fact, Parliament has frequently given up sovereignty over territory in the process of winding up the Empire. Initially, it was argued that the self-government statutes in the Dominions were merely a form of devolution and that, in theory at least, Westminster could resume its authority. Arguments continued in the various Dominion Conferences, where the Irish Free State was often in the lead in pressing for a wide understanding of self-government. The Statute of Westminster (1931) appeared to give up authority over the self-governing Dominions but a legal pedant could still argue that the British Parliament could repeal that as well. In any case, the Statute still contained provisions for Parliament to legislate for the Dominions in various ways, albeit with the consent of the relevant Dominion parliament. Over time, however, it was understood that the former Dominions (including Ireland) were independent and sovereign states. As it happened, even Dicey agreed that a sovereign parliament could surrender its sovereignty, but only by transferring power wholly or partly to a new sovereign body (Wade 1959).

UK political leaders have also made what, by international standards, are remarkable concessions on the right of the component nations to secede from the Union. Conservative Prime Minister Major (1993) declared that no nation could be kept in a union against its will, while his predecessor, Margaret Thatcher (1993: 624) conceded that

> [a]s a nation, they (the Scots) have an undoubted right to national self-determination; thus far they have exercised that right by joining and remaining in the Union. Should they determine on independence no English party or politician would stand in their way, however much we might regret their departure.

Prime Minister Theresa May (2019) said much the same thing. In 2012, Conservative Prime Minister David Cameron concluded the Edinburgh Agreement with the First Minister of Scotland, allowing a referendum on independence with a promise to respect the result. Subsequently, unionist politicians resisted another referendum, not on the ground that Scotland does not have right to self-determination but that the time is not right or that people do not want one. David Miller's (1995, 2000) argument that, because of their shared experiences, the nations do not have the moral right to secede thus finds little support in the political class.

The idea that Northern Ireland was free to leave the United Kingdom and unify with the rest of the island was implicit from the Treaty of 1922. The Ireland Act of 1949 repeated it in a negative way by stipulating that it could happen only with the assent of the Parliament of Northern Ireland. The Sunningdale agreement (1973) provided for a border poll. In the Downing

Street Declaration of 1983, the UK Government made a concession which, by international standards, is quite extraordinary:

> The Prime Minister, on behalf of the British Government, reaffirms that they will uphold the democratic wish of the greater number of the people of Northern Ireland on the issue of whether they prefer to support the Union or a sovereign united Ireland. On this basis, he reiterates, on the behalf of the British Government, that they have no selfish strategic or economic interest in Northern Ireland. Their primary interest is to see peace, stability and reconciliation established by agreement among all the people who inhabit the island, and they will work together with the Irish Government to achieve such an agreement, which will embrace the totality of relationships. The role of the British Government will be to encourage, facilitate and enable the achievement of such agreement over a period through a process of dialogue and co-operation based on full respect for the rights and identities of both traditions in Ireland. They accept that such agreement may, as of right, take the form of agreed structures for the island as a whole, including a united Ireland achieved by peaceful means on the following basis. The British Government agree that it is for the people of the island of Ireland alone, by agreement between the two parts respectively, to exercise their right of self-determination on the basis of consent, freely and concurrently given, North and South, to bring about a united Ireland, if that is their wish. They reaffirm as a binding obligation that they will, for their part, introduce the necessary legislation to give effect to this, or equally to any measure of agreement on future relationships in Ireland which the people living in Ireland may themselves freely so determine without external impediment. They believe that the people of Britain would wish, in friendship to all sides, to enable the people of Ireland to reach agreement on how they may live together in harmony and in partnership, with respect for their diverse traditions, and with full recognition of the special links and the unique relationship which exist between the peoples of Britain and Ireland.
>
> (http://cain.ulst.ac.uk/events/peace/docs/dsd151293.htm)

Later, the Good Friday Agreement provided for secession from the UK and unification with Ireland by local referendum. The case of secession thus appears clear, and nobody seems to have questioned whether the UK Parliament could legally have surrendered its sovereignty over Scotland had the 2014 referendum resulted in a vote for independence.

The matter of 'internal' self-determination, or whether the nations have the right to negotiate their own position within the Union, may be rather different. Major (1993) and Thatcher (1993) matched their acceptance of a hypothetical secession with an insistence that, if they remained in the UK, Scots must accept the rules; there was no right of unilateral devolution.[4] This seems slightly perverse, that unionists would accept the radical option but not the one that keeps the Union, but it is at least consistent in preserving the principle of national sovereignty. On this reasoning, devolution, when it came, was a gift of Westminster, not an act of self-determination. Once again, not everyone is convinced. Devolution was carried out by local referendum in the three territories, while clauses in the Scotland (2016) and Wales (2017) Acts, later stipulated that their legislatures could be abolished only by local referendum.

The arguments about this have become very confused. In 1989, the Scottish Constitutional Convention, composed of representatives of the Labour, Liberal Democrat and Green parties, but not the Scottish National Party, along with representatives of civil society, issued a Claim of Right insisting on 'the sovereign right of the Scottish people to determine the form of government best suited to their needs' (Dudley Edwards 1988). Yet, while all but one of the Scottish Labour MPs signed up to the Claim, the Scotland Act passed by the Labour Government in 1998 made it clear that sovereignty remained at Westminster. Tony Blair, in a Diceyan moment, even claimed that 'sovereignty remains with me as an English MP' (Brogan 1997). In 2012, the Labour and Liberal Democrat parties in the Scottish Parliament reaffirmed the 1989 Claim of Right which 'acknowledges the sovereign right of the Scottish people to determine the form of government best suited to their needs' (Scottish Parliament Official Report, 26-01-2012). The Conservatives voted against on the grounds that the only right the Scots had was to leave the UK, not to decide on their terms of continuing membership. By 2018, a motion presented in the House of Commons recognizing the Claim of Right of 1988 was accepted by all parties (Hansard, Vol. 644, 04-07-18). The unionist parties argued that the Scottish people had settled this issue in the referendums of 1997 and 2014 but in doing this they (perhaps unwillingly) conceded that the Union was not indivisible and that Scotland did constitute a political *demos*. Some said that the resolution was about devolution, which had been realized, so that it was no longer a live issue. Labour argued that it was time to talk about other things, although their shadow Secretary of State for Scotland did

[4] Gallagher's (2020) claim that accepting secession meant recognizing shared sovereignty is thus not germane. To the contrary it reinforces the traditional sovereignty doctrine.

say that a future Scottish Parliament would have the right to hold another independence referendum (Hansard Vol. 644, 04-07-18); this was later withdrawn under pressure from the party leadership.

The same ambivalence characterizes the settlement in Northern Ireland. UK Governments have insisted that Westminster sovereignty is unabridged, while nationalists claim that the polity of Northern Ireland is only legitimate under the conditions of the Good Friday Agreement (Coakley and Todd 2020). The renunciation by Ireland of its claim over the North was made on the understanding that it would have a role in setting the future of the province. Nationalists also claim that, as key parts of the GFA are in an international agreement deposited with the United Nations, it is entrenched against Westminster. Under the St Andrew's Agreement (2006) the UK Government surrendered its ability to suspend the self-governing institutions in Northern Ireland, a power which nationalists and the Irish Government had never accepted, although in theory Westminster could still use primary legislation to do so. More widely, it is argued the settlement was grounded in the fundamental principle of consent, built into the institutions, which should be used as a key for interpretation (McCrudden and Halberstam 2018).

These arguments have come in the context of more general questioning of the principle of parliamentary sovereignty. There was a lively debate about sovereignty during the UK's drawn-out efforts to join the (then) European Economic Community in the 1960s and 1970s. Claims by Eurosceptics that the matter was not discussed at the time are simply wrong, although it is true that UK governments did not defend the idea of shared sovereignty, and assured the public that the independence of the state was not threatened. The principle of the primacy of EU law had already been established by the treaties and judgments of the Court of Justice of the European Union (CJEU), meaning that a valid European law would take precedence over an existing UK law. This is, at a stretch, compatible with the view that UK sovereignty has not been breached, as it can be argued that the European Communities Act of 1972 delegated this power and, like the devolution statutes, it could be repealed. The more difficult case was where a new UK statute is found to be in breach of a previous EU enactment. In the *Factortame* case, it was argued that provisions of the Merchant Shipping Act (1988) were contrary to EU law. After the case had dragged on over a decade, the House of Lords, guided by the CJEU, decided that the European law should prevail. This was a landmark case but, arguably, did not affect the matter of supremacy, since the matter at stake concerned the detailed application of the relevant laws and not a head-on challenge to European law. In any case, the UK retained the right to withdraw from the EU altogether; indeed, the Lisbon Treaty (2008) provided a mechanism to do so.

Others argued that membership of the European Union did modify our understanding of sovereignty by creating a distinct and self-referential legal order. MacCormick (1999) argues that Europe brought with it a new rule of recognition, confirmed in *Factortame*, by which an otherwise valid law passed by Parliament could be disapplied by a new constitutional interpreter, the Court of Justice of the European Union. The United Kingdom could escape this by withdrawing from the European Union but, as long as it remained a member, its sovereignty was curtailed.

The Human Rights Act of 1998, which incorporated the European Convention on Human Rights (ECHR) into UK law, posed another challenge. The devolution statutes had already incorporated the Convention into devolved law, allowing the courts to strike down statutory provisions which infringed it but that merely reinforced the idea that the devolved legislatures are not sovereign. The courts were not given the power to strike down Westminster laws, but a provision was introduced allowing ECHR matters to be raised in court proceedings. If the law was found to be in breach of the Charter, Parliament was invited to use a fast-track procedure to change it.

Westminster also appeared to limit itself in the European Union Act (2011), which stipulated that any changes in the EU treaties extending the competences of the EU should not be approved unless supported both by Parliament and by a majority of those voting in a referendum.[5] Unlike in the Human Rights Act or the devolution statutes, there was no provision for Parliament to override these requirements short of repealing the Act itself. Nor was there any suggestion that such referendums were only advisory to Parliament; the provision for dual support by Parliament and the voters strongly indicates that they were not.

There are also provisions for Parliament to alter its own internal requirements for legislation. The Parliament Acts of 1910 and 1949 curtail the rights of the House of Lords, allowing it only to delay most legislation and not to do even that with money bills. This might be seen as a mere change in internal parliamentary procedure but the 1949 Act was belatedly challenged in 2005 (*Jackson v Attorney General*) on the ground that the Act could not be used to change its own provisions (by shortening the delay period). The challenge was not sustained. Provisions giving English MPs the right to decide whether bills

[5] It also listed a further range of issues in which ministers could not vote in the Council without parliamentary approval.

affecting only England should proceed, on the other hand, were put into the standing orders of the House of Commons rather than primary legislation.

Squaring the Circle

It was in this contested environment that the Millennium devolution legislation arrived, allowing of two interpretations. On the one hand, they are the gift of a sovereign Parliament, which can take them back or override them at any time; this requires the prior acceptance of parliamentary sovereignty. On another reading, they are seen as the latest articulation of a union of nations, building upon historical understandings and divided, or at least contested, sovereignty. Since the United Kingdom does not have a codified constitution, there is no requirement to resolve the issue. Instead, the sovereignty question can remain, as it always has been, subject to competing interpretations. The United Kingdom is not alone in entertaining such constitutional ambiguities, which occur even in elaborate written constitutions (Foley 2012), but is perhaps an extreme example. One way of dealing with them is by abeyances (suspension of argument) and silences, that is avoiding the matters as long as they are not pressing (Foley 2012; Schertzer 2017). Another device is the constitutional conventions unwritten understandings that serve to fill the spaces in statutory or codified provisions. Foley's (2012: 38) observation sums up the UK constitutional tradition well: 'The "understandings" only remain understood as long as they remain sufficiently obscure to allow them to retain an approximate appearance of internal coherence and clarity while . . . accommodating several potentially conflicting and quite unresolved points of issue.' Devolution has brought some of them into the open.

A. V. Dicey himself was one of the most influential contributors to the idea of conventions (Wade 1959), including those governing the workings of the Union and how it differs from a unitary state. So Dicey (1959: 66) recognizes that 'the statesmen who drew and passed this article (of the Irish Act of Union) meant to bind the action of future Parliaments is apparent from its language. That the attempt has failed of success is apparent to everyone who knows the contents of the Irish Church Act, 1869.' Similarly, for Scotland:

> [L]ogically, there is a contradiction between the creation of a really sovereign legislature which nevertheless cannot repeal the whole or certain parts of a statute which creates this sovereign power . . . the enactment of laws which are described as unchangeable, immutable or the like, is not

> necessarily futile... It represents the conviction of the Parliament which passed the Act of Union that the Act for the security of the Church in Scotland ought to be morally or constitutionally unchangeable, even by the British Parliament... A sovereign Parliament, in short, though it cannot be logically bound to abstain from changing any given law, may, by the fact that an Act when it was passed had been declared to be unchangeable, receive a warning that it cannot be changed without grave danger to the Constitution of the country. (Dicey and Rait 1920: 253–4)

The devolution settlements rest heavily on conventions. A central theme is that of consent but it is interpreted in confusingly different ways. The Legislative Consent (or Sewel) Convention was introduced during the debate on the Scotland Bill when Lord Sewel declared that he expected a convention to develop by which Westminster would not normally legislate in devolved matters without the consent of the relevant legislature. This was later incorporated into a memoranda of understanding with the devolved bodies. It was also extended to include changes to the competences of the devolved bodies. There was no provision for what would happen if consent were to be refused. Powers to transfer additional competences by statutory instrument are, under the devolution acts, subject to consent by the devolved legislature. Other statutory instruments are not formally subject to the consent provision, although there has been consultation (House of Lords Select Committee on the Constitution 2020). Another consent mechanism was introduced in the European Union Withdrawal Act of 2017, concerning the allocation of powers repatriated from the EU. The Act stipulated that the UK Government could use a statutory instrument to reserve some of the otherwise devolved powers coming back, but that this would be subject to a consent mechanism. This time the effect of the mechanism was spelt out in full. If the devolved legislature consents, the instrument is valid; if it refuses consent, it is valid; and if it takes no decision, it is valid. Again, one might argue that this does not change the law but it does break that very uncertainty about consequences which is an important feature of how constitutional conventions really work (Foley 2012).

There are two ways to read the various consent mechanisms. One is as a mechanism to allow the two levels of government to work together and avoid matters falling in the gap between their legislative provisions. This is the main use that has been made of it under governments of all parties. The other reading is that it is a means of safeguarding the powers of the devolved legislatures against Westminster encroachment.

It was to strengthen the latter aspect that the UK Government agreed, as part of the new settlement following the Scottish independence referendum of 2014, to put the convention into statutory form. This was duly done in the Scotland Act of 2016 and the Wales Act of 2017 as a rider on the clause asserting Westminster sovereignty, reading: 'But it is recognized that the Parliament of the United Kingdom will not normally legislate with regard to devolved matters without the consent of the Scottish Parliament (National Assembly for Wales).' The political objective was to suggest that the convention was being entrenched but it was entrenched only as a recognition of a convention, which did not change its legal status. Indeed, one could argue that putting it on a statutory footing suggested that it could be repealed by Parliament, so weakening it.[6] A convention is part of a broad set of constitutional understandings that underpin the workings of our institutions, including parliamentary sovereignty itself. Another weakness was the retention of the word 'normally' in the statutory version. No indication was given of what was to be considered abnormal and it was left to the UK Parliament (in practice the Government) to decide the matter unilaterally. Another clause in the acts provided that the Scottish Parliament and National Assembly for Wales respectively are a permanent part of the constitution and could not be abolished except following a referendum in the nations concerned. Like the provision of the European Union Act 2011 requiring a referendum before more powers could be transferred to the European Union, this is unqualified but, unless it is taken to limit the authority of the UK Parliament, it lacks any binding force.

Interpreting the Constitution

The Millennium settlement has consequently been a highly contested matter. On the one side, authority and stability are given by the principle of parliamentary sovereignty, but this turns out to have weak foundations. On the other, there are broader, epistemic arguments about the meaning of the constitution and the way it emerged from statute law, common law, conventions and politics as a broad and contested field. Yet there is no authoritative interpreter or arbiter. The Supreme Court since its foundation has sought to keep

[6] In a further twist in the argument, O'Neill (2017) suggested that it could mean that judges could overrule Parliament were the latter to legislate to bind itself by seeking to entrench the Sewel convention.

within the bounds of parliamentary statutes and declined to enter into wider epistemic reasoning. Generally, judges have drawn back from a bold interpretation of the devolution statutes and tended to treat them as ordinary laws such as those governing municipal government (Tomkins 2015). Some judges have played with ideas, especially in *obiter dicta*, that is general commentary arising from cases but not affecting the resolution of the case in hand, but tend to revert to hard law in deciding cases. Academic commentators have ranged wider but without coming up with a shared doctrine on the Millennium settlement. Litigants in cases have sought to broaden out their challenges by invoking constitutional principles. So, issues of sovereignty have been intensively debated since the late twentieth century and have increasingly come before the courts but without resolution.

What we are left with it is a tantalizing series of suggestions that devolution may have changed the way that sovereignty and parliamentary supremacy work, but a reluctance on the part of the judges to take the matter beyond speculation. Lord Steyn (2005: 102), in *Jackson v Attorney General*, remarked that membership of the European Union, the European Convention on Human rights and devolution meant that

> the classic account given by Dicey of the doctrine of the supremacy of Parliament, pure and absolute as it was, can now be seen to be out of place in the modern United Kingdom; nevertheless, the supremacy of Parliament is still the *general* principle of our constitution.

Lady Justice Arden (2015), later a judge of the Supreme Court, went further and argued in an academic publication that the devolution statutes were constitutional, that UK devolution was of a federal nature, and the judges should look for guidance to foreign federal jurisprudence.

Some safeguards for the devolution settlement have emerged from the courts. One is the doctrine of the constitutional law, a statute which is not entrenched but is protected from implied repeal. If a subsequent statute conflicts with a constitutional law, it does not repeal the conflicting clause unless Parliament expressly states so. In *Thoburn v Sunderland City Council*, Lord Justice Laws (2002), declared that the European Communities Act is such a constitutional law. Lord Hope (2012b) subsequently declared the Scotland Act to be a constitutional law and thus not subject to implied repeal. Neither of them, however, accepted that Parliament could not amend or repeal either Act if it chose expressly to do so. Indeed Laws (2002, para. 59) made a very strong statement of the traditional doctrine that Parliament could not limit its own sovereignty even if it wanted to do so. Just in case the point was not understood, the European Union Act (2011) included a declaratory clause to the same effect with respect to EU law.

Another move is to recognize the devolved bodies as enjoying broad powers, to be interpreted generously, raising them above the level of municipal governments, even though both are creatures of statute. Municipal governments are subject, in the exercise of their political judgment, to common law standards of irrationality, unreasonableness or arbitrariness. *Robinson v Secretary of State for Northern Ireland*) concerned the procedure for electing the First Minister and whether strict adherence to the working of the Northern Ireland Act was necessary.[7] A narrow majority of the Law Lords agreed that the Act was a constitutional provision giving the Assembly broad powers, to be interpreted generously. Regard had to be paid to its underlying purpose, to achieve cross-community consent in government (House of Lords 2002). Lord Hope (2012a), in *Imperial Tobacco,* interpreted the Scotland Act as establishing a full parliament with broad legislative competences. On the other hand, this did not mean that it should not be interpreted just like any other statute;[8] the other judges agreed. Hope (2011) had given a similar judgment in the case of *AXA General Insurance v Lord Advocate*. The judges in *AXA* agreed that the Scottish Parliament, in making its political judgments about policy, should not be subject to the irrationality test.

Judges and commentators have also played with the concept of common law constitutionalism. This is an old idea, that Parliament itself is the creature of the common law, which provides the basis for its authority. Judges have opined that, if Parliament were to breach fundamental principles of the rule of law, then the courts might have to intervene. These ideas have always been rather speculative and hypothetical and have not affected the resolution of cases. They could, indeed, provoke a constitutional revolution if they did. More plausibly, however, it has been suggested that the courts might disallow devolved legislation in conflict with these principles (Anthony 2015; McCorkindale, McHarg and Scott 2017).

The constitutional law of devolution has remained underdeveloped because politicians have generally preferred to keep matters out of the courts. Most of the challenges to the competence of devolved legislatures have been raised by

[7] Precisely, whether a First Minister and a Deputy First Minister could still be elected after the statutory period had expired.

[8] 'the description of the Act as a constitutional statute cannot be taken, in itself, to be a guide to its interpretation. The statute must be interpreted like any other statute' (Hope 2012a).

private parties under European Union law or the European Convention on Human Rights (ECHR). The first case not concerning European law (*Robinson v Secretary of State for Northern Ireland*) was in Northern Ireland in 2002 and the first case in Scotland not involving European matters was *Imperial Tobacco v Lord Advocate* (2012). The first case referred by the UK Government concerning the Scottish Parliament was not until 2018 and concerned procedures for withdrawing from the European Union (the Scottish Continuity Bill). By contrast, three cases were referred by the UK law officers shortly after the National Assembly for Wales had gained legislative powers (2012–14).

The most serious test of the Sewel Convention was in *Miller v Secretary of State for Exiting the European Union*, decided in 2017 (Douglas Scott 2018; McHarg 2018). Gina Miller had challenged the UK Government on the grounds that parliamentary approval was needed to trigger Article 50, starting the process of withdrawal from the EU. The Scottish Government in the person of the Lord Advocate, along with the Counsel General for Wales joined the case to argue that, because Brexit would alter the powers of the devolved bodies,[9] legislative consent was necessary. When Miller lost in the Divisional Court in England, she appealed to the Supreme Court. At this point, a set of cases arising from Northern Ireland was included in the appeal. This was the occasion for rehearsal of the broad debate about the Union, dating back to 1707.

It was not claimed that Scotland or Northern Ireland could veto Article 50, merely that it would require the legislative consent procedure to be taken seriously. The Lord Advocate (2016), for the Scottish Government, deployed a wide epistemic argument. The essence was that Article 50 stipulated that withdrawal must be in accordance with the constitutional requirements of the state concerned. In the UK, this includes a wide body of law, including the Claim of Right of 1689 and the Acts of Union of 1706/7, thus rooting a distinct argument in Scottish, rather than English or UK constitutionalism. He cited Lord Cooper's dictum in *MacCormick v Lord Advocate* (1953) that the unlimited sovereignty of Parliament does not apply in Scotland, and the various judicial suggestions that the sovereignty of the UK Parliament is not, if it ever was, absolute. While the UK Government did indeed enjoy prerogative power in conducting international relations, the internal extension of those could not be assumed to be the same in Scots law as in that of England & Wales. He further claimed that conventions do form part of the law of the UK

[9] At a minimum, the provisions binding them to observe EU law would have to be removed.

constitution. Treading a fine line, he conceded that, were Parliament to pass relevant legislation without consent, the courts could not decline to recognize its validity but, on the other hand, they could identify what the constitutional requirements were, as required by the relevant passage in the EU treaties.

The UK Government might have confined its case to the narrow grounds that Brexit was a matter of international relations, which is reserved, or that it was not a 'normal' situation within the scope of the Sewel Convention. Instead, the Advocate General (for the UK Government) argued that Sewel was merely a 'political' device of no concern to the courts. The UK Supreme Court (2017) agreed; in effect, it declined to enter into constitutional reasoning and fell back on the Diceyean doctrine of parliamentary supremacy as a simple empirical fact. The Northern Ireland arguments were briskly dismissed and the Sewel Convention was interpreted as a device to promote cooperation and 'harmonious relationships' rather than to protect devolved competence. Against the post-2016 understanding that the UK might be evolving in a federal direction, this took matters back to the early Dicey.[10] O'Neill (2017) notes, 'As a constitutional court for the United Kingdom tasked with ascertaining the constitutional law of the United Kingdom, the Supreme Court might have at least adverted to these other constitutional traditions within the polity.'[11] Instead, the case was argued within what (McCrudden and Halberstam (2018) call a 'London-based legal interpretive community' and what political scientists would call an 'epistemic community' that was insensitive to these questions. It thus passed on the opportunity to function as a truly constitutional court.

Law, Politics and Constitutionalism

The Diceyan tradition has been to define the constitution in narrow, legal terms and to consign the difficult and ambiguous questions to the realm of 'politics.' De Montpensier (1966) thus wrote that 'the word constitutional seems to me to blur two separate logics, that of law and that of politics, and the logical translation from one logic to the other is often unnoticed.' The Supreme Court judgment in *Miller* goes in the same direction. Yet this

[10] That is the supporter of Westminster rather than popular sovereignty.

[11] Illlustrating that the legal arguments can be played both ways, elsewhere O'Neill (2011) has written that 'The UK is a unitary state, not a federation. This remains the case even after devolution. Power devolved from the Westminster centre is power retained rather than power ceded, and sovereignty divided.'

distinction between law and politics has come under wide criticism as has the idea that these two exhaust the sources of legitimate authority. (Grégoire and Webber 2010; Tomkins 2013; Loughlin 2017; Loughlin and Tierney 2018). Constitutionalism cannot be reduced to either but is a form of meta-politics that seeks to set the terms for day-to-day political exchange. It employs a wider epistemic approach to the rules of the game, drawing on law, convention, practice, history, precedent and normative principles as well as practice and interpretation in a complex account of power and authority (Foley 2012; Elliot 2015). Conventions are not to be dismissed as 'just political' but as Mitchell (1968) argued, may be themselves a form of law. In the absence of revolutionary upheaval, they are the means by which constitutions evolve and they then sometimes crystalize into, or are codified in, statute law. Seen this way, conventions are not subordinate to legal norms but part of the foundation of legal order; as Galligan and Brenton (2015: 417) put it 'conventions are more fundamental than laws'. Indeed, the doctrine of parliamentary sovereignty itself might be argued to rest upon convention.

Elliot (2015) similarly distinguishes between legality and constitutionality while Himsworth and O'Neill (2015: 18) cautiously suggest that '[a]lthough this could never be directly restrained by a court' a Westminster Act ignoring the Legislative Consent (Sewel) convention 'might well be regarded as unconstitutional'. Douglas-Scott (2019) argues that the UK Government's ignoring the refusal of legislative consent to the EU Withdrawal Act was legal but unconstitutional.

This is consistent with the post-sovereignty perspective (MacCormick 1999; Keating 2001) that sovereignty can no longer be considered an unquestioned foundational principle, which cannot be shared or divided. Instead, there can be multiple sources of authority, not necessarily commensurate and not always leading to a definitive outcome. Sovereignty is not something that exists or a predicate applicable to individual entities, but as a set of relationships, based both on power and on norms that may be shared or contested (Loughlin 2003). The outcome is a form of constitutional pluralism that creates a space for new forms of constitutional reasoning and negotiation (Tierney 2004). Walker (2003), noting that sovereignty claims are still very much alive, calls this 'late sovereignty', but the substantive point is similar. Sovereignty thus ceases to be a trump card to be deployed in arguments about authority. Strange to relate, even Dicey can be invoked in favour of a post-sovereign interpretation. So, he and Robert Rait conceded that 'the further dogma of Augustinian jurists that in every State there must of necessity exist some absolutely sovereign power is not true'. They then dismiss the point, insisting that '[w]hether this condition of things may or may not be called a condition of divided sovereignty is a question of words and of no great importance' (Dicey and Rait 1920: 100).

There is an obvious connection here with the conception of the UK as a union of territories and peoples whose original prerogatives were not extinguished by the acts of union. Similar arguments are made in Spain for historic rights, which pre-date the 1978 Constitution, against the centralist argument that all rights derive from that constitution as the sovereign expression of a unitary people (Herrero de Miñon 1998; Herrero de Miñon and Lluch 1998). The outcome is not necessarily a doctrine of secession (which is what Spanish unionists fear) since the UK arguably has that, but a principle of internal self-determination whereby the nations can negotiate their position within the Union.

The courts' reluctance to engage in deeper constitutional reasoning contrasts with the Supreme Court of Canada, which has taken conventions seriously. The issue received a full airing in the Patriation case, concerning the 1982 Constitution, adopted without the consent of Quebec. In that case, the majority of judges refused to enforce a convention, but not without dissent (Russell et al. 1982). Since then, the Court has moved on to a wider epistemic interpretation of the constitution as based on a broad series of values and practices, from which specific decisions might be derived (Schertzer 2017; Brouillet and Mullen 2018).[12] It has also brought back the idea of the constitutional compact (Grammon 2016). This is not to treat conventions as though they are positive law but rather to bring them into a process of debate and provide guidance to political actors. Understood in this way, conventions work only when they do not have to be enforced as hard law.

The Supreme Court of Canada's (1998) ruling on the possible secession of Quebec, which has attracted wide international interest, goes in the same direction. Invited to pronounce on whether Quebec had the right to secede, it declared that this was not encompassed by the constitution. Rather than resting on this narrow interpretation, however, it engaged in wider reasoning, noting that the constitution itself was embedded in normative principles of democracy. Its conclusion was that, if any province decided, by a clear referendum majority on a clear question, that it wished to secede, Canada would be obliged to negotiate. Having stated these principles, the court then handed

[12] The Supreme Court stated in 1981 during the patriation of the Constitution that "constitutional conventions plus constitutional law equal the total constitution of the country". https://www.thecanadianencyclopedia.ca/en/article/constitutional-history

the matter back to the politicians. A similar argument might be made about Scottish secession. According to law, the Scottish Parliament does not have the power to stage a referendum on independence, the Union being a reserved matter. Broader epistemic reasoning, however, might start with the proposition that the right of self-determination for Scotland has long been recognized. If that is so, then there must be a way for that to be realized. Broader principles built into our understanding of the constitution suggest that the this must be done democratically. The procedure of gaining a parliamentary majority (especially in a proportional representation system) on a promise to hold a referendum and then holding that referendum would meet that test. While not everyone might agree, this at least looks like a plausible argument to the effect that such a referendum, while not strictly legal, could be constitutional.

It is not that the courts and governments pay no attention to convention in relation to other aspects of the constitution. Conventions governing the Monarch and the House of Lords are taken very seriously. In another Brexit-related case, indeed, the UK Supreme Court (2019) disallowed the Government's advice to the Queen on the prorogation of Parliament on the grounds that it had not given adequate justification for its action. The case was widely seen as restoring the balance between the executive and legislative branches of government and thus not revolutionary in its scope. What was more interesting is the way that the Court took the opportunity for some extended constitutional reasoning, arguing that '[a]lthough the United Kingdom does not have a single document entitled "The Constitution", it nevertheless possesses a Constitution, established over the course of our history by common law, statutes, conventions and practice' (UK Supreme Court 2019, para. 40). This appears to be at odds with the dismissal of the Sewel Convention—and conventions in general—and the refusal to engage in broader constitutional reasoning in *Miller*. On the other hand, it might merely reinforce the basis of the constitution in the monarch-in-parliament doctrine while discounting the territorial dimension.

The Supreme Court has also made gestures in the direction of popular sovereignty. In the prorogation case, it accepted the outcome of the Brexit referendum as binding even though it was, in a legal sense, undoubtedly advisory: 'Technically, the result was not legally binding. But the Government had pledged to honour the result and it has since been treated as politically and democratically binding. Successive Governments and Parliament have acted on that basis' (UK Supreme Court, 2019, para 7). This looks a bit like Diceyean reasoning, except that the word 'binding' takes the argument a step further away from mere prudence and political calculation. In a later passage, speaking of the decision to leave the EU they argue that '[t]he people have decided...' (UK Supreme Court, 2019, para 57). This seems to mirror the late Dicey, suggesting perhaps that we have not moved forward in a hundred years.

If the doctrine of parliamentary sovereignty is no longer adequate to secure legitimacy and stability across a complex system, there is not the consensus necessary to move to a different paradigm such as a balanced federal system. Instead, the challenge is to manage constitutional pluralism and the absence of shared *demos* and *telos* across the nations. In these circumstances, constitution-making is not about finding a definitive fix but about accommodation on normatively acceptable terms. Such an interpretive approach does not mean that any theory is as good as any other, or that it is all a matter of individual preference (Lakin 2018).

There are two other factors of relevance to the UK case. One is what Burgess (2012) identifies as a federal spirit of self-restraint: damage limitation, the obligation to take the others into consideration; moral imperative to observe the unwritten norms of the constitution; and political empathy, which includes partnership, friendship, understanding, mutual trust, respect and good faith. The second concerns power. The Westminster doctrine of sovereignty conflates what are seen, in some other legal traditions, as two issues: the sovereignty of the state and the organization of authority within it (Troper 2012). So parliamentary sovereignty has been expanded to encompass the different matter of omnicompetence and supremacy (Loughlin and Tierney 2018). In turn, Westminster governments have always conceived of sovereignty and unity as a mechanism for centralization (Armstrong 2003). While there is a lot of talk about the need for respect and understanding among the various orders of government in the United Kingdom, less is said about power. Since the advent of devolution, UK governments have been quite forbearing and have allowed the nations considerable latitude in steering their own policy directions in devolved matters. Yet the ultimate power rests at the centre and devolution remains a series of exceptions to the rule, rather than a radical transformation of the nature of the state.

5

Union at the Centre

Self-Rule and Shared Rule

Scholars of federalism identify two characteristics: self-rule, in which the federated units run their own affairs, and shared rule, in which 'orders of government'[1] deal together with common concerns affecting the state as a whole (Elazar 1987; Burgess 2012). While the UK settlement provides for extensive self-rule, shared rule is almost completely absent. The 1999 devolution settlement introduced radical changes in government at the territorial periphery but changed almost nothing at the centre. Consequently, the constitution could be seen at the periphery as quasi-federal while, at the centre, it remained unitary. While the rather broad and clear demarcation of competences allows the devolved governments considerable scope in policy matters, they lack the means of influencing wider state policies that mark many federal systems. In one sense, we could say that, in relation to devolved matters, the UK has no centre, only a set of concurrent governments. In another sense, it has a centre, which is England, which remained an integral part of the central state and whose weight will always dominate the whole without needing separate institutional expression. There is a similar ambiguity about hierarchy. Most competences belong clearly to one level or the other and there is no hierarchy of laws such that in case of contradiction those of Westminster would prevail. On the other hand, the settlement explicitly conserved the principle of parliamentary sovereignty and supremacy, so that Westminster can choose to override the devolveds by changing the devolution legislation itself or passing a 'protected enactment'. A similar situation exists on the executive side. There are no central departments covering devolved matters but, rather, formally co-equal governments with specified territorial reach, but English departments are not designated as such.

This all makes the centre both potentially dominant, should it choose to exercise its supremacy powers, and practically weak in that it lacks the

[1] This sounds less hierarchical than 'levels' of government.

State and Nation in the United Kingdom: The Fractured Union. Michael Keating, Oxford University Press (2021).
 DOI: 10.1093/oso/9780198841371.003.0005

machinery to intervene at the periphery. For much of the time, this has been of little concern to the centre, which has been content to allow the devolution as a set of exceptions that had little impact on the whole. Over time, however, UK Governments have become more concerned about the centrifugal tendencies of devolution, the lack of mechanisms to bind the nations into the Union, the lack of visibility of the UK itself and the lack of appreciation of what it does. This has focused attention on what is seen as the missing element in the settlement, the articulation of the two levels and two-way influence between them.

Linking the Levels

In some federal and devolved systems, a second chamber of Parliament represents territorial interests. The German Bundesrat consists of delegates from the regional governments. Just over a quarter of the members of the Spanish Senate are chosen by the regional legislatures. Canadian Senators are appointed by the Prime Minister but are deemed to be from specific provinces. United States Senators are elected from each state although they do not represent state governments. There is nothing equivalent in the United Kingdom.

Discussions about the future of devolution have often included proposals for a chamber of the nations and regions to replace the House of Lords. Yet the reverse has rarely been true. While reform of the Lords has been discussed since the early twentieth century, none of the official proposals[2] included a territorial element. Although the Wakeham Commission (Royal Commission on the reform of the House of Lords, 2000) was originally tasked with including provision for the nations and regions, the report and subsequent recommendations made no reference to them. Nor did the proposals in 2011 from the Liberal Democrat–Conservative Coalition Government or the various resolutions put to the House of Commons. Only England received any recognition in the 2011 proposals and the reforms of 1999,[3] in the strange provision that bishops of the Church of England would still be present.

Some countries also have mechanisms for the representation of nations and regions in the central executive. Belgium has formal mechanisms requiring parity of French and Flemish speakers. Elsewhere, the provision is more

[2] In 1911, 1968, 1999, 2007 and 2011.

[3] Which removed most of the hereditary peers.

informal, as in Canada where federal cabinets always where possible have a significant presence from Quebec and from the West. Before devolution, there was a pale reflection of this in British practice (Keating 1975). From the Second World War until the 1980s, there was a Scottish MP in the Ministry of Agriculture. In the 1970s, this was extended to the Department of Energy following a promise by Labour leader Harold Wilson. Labour Governments before 1979 always found place for a Scottish mining MP. Overall, however, Scottish MPs were under-represented at the centre until the 1990s. There followed a period in which they were over-represented in Labour Governments and even, in proportion to their numbers, in Conservative ones. This phase ended in 2010, since when there has only been one Scottish MP apart from the Secretary of State for Scotland, in the Cabinet (a Liberal Democrat). With the deepening of devolution, there has been some speculation about whether it would ever again be possible to have a Scottish (or perhaps Welsh) MP as Prime Minister. Northern Ireland MPs have not served in UK Governments since the 1960s.

Political parties provide another mechanism for input. None of the British parliamentary parties has had a significant territorial caucus, since the failure of the Radical Liberals to establish a 'Welsh Party' in the 1880s. There are internal party groups but these rarely take a distinctive policy line and they are in no way comparable to the organized factions seen in both Conservative and Labour. After their wipe-out in Scotland at the General Election of 1997, there was recurrent talk that the Scottish Conservatives might revert to their pre-1965 status as an independent party with a stronger commitment to Scotland, but this was rejected both by the UK leadership and by the party in Scotland. When, in 2017, they regained a significant number of seats in Scotland, there was speculation that they might operate as a discrete group with leverage over government, but that did not happen. On the Labour side, there has never been a cohesive Scottish group, as opposed to a capacity for lobbying. Northern Ireland has its own party system and the formal link between the Ulster Unionists and the Conservative Party was broken in 1974. Since then, both Labour and Conservative governments have bargained with both Ulster Unionists and nationalists when they lacked majorities, culminating in a formal arrangement between the Conservatives and the Democratic Unionists between 2017 and 2019.

For the first two decades of devolution, this posed few problems as UK governments had little interest or political incentive to intervene in devolved matters.

Mechanisms to govern intergovernmental relations were put in place after 1999 but mostly atrophied for want of use. There were Memorandums of Understanding concerning overlapping policy fields, which were largely uncontentious. Joint Ministerial Committees (JMCs) of the UK and devolved governments were to attend to common and overlapping issues but fell into disuse for lack of anything substantive to discuss. Issues were, instead, handled in bilateral discussions among departments. The only JMC that did meet regularly was that on Europe, to agree a common line to be taken in the Council of the European Union. The arrival in government of the SNP and the Scottish referendum of 2014 prompted a rethink, including a relaunch of the moribund JMC system. An additional committee was later struck to consider Brexit-related matters (JMC European Negotiations).

Whatever the format that joint committees have used, a fundamental principle is that the UK Government retains the last word. Committees are thus, essentially consultative, without substantive power. They also embody the principle that the UK speaks both for the centre and for England so that when it does have the last word, it can look like England overruling the other nations. There are no institutions independent of government to provide data and analysis or to broker solutions among the various governments, as happens in many federal or quasi-federal systems. The Royal Society of Edinburgh (2018) suggested a statutory basis, with stronger joint JMCs, accompanied by a secretariat which would have the responsibility of providing a common database for discussions and a capacity for brokering solutions. The House of Commons Public Administration and Constitution Committee (2018) also proposed the creation of a secretariat separate from the governments. In the absence of mechanism such as this, when issues enter the inter-governmental arena, elements of hierarchy reappear.

Brexit greatly extends the scope of intergovernmental relations by repatriating from Brussels competences that ensured coherence across the UK (Chapter 6). It also extends the scope of international agreements (both with the EU and with third countries) in areas previously covered by European provisions. Trade agreements these days are about a lot more than trade in the traditional sense, extending to product standards, environmental provisions, labour standards and other matters, many of which are devolved. The devolution statutes contain provision for UK ministers to force devolved ministers to give effect to the UK's international obligations, which was seen at the time as a last-resort safeguard. They do not, however, oblige the devolved legislatures to make any changes in law to implement international agreements. This has opened up a whole new set of areas at the boundary of reserved and devolved competence. Foreign trade and international agreements are reserved; much of their implementation is devolved. The effects of Brexit on the settlement are discussed more fully in Chapter 6.

Reforming the Centre

The way that devolution unfolded meant that there was never a clear focus for devolution issues in Whitehall. At times of constitutional difficulty, the central apparatus has been strengthened and initiatives launched to sensitize Whitehall departments to devolution. In 2019, the Prime Minister assumed the symbolic title of Minister for the Union. When matters have stabilized, the apparatus has been run down again and predominantly English Whitehall departments allowed to forget about the devolved implications of their own policies. Responsibility for the devolved settlement has moved around among ministers and departments, often located in the Cabinet Office.

A decision was taken in 1999 to retain Secretaries of State for Scotland, Wales and Northern Ireland, at least part-time until the settlement bedded down; proposals were mooted to merge the territorial Offices into a single department for devolution or constitutional affairs. In the meantime, shorn of their spending and administrative responsibilities, the task of the renamed Scotland and Wales Offices was largely political. They did not, as envisaged in the 1970s' devolution proposals, have a tutelary role, monitoring the devolved administrations and seeking to keep them in line. With the challenge of the SNP in Scotland and the series of constitutional changes in Wales, the Secretaries of State became full time again and started to increase their staffing. The Northern Ireland Office had more to do in managing the Good Friday Agreement and governing the territory during periods when the Stormont institutions were not in operation.

The Scottish independence referendum prompted the UK Government to the realization that it lacked a visible presence in Scotland, except for the less gratifying tasks of tax collection and welfare. Inspired by the Canadian response to the 1995 Quebec independence referendum, a decision was then taken to raise the UK profile in Scotland. As part of a programme of thirteen 'hubs' across the UK, government offices were consolidated in city-centre sites in Edinburgh, Cardiff and Belfast. In 2019 a further review was launched into the UK Government's 'union capability' including the role of the territorial offices. Attention also turned to spending in the devolved territories.

Although initially the devolved governments received almost all their funding from the UK, the block allocation formula meant that this could not be used as a mechanism for control. While Gordon Brown, as Chancellor of the Exchequer, could impose centralizing Public Service Agreements on Whitehall departments, these could not, for constitutional reasons extend to the devolved administrations. There have been some instances of formula by-pass but the Treasury has generally preferred to use the block funding mechanism as the best means of expenditure control.

Politically, this created the problem that the UK had the hard task of raising taxes while the devolved governments had the more gratifying role of spending the proceeds. Even where the UK does spend money, reserved competences do not include the more electorally appealing forms of spending. In the aftermath of the Scottish independence referendum, again inspired by Canada, it looked for more opportunities to put a Union flag on spending projects. The area of economic development, which is a shared responsibility, was a good place to start. There was also a search for ways to spend money directly in the devolved territories, without passing through the devolved governments and the block grant formula (Torrance 2020b).

One move was to extend into the devolved territories City Deals and Growth Deals, an English intergovernmental programme aimed at regeneration, initially of urban areas but later extended to the entire country. The formula is an old one, aimed at 'joining up' different capabilities and competences to focus on the needs of places. There is, however, an underlying purpose. In England, they were aimed at addressing a fragmented urban government system and co-opting local elites into centrally directed strategies (Moran, Tomaney and Williams, 2018). Power was to be shifted into the hands of elected metro-mayors working with the centre. The constitutional situation of the devolved governments is very different, but there is also a political logic—to lever devolved budgets behind UK Government priorities, to insert the centre back into local policy-making networks and to gain higher visibility for UK moneys. The first one in Scotland came from an approach from Glasgow City Council to the UK Government around the time of the independence referendum. The Scottish Government then came on board and eventually the programme was rolled out for the whole of Scotland. Deals were agreed in Wales from 2016 and Northern Ireland in 2019. The essentially political logic of the strategy can be gauged from the small amounts of money involved (Chapter 8).

Brexit provided further opportunities for the UK Government to control spending in the devolved territories, as agricultural funding and regional development and social funds come back from the EU. The decision was taken not to roll these into the block grant, but to set up dedicated funds allocated from the centre.

The Emergence of England

One obstacle to the emergence of a federal-type centre in the UK remains the fact that the central Government and Parliament double up as those of England. In so far as England has emerged institutionally, it is by subtraction. From the nineteenth century, administrative devolution to Ireland and Scotland and, later, Wales, left key departments in Whitehall administering only England. An idea of the balance of responsibilities can be gained by looking at the percentages of equivalent expenditure used in the Barnett Formula. On this measure, Education and Local Government are 100 per cent devolved so that the Whitehall departments are entirely English. Health, and Environment, Food and Rural Affairs are over 99 per cent devolved, so that Whitehall has some residual responsibilities. Business, Innovation and Skills straddles English and UK competences, being two-thirds devolved. Justice and Home Office responsibilities are 100 per cent and 90 per cent respectively limited to England-and-Wales. There is, however, no formal recognition that some departments are wholly English and thus effectively territorial departments. They are not seen in any respect as speaking for England as opposed to the UK as a whole. Similarly, Cabinet committees mix English, British, England-and-Wales and UK responsibilities in various proportions, but without recognizing an explicitly English dimension across them (Gallagher 2018). Yet, no UK government department has England in its title and even in Scotland, Wales and Northern Ireland the ministers are usually referred to as 'UK' rather than 'English'. This has added to public confusion about responsibilities and has led Whitehall ministers and civil servants often to forget that they represent only one territorial component of the Union.

England is more visible in the nomenclature of government agencies. During the 1900s, under a firmly anti-devolution Conservative Government, administrative devolution was extended to a number of agencies, which were divided into their national components, with an explicitly English element. The Arts Council of Great Britain had been established after the Second World War and in the 1960s Scottish and Welsh committees were set up within it. In 1994 the Council was abolished altogether and replaced with separate English, Scottish and Welsh equivalents. This is a striking move in international comparison, as there was no longer any state-wide body for the culture and the arts, an important influence in nation-building. In 1996 Sport England was created alongside equivalent bodies for Scotland and Wales but with a separate UK Sport agency. In 1992, university funding was administratively devolved and an English body created. The trend continued after devolution. The Environment Agency shed its Welsh responsibilities in 2013, so becoming an English body. The British Broadcasting Corporation (BBC), seen by its Scottish first director general in the 1920s as a custodian of a British national ethos, has retained an internal 'nations and regions' formula, and demands for the devolution of broadcasting regulation have been resisted. At the same time as this slow institutional emergence, there has been a debate about the political existence of England.

The political subtraction of England from the UK has been similarly uneven. Englishness has long been an implicit presence (Aughey and Berberich, 2011; Kenny 2018). It may have emerged since devolution but has not given rise to specific constitutional demands, but is rather a demand for recognition as a constituent nation rather than anything analogous to movements in Scotland, Wales or Northern Ireland. Indeed, the prime expression of English nationalism may be not secession from the UK but Brexit, a repudiation of the concept of union and power-sharing and a demand to 'bring back control' or sovereignty (Wellings 2011). This association of Euroscepticism with Englishness occurred just at the time that the nationalisms of the periphery were adopting Europe as a framework for their own aspirations. The shift of Euroscepticism from parliamentary to popular sovereignty (Douglas-Scott, 2017) expressed in the referendum implied the existence of a single *demos*, but the solid Remain majorities in Scotland and Northern Ireland reinforce the idea of Brexit as an English project. With the English comprising the overwhelming majority of the population, there is little danger of their being outvoted in a referendum, but there is evidence that many of them would dispense with Scotland and Northern Ireland if that were the cost of leaving the EU (Chapter 10).

Balancing the Union

The Scottish Question is about the relation of Scotland to the United Kingdom. The Northern Irish Question is about the relationship of Northern Ireland to Great Britain and to Ireland, and relations between its own communities. There is no such clear definition of the English Question and hence answer. Until at least the question is clarified, the prospects of balancing the Union and reforming that centre must remain elusive. One approach is to balance the Union by making England a devolved nation and creating a new, 'federal' level above it. This recalls the Home Rule All Round of the early twentieth century, with national legislatures under an 'Imperial Parliament' acting as a federal legislature. While nobody talks about 'imperial' matters, the objections to the idea of symmetrical devolution have hardly changed (Russell and Sheldon 2018). There has never been significant support for it among politicians or citizens in England, which is hardly surprising, given that England has an overwhelming presence in Westminster. A federal arrangement would actually reduce this dominance by confining English affairs to a second-level parliament, subordinated to a federal constitution.

Another standard response is to divide England into regions, which would have their own devolved governments (Torrance 2014). This idea, which goes back to the early twentieth century (Keating 1982), has merit in its own right, as England is one of the most centralized jurisdictions in Europe but that has nothing to do with England's place in the Union constitution. Nobody has ever advocated legislative powers or the reserved powers model for English regions, or the abolition of the main domestic departments in Whitehall, which is what would be required to put them on a par with Scotland, Wales and Northern Ireland. In a piece of linguistic stretching, the term 'devolution' has been applied to the reform of government in English city regions, but this has almost nothing in common with the devolution to the smaller nations of the UK. English regional and city-regional government is a saga that has been going on since at least the 1960s, with regular cycles of consolidation, fragmentation and reinvention without ever arriving at a stable configuration.

Given the lack of support for an English Parliament, attention has focused on an English dimension at Westminster itself. Named after the constituency of anti-devolution Scottish MP Tam Dalyell in the 1970s, the West Lothian Question is the anomaly that, after devolution, Scottish MPs would be able to vote on purely English matters while neither they nor English MPs could vote on the same questions in relation to Scotland. The issue had given Gladstone sleepless nights when elaborating his Irish Home Rule bills. The matter particularly preoccupied Conservatives, worried that a future Labour Government reliant for its majority on Scottish MPs could impose policies on England. While the argument looks persuasive in principle, in practice, the danger was remote. Only briefly, between 1964 and 1966 and between the two general elections of 1974, have Labour governments depended on Scottish MPs for their existence.[4]

One idea is to create an English Parliament within Westminster by giving English MPs dual mandates (Denham 2018). A more modest solution is to forbid Scottish, Welsh and Northern Irish MPs from voting on purely English

[4] With a small majority in the first case and as a minority government in the second.

matters, a formula known as English Votes for English Laws (EVEL). However it is done, this raises a number of practical objections (Glover and Kenny (2018a, b). It might be difficult to separate out purely English matters: there are overspills from England into the other nations, and votes on English priorities influence devolved spending via the Barnett Formula. These might rather easily be addressed by reforming procedures and creating a clearer English jurisdiction, or by replacing the Barnett Formula with something more defensible. A more intractable issue is composition of the executive, since Scottish MPs would still participate in deciding who were ministers, including in 'English' departments. Unionist objections, however, go deeper than this, suggesting that (EVEL) would violate the principle of equality of MPs and the Union itself. Bogdanor (2007) complains that governments could not count on solid majorities for their legislation, although proportional representation[5] would have the same effect. Hazell (2008) also feared for the Union were EVEL to be introduced. Russell and Lodge (2006: 87) argued that EVEL would raise questions about the nature of the Union itself, based on the principle that all MPs, 'as members of a single parliamentary body, can vote on all matters, regardless of their territorial application'. One might equally argue that there are already two classes of MP: those who can vote on domestic matters concerning their own constituencies and those who cannot.

The matter was addressed in the wake of the 2014 Scottish independence referendum, when David Cameron promised something for England to compensate for the attention given to Scotland. The pledge was widely criticized for encouraging an inchoate English nationalism and tinkering unnecessarily with the Union, as well as diluting the concessions to Scotland but Cameron proceeded with EVEL after gaining a majority at the 2015 General Election. The outcome was modest (Glover and Kenny, 2018b). An English committee can vote on bills concerning only England and, effectively veto them. This deals only with the issue of policies being imposed on England but does not allow English MPs to initiate policy, so addressing only half of the question. What is more significant is the questions it raises about the Union and the lack of a federal or a central level. EVEL was opposed by both nationalists and unionists. The SNP complained that it made Scottish MPs 'second class citizens' and that many English issues had knock-on effects in Scotland, including financial consequences (Scottish National Party, 2015). Far from accepting EVEL as a quid pro quo for more powers to Scotland, they then abandoned

[5] Which Bogdanor (1984) has supported.

their previous practice of abstaining on English issues. Previously this had made little difference, but from 2015 they had a significant presence in Parliament. Labour MPs complained about the downgrading of Scotland's parliamentary presence and claimed that it was a Conservative fix. In practice, EVEL in the form adopted does not seem to have had much effect on anything, suggesting that it was more a small gesture directed at English grumbling than a real effort to rebalance the Union.

The impossibility of disentangling England from the centre goes to the heart of the conundrums underlying the devolution settlement. There is no agreed *telos* but rather a series of responses to differentiated demands across the Union. English opinion is not hostile to devolution to the periphery (Chapter 10) but does not want it for itself; rather, there is an appeal for some form of recognition. The argument in Scotland, where it is not about independence, focuses on more powers to be exercised autonomously. In Wales, there are well-developed proposals for cooperative federalism, with large areas of shared competences, in which the nations would have a say (Welsh Government 2017a, b). There is no shared vision for what the centre might look like. For twenty years, the weakness of the centre, of intergovernmental cooperation and of frameworks for addressing common issues was compensated by membership of the European Union, which did provide such an overarching frame. Withdrawal from the EU has exposed this absence in the constitutional provision and created further conflicts over the nature of the domestic settlement.

6

Between Two Unions

Europe as a Union

Home Rule debates in the late nineteenth and early twentieth centuries played out in the context of Empire and the emerging Commonwealth. Devolution, a hundred years later, came about while the United Kingdom was part of another overarching body, the European Union. The implications of membership of the European Communities was a background factor in the devolution debates on the 1970s; the minority report of the Kilbrandon Commission considered that it made legislative devolution impossible (Crowther Hunt and Peacock 1973). By the twenty-first century, the issues had become deeply entangled.

There have been protracted debates about the nature of the European project. For some, it is the germ of a future federation. Neo-functionalist theories argued that integration would produce a self-sustaining dynamic as spillovers from one field influenced others. On the other side, intergovernmentalists see the European Union (EU)[1] as an association of sovereign nation-states pursuing their own self-interests. Far from being a threat, the EU is the saviour of the nation-state (Milward 2000), giving it an external support system in a precarious world, and letting it offload some of the more difficult tasks of governing.

Both perspectives yield useful insights, but both are strongly moulded by the legacy of statehood, whether federal or unitary. The EU is better approached as a plurinational union in the sense discussed in Chapter 1. It has a purpose or *telos*, but this is rather contested. From the beginning, the treaties proclaimed the aim to be an 'ever closer union of the peoples of Europe', a phrase that has been parsed endlessly. The first concern was security, but efforts to forge a defence union failed and collective security was subsumed into the transatlantic NATO alliance in the context of the Cold War. Attention then turned to economics and the development of a regulated market order. The EU's origins as an economic union, culminating in the

[1] We will call it this for consistency although the terminology has changed over the years.

State and Nation in the United Kingdom: The Fractured Union. Michael Keating, Oxford University Press (2021).
 DOI: 10.1093/oso/9780198841371.003.0006

commitment to a full internal market and then a currency union, has marked its vocation and its institutions. The internal market is predicated on the elimination of barriers to the free movement of goods, services, capital and people. The single currency regime has constitutionalized strict economic criteria, notably about budget deficits and debts. The Commission and the Court of Justice have been particularly assiduous in enforcing market competition to the point that critics on the left have seen it as a form of embedded neo-liberalism.

Yet the market-driven conception has been challenged by the concept of 'social Europe'. While the welfare state has remained overwhelmingly a national responsibility, there is a concern to avoid a European 'race to the bottom' in taxation, regulation and social welfare, threatening national social compromises (Bartolini 2005). In practice, social measures have focused on matters close to the economy, such as labour market issues and working standards. Gradually, the social dimension has been valued in its own right, although its importance has waxed and waned over time. A similar rationale was later used to elaborate European environmental policy.

These competing visions have influenced the institutional development of the Union. If it is to be a mere free-trade area, then all that may be required are regulatory institutions to assure market conditions. Even then, however, securing an integrated internal market could require stronger mechanisms. It was Margaret Thatcher who accepted qualified majority voting as the only way to secure the Single Market programme in the 1980s. If the EU is to assume a broader policy role covering social and environmental matters or security, then stronger institutions approaching a European government might be indicated. That, in turn, has posed the question of the 'democratic deficit' as power shifts from elected national governments to remote and non-accountable European agencies.

One response is to argue that, ultimately, it is the member states with their own democratic procedures that are in charge, and that shortcomings can be addressed with stronger provisions for national accountability. Another is to strengthen democratic mechanisms at the European level, notably the European Parliament, whose remit has indeed been extended considerably. This in turn encounters the objection that there is no European *demos* and no public space to deliberate policy choices and arrive at conclusions. The response to this, in turn, is that unions do not depend on a single *demos* but operate complex forms of 'demoicracy' (Nicolaïdis 2012, 2013) (Chapter 1).

As for *ethos*, the architects of the European project consciously embraced universal values, including the defence of democracy and human rights. The

(Maastricht) Treaty on European Union introduced the concept of European citizenship, not to displace national citizenship but rather to give expression to the complex and multilevel nature of citizenship in the modern world, where citizenship of a nation-state does not exhaust the possibilities (Bauböck 2018). It also provided a direct link from the Union to the citizen. The EU Charter of Rights reinforced the common *ethos*, as does the requirement of member states to subscribe to the European Convention on Human Rights and the EU's own adherence to it.

There have been prolonged arguments over the locus of sovereignty in the European Union, where it does lie and where it should. On the one hand are those who insist that it remains with nation-states, who merely lend power to the EU. On the other are analysts who believe that the EU itself has taken on at least elements of sovereign authority (MacCormick 1999), a matter to be celebrated or deplored according to one's political predilections. They point to the supranational principle and the supremacy of European over national laws in areas of EU competence. This takes us to the post-sovereign perspective or shared and divided, rather than unitary authority (Chapter 1). For some states, indeed, EU membership actually enhances effective sovereignty. Germany's integration into Europe was the price of recovering its sovereignty after the Nazi experience and the Second World War. Europe was a vital underpinning for recovered democracy in Spain, Greece and Italy. France reconciled Europe with its sovereignty through the doctrine of *l'Europe des patries*, an intergovernmental vision, with common policies but playing down shared sovereignty.[2] For small member states, including Ireland, European membership enhances national sovereignty, allowing them an influence they would lack as fully independent actors, although there are tensions here.

An attempt to put the EU on a sounder constitutional footing was made in the Constitutional Convention from 2001 to 2003. This provoked a debate about *telos*: whether the European *ethos* should be defined as Christian, multicultural or secular; and the existence or not of a European *demos*. The UK objected to any teleological language referring to federal union. Towards the end of the Convention, member states moved in to take a stronger steering role and an institutional compromise was reached. The draft constitution provided a target for Eurosceptics and other oppositional forces and did not survive referendums in France and the Netherlands. Such was the perceived need to change, however, that member states salvaged the functional parts, stripping out much of the normative language and emotive trappings, and passed

[2] There are, of course, different variations of this, more or less nationalist in inspiration.

it as the Lisbon Treaty. Thereafter, the European Union has tended to avoid grand designs, ambitious commitments to a new constitutional order and the idea of a European people, in favour of practical measures.

From the 1980s, the argument over whether Europe or the nation-state would or should predominate was enlarged by a debate over the link between Europe and subnational territories (Keating and Jones 1985). Regionalists, minority nationalists and localists have seen the EU as an opportunity to weaken the nation-state, while retaining an overarching economic and political framework. For some nationalists, Europe provides a framework for secession, swapping the confining states in which they are a minority for a larger community, in which the external costs of independence are taken care of and continued access to wider markets is ensured. Others take a post-sovereign perspective, in which sovereignty is shared and pooled, not just between Europe and the states but in a multilevel federalism (Keating 2017a). There are utopian visions of a Europe of the Peoples in which the 'artificial' states will give way to more authentic communities as the building blocks of the new order.

A Europe of the Regions movement achieved some success during the 1990s and 2000s. A Committee of the Regions provided consultative input to European policy proposals. Regional governments, where they have a ministerial structure and their state law permits, may represent their member state (but not themselves) in the Council of the European Union. The EU treaties now contain reference to local and regional levels as part of the European system and of democratic representation, and the principles of subsidiarity and proportionality are extended to them.[3] Territorial cohesion is inscribed in the treaties alongside economic and social cohesion. The EU has emphasized the need to include local government and civil society in the administration of its cohesion policies but has scrupulously refrained from telling member states how to organize their territorial government.

The EU, together with the Council of Europe, recognizes that minorities within states deserve protection; this is part of the criteria for admission of new states. Yet they tend to confine protection to *individuals* belonging to minorities and stop short of advocating self-government as a collective right of groups. Leaders of both the European Commission and the European Council will defer to member states and have spoken out against secessionist movements, whether they are proceeding unilaterally, as in Catalonia, or even

[3] This means that action should be taken at the lowest level possible and that European regulations should only have sufficient detail to fulfil their purpose.

in accordance with procedures agreed with their state, as in Scotland.[4] Ideas that the EU would lead to a 'Europe of the Peoples' and a radical recasting of statehood remain the illusion they always were. Yet the European framework has shaped the management of territory and the accommodation of nationalism in important ways, not least in the United Kingdom.

Reconciling the Two Unions

The United Kingdom has had a difficult relationship with the European project (Gros-Fitzgibbon 2016), largely because its leaders have refused to accept the supranational principle or any compromise with the doctrine of parliamentary sovereignty. Opponents of EU membership have repeatedly argued that it was originally confined to economics, with political union brought in later by stealth; this was a prominent feature of the 2016 Brexit campaign. In fact, issues of sovereignty lay at the heart of British attitudes to Europe from the beginning; Hugh Gaitskell (1962) famously warned that it would mean the end of 1,000 years of British history (ignoring the fact that Britain only dates from 1707). UK governments have preferred an intergovernmental Europe and have seen federalism as a centralizing principle—even as they opposed internal federalization of the United Kingdom for the opposite reason. After accession, successive UK governments skirted around the issue to avoid facing the question of principle. The courts went along with the idea that European laws prevailed because Parliament had provided for this in the European Communities Act, not because it had surrendered sovereignty (Armstrong 2017). Although the primacy of EU law had been established by 1964 (in the Costa case), it was not until 1991 (in *Factortame*) that the courts disallowed a UK law on the grounds that it violated European provisions. Ironically, it has been argued that it was not until the EU Withdrawal Bill of 2018 that the principle of supremacy of EU law was formally accepted by the UK Government. In practice, however, UK Governments avoided any breach of EU law.

The essential premise of the movement for UK withdrawal from the EU was that its supranational features were incompatible with the principle of parliamentary and national sovereignty. So, the foundation of the Brexit

[4] In an interview on British television (Andrew Marr Show, 16-02-2014), José Manuel Barroso declared that it would be 'extremely difficult, if not impossible', for an independent Scotland to join the EU, even though the UK Government had agreed to the referendum process.

campaign of 2016 was to restore the sovereignty of the nation-state, to 'take back control'. This entailed a rebordering of the UK state.

A different perspective is opened, however, if we conceive of both the UK and the EU as plurinational unions, in which *demos*, *telos* and *ethos* are contested. They are neither unitary states nor federations but share some federalizing tendencies. Their purpose variously includes economic competition, social cohesion, democratic consolidation, security and convenience. They have supporters both on the right and the left, and efforts to reduce them to a singular or coherent set of ideas merely provoke disagreement. In both cases, ideas of the nature and purpose of the union differ from one part to another. Neither has resolved the issue of sovereignty but are able to put it in abeyance when necessary. None of these means that the unions cannot work well for their members as long as diversity, not only in culture and identity but also in the meaning and purpose of union itself, is recognized.

In this perspective, the two unions, far from being in contradiction, are a good fit and provide complementary ways of understanding and managing political authority. Indeed, the European frame for long underpinned the devolution settlement, compensating for some of the abeyances and gaps in the constitutional architecture. In the first place, Europe provides a discursive space for concepts of shared and divided sovereignty, which chime with domestic arguments. This is not to say that either union has a precise vision of sovereignty. On the contrary, it is the very fact that different accounts of the foundations of political authority can coexist that is the contribution to stability. Labour-led governments in Scotland and Wales played the Europe-of-the-Regions game in the 2000s, projecting their nations beyond the UK frame while containing separatist impulses. Intellectuals like Neil MacCormick (1999) deployed ideas of post-sovereignty and multilevel order to explore middle-ways between union and independence. The SNP, while earlier expressing favourable views towards Europe, opposed membership in the 1970s on sovereignty grounds. In the mid-1980s they changed tack again, adopting the slogan of independence-in-Europe, albeit an intergovernmental rather than a federal Europe. This allowed them to soften the representation of independence in the Scottish referendum campaign of 2014, where Europe was presented as one of the five unions in which an independent Scotland would remain, the others being the monarchical, monetary, defence and social unions. Post-sovereignty and pro-European thinking has long been strong in Plaid Cymru and their periodic swings towards independence have been accompanied by a strong European commitment.

The strongest manifestation of European post-sovereignty thinking is in the Northern Ireland settlement. While the republican nationalists of Sinn Féin were long Eurosceptics and opposed every European referendum in the Republic of Ireland, the moderate SDLP were staunchly pro-Europe. Unionists, who already tended to oppose the European project as a threat to sovereignty and some of whom associated it with Catholicism, were sceptical. The potential of European integration in both the UK and Ireland to reframe the Northern Ireland question had been noted during the debates around the Sunningdale agreement, concluded just as both countries were entering the (then) European Communities (Dorr 2017). Europe also received mention in the Anglo-Irish Agreement and the Downing Street Declaration. The hope was that fixed identities would soften, if not disappear, within a common supranational framework, that the border could be opened up for travel and commerce, and that cross-border institutions might flourish. The Good Friday Agreement can be considered post-sovereigntist in that it suspends belief in sovereignty and diffuses it across multiple levels. The GFA in effect suspended the conflict about the *telos* by conceding that both aspirations were legitimate and allowing them eventually to be resolved by referendum. Citizens are invited to adopt any identity or combination of identities and these are given institutional expression. While Northern Ireland remains within the UK, the role of the Republic of Ireland in determining its future is recognized. So while the EU did not play much of a direct role in the Irish peace process and there is not a lot about Europe in the GFA, EU membership was a vital background factor in the new thinking that underpinned it and in shaping the attitudes of both the UK and Irish governments.

The most profound effects of Europeanization were felt at the border between Northern Ireland and the Irish Republic (Anderson 2018, where a combination of the historic Common Travel Area, the GFA and the European Single Market permitted the dismantling of infrastructure and the abolition of controls. EU membership and the Single Market permitted the emergence of all-Ireland markets in agriculture and energy, while public services such as health could be organized on a cross-border basis; the provisions on the union in the GFA ensured that these could not be exploited as insidious routes to Irish unification. The border was not abolished; on the contrary, it was for the first time recognized by all sides. It was, however, as far as possible, emptied of substantive meaning. Relations between the two communities and their political representatives remained tense but the territorial expression of these competing identities as exclusive claims on territory had almost ceased to be an issue by the time of the Brexit referendum in 2016.

At the border itself, identities and social relationships could recompose in complex ways without always been forced into the straitjacket of the competing territorial-national projects (Hayward 2018; Todd 2018).

While EU membership met opposition in both the UK and Ireland (Keogh 1997) on sovereignty grounds, there was a strong and growing view in Ireland that it had actually enhanced the country's effective sovereignty. Ireland's trade was diversified away from Great Britain and, as a small independent European state, it was able to exercise influence in a wider polity. Common membership of European institutions also allowed British and Irish ministers to meet on a regular basis on terms of equality, which has been credited with easing cooperation over Northern Ireland.

In concrete ways, EU membership allowed for a more expansive and permissive devolution internal settlement than might otherwise have been possible or was offered in the failed devolution proposals of 1978 when the UK was within the European Communities but the Single Market programme had not been elaborated. Policies across a range of fields, including agriculture and fisheries, environment and regional development were both devolved and Europeanized, with UK responsibilities largely confined to forging a common position in European negotiations. Whatever discretion was available to member states in the implementation of policy was extended to the devolved UK administrations. In some cases, indeed, there was sometimes more commonality at the European level than within the UK. EU undergraduates at Scottish universities did not pay fees because they had to be treated as domestic students; English, Welsh and Northern Irish students in Scotland do pay. More broadly, the European framework provided a single or internal market within the United Kingdom itself (Chapter 8), harmonizing or providing mutual recognition for regulation across a range of devolved matters.

Or course, EU membership did constrain the exercise of devolved powers. Not only must devolved governments and legislatures act within EU law, but the UK needed to present a single position at the Council of the European Union where rules are adopted. The formal mechanism for this was the Joint Ministerial Committee (Europe) representing the devolved and UK governments, but on which the UK had the last word. Devolved ministers were also allowed, at the invitation of the UK, to participate in the UK delegation to the Council of the EU, but only to represent the UK as a whole, not their own particular interests.

If the UK Government thus remained master of the game, these arrangements did draw devolved governments into European policy networks. They were present in Brussels, they had extensive contacts with the Commission, and were embedded in European-wide policy communities. They were active in pan-European networks of sub-state governments such as the association of Regions with Legislative Powers (RegLeg) and sectoral bodies. Elaboration of policy within these multilevel networks shifted the focus away from bilateral negotiations between the UK and devolved institutions and served to diffuse influence and reduce confrontation. In this way, UK borders were loosened and opened.

Human and Citizen Rights

Rights and citizenship is one of the central issues in the constitution of unions (Chapter 1). On the one hand, equal rights are an expression of the *ethos* or normative content of union and of citizenship. On the other hand, if they are linked expressly to nationality, they risk the alienation of minorities who may not identify with the whole. In Quebec, the Canadian Charter of Rights has aroused some opposition, not because of its substantive content but because it is seen as a centralizing and Canadian nationalist measure. Historically, the United Kingdom has lacked a tradition of legally enforceable citizen rights, relying instead on the political process. Conservatives have not favoured restraining parliamentary sovereignty, while the left has been suspicious of putting power in the hands of judges and feared that rights might be exploited by the powerful to defend their privileges against progressive governments.

These attitudes have changed since the 1960s and constitutional reformers have tended to favour entrenched rights, enforceable by the courts. The first charter of rights, however, was not a British one but the European Charter for the Protection of Human Rights and Fundamental Freedoms (ECHR), incorporated into UK law in the Human Rights Act of 1998 but into the devolved statutes in a stronger form allowing courts to strike down devolved legislation (Chapter 3). From 2009, the Charter of Fundamental Rights of the European Union came into effect, in spite of the efforts of the UK Labour Government to opt out. Although it only applies to EU law, its implications exceed that, given the intricate connection between EU and national law. It goes beyond the ECHR in including important political and social rights and, although the rights are often expressed in rather general terms, it is part of EU law, so that rulings made under it are binding both on member states and sub-state authorities.

These provisions have come under attack from the left and (mainly) from the right, for curtailing parliamentary sovereignty and putting power in the hands of judges. Eurosceptics take particular offence at the idea that a court of 'foreign judges' (the European Court of Human Rights in Strasbourg or Court of Justice of the EU) has the last word on cases. For adherents to the plurinational rather than the Westminster view of the constitution, however, a central merit of the system is that it detaches the question of rights from that of nationality. Instead, rights are expressed as universal in principle and enforceable in a European legal arena. This makes the European Convention and Charter acceptable in Scotland, where a substantial part of the population do not regard themselves as British. It is crucial in Northern Ireland, where the division is more pronounced and the minority community has memories of the failure of successive UK governments to protect them from discrimination under the old Stormont regime.

While laying down general principles of rights, the Convention and the practice of the Strasbourg court has been to respect the traditions and autonomy of national judicial and political systems and enter into dialogue with them. It will frequently issue opinions on contentious issues and then refer them back to national courts for final resolution. This has opened up another multilevel discursive space for consideration of public policy matters and the balance between public power and private rights. Indeed, most of the challenges to the competence of the devolved bodies have come under EU or ECHR provisions rather than the devolution statutes themselves. While ECRH and the EU Charter of Rights proved politically contentious in England, they aroused much less opposition in the devolved territories. As we will see in Chapter 7, efforts to replace European provisions with a UK Bill of Rights have raised serious constitutional problems.

Brexit

The 2016 referendum on UK withdrawal from the EU consequently delivered a shock to the system as the component nations were pulled in different directions. In Scotland, all the parties in the Parliament[5] favoured Remain, although there was some internal dissent. The same was true in the National Assembly for Wales with the exception of the United Kingdom Independence Party. In Northern Ireland, the historically Eurosceptic Democratic Unionist Party (DUP) came out for Leave while the smaller Ulster Unionist Party favoured Remain, at least until after the referendum. The moderate nationalist

[5] SNP, Conservative, Labour, Liberal Democrat and Green.

SDLP remained pro- European while Sinn Féin abandoned its historic Euroscepticism to campaign for Remain, on the grounds that leaving the EU would mean a return of the border ('repartitioning Ireland') and threaten the gains of the Good Friday Agreement. The outcome was a 52 per cent majority across the UK for Leave, spawning the slogan 'the British people voted to leave the EU' (May 2019a). Yet, while both England and Wales voted to leave, 62 per cent in Scotland, and 56 per cent in Northern Ireland voted to remain (Hobolt 2016). This immediately posed the question of the relevant *demos* and whether there were different mandates across the Union. It also posed serious questions about the devolution settlement, given its reliance on the European framework, a matter given little attention in the campaigns in England (Rawlings 2017). Doing nothing was not an option since, at a minimum, the requirement for the devolved institutions to work within European law would have to be removed. Something would also have to be done about the Irish border (Murphy 2018) and, more broadly, the hardening of the UK borders would reduce opportunities for devolved nations to operate in European space. Brexit thus unleashed contradictory forces: centrifugal pressures towards disintegration of the Union as the component parts found their own place in Europe and the world; recentralization as the UK was recomposed as a sovereign and unitary nation-state; or reconfiguration and increased asymmetry across the Union. Prime Minister Theresa May promised a 'red, white and blue Brexit' (*Guardian* 2016) suggesting both a unity of purpose and the inclusion of the devolved nations. Yet, while a new Joint Ministerial Committee (European Negotiations) was established, its role was consultative rather than decision-making. As a matter of foreign relations, Brexit was seen in London as an exclusively reserved matter.

Disintegration

Immediately after the referendum, the SNP Government in Scotland demanded a new independence referendum on the ground that Scotland being taken out of the EU against its will constituted the 'material change of circumstances' which they had said in their 2016 Scottish election manifesto would legitimate another vote. Sinn Féin talked up a border poll on Irish unification as envisaged under the Good Friday Agreement. Neither was an immediate success, for two reasons. First, while the secession of Scotland and Northern Ireland would keep borders with the EU open, it would impose a hard border with the remainder of the United Kingdom, which was much more important as a trading partner. This undermined the attraction of the Scottish 'independence in Europe' proposals of 2014 which would have left both borders open. In Northern Ireland, similarly, unification would abolish the intra-Irish border but impose a new one between Ireland and Great Britain, undermining the GFA which had kept open boundaries on both sides.

The second key factor was the state of public opinion (discussed more fully in Chapter 10). Brexit did increase support for secession but not decisively. In spite of the clear message of the SNP, there was no stable connection among the Scottish electorate between independence and being in Europe, and in 2016 almost a third of independence supporters voted Leave. Indeed, no combination of Yes/No to independence and Remain/Leave to Europe commanded anything like a majority (Prosser and Fieldhouse 2017). The independence referendum gambit cost the SNP votes and seats in the snap General Election of 2017, which appeared to close the issue. As the Brexit debate was drawn out over the following two years, however, matters changed. While the Labour Party prevaricated over support for a second referendum to overturn Brexit, the SNP came down firmly in support. It also doubled down on support for a second independence referendum. The Scottish Conservatives, for their part, doubled down on refusing another independence referendum and (changing their position since 2016) pressing ahead with Brexit. Public opinion started to realign, with support for independence correlating more with Remain. This polarization played to the advantage of the SNP, who recovered votes and seats at the General Election of 2019, scoring 45 per cent, while the Scottish Conservatives' lost both votes and half their seats. Yet there was still not a convincing majority for independence.

The majority Remain vote in Northern Ireland showed sharp divisions between the two communities. Almost ninety per cent of nationalists voted to remain, compared with just a third of unionists (Garry 2017b). The issue had therefore caused a much deeper division within Northern Ireland than between the province and the UK as a whole. While Protestants remained firmly unionist, there was a move back among Catholics to support for Irish reunification (Chapter 10). Unification began to be talked about in both parts of Ireland as a serious prospect, for the first time in some years.

Even in Wales, which had voted Leave, there was concern about the constitutional implications of Brexit. The term 'indy-curious' began to be used for Remainers who, while not supporting secession, had seen their faith in the Union shaken (Trystan 2019).

Recentralization

While one effect of Brexit was centrifugal, another went in the opposite direction. The central thrust of Brexit was to take back control to a sovereign Parliament. After the referendum, this quickly transmuted into a claim for popular sovereignty and Theresa May's dictum that the British people had spoken. If the idea of parliamentary sovereignty is difficult in a plurinational union, that of popular sovereignty is even more so, given the absence of a single *demos*. Yet this idea of a unified mandate was to underpin the strategy of UK Government up to and beyond the point of departure.).

The issue was joined in a practical way over what would happen to matters such as agriculture, fisheries, environment, regional economic development and, in Scotland and Northern Ireland, large parts of Justice and Home Affairs, which were devolved but subject to European law. There was wide agreement that, with the European framework gone, there would need to be some mechanism to deal with common problems and externalities in these fields. There was a major difference on how this might be done, exposing a serious contrast in interpretations of the settlement. The UK Government's (2017b) view was that the devolved governments 'are responsible for implementing the common policy frameworks set by the EU' rather than making policy. So, 'when the UK leaves the EU, the powers which the EU currently exercises in relation to the common frameworks will return to the UK' (UK Government 2017b). This was disputed by the devolved governments, which pointed out that these competences are not reserved in the devolution acts and therefore devolved. The EU frameworks have no counterpart in the UK constitution and would cease after Brexit. In pursuit of its interpretation, the UK Government proposed, in the first draft of the EU Withdrawal Bill, that all the relevant powers under the heading of 'retained EU law' would revert to Westminster. Since, it argued, the powers had never really been devolved, no 'decisions' currently taken by the devolved governments would be brought back to Westminster. In due course, some of the competences might be 'released' back so that the devolved bodies might actually gain powers (UK Government 2017a). The result was a major clash between the UK Government and the devolved legislatures (including the Scottish and Welsh Conservatives) which refused legislative consent under the Sewel Convention. Eventually, the UK Government backed down and agreed to drop the sweeping reservation of competences but retained the power to take back through statutory instrument such matters as might be necessary.[6] On this basis, the National

[6] As explained in Chapter 5, this was a novel version of the consent mechanism.

Assembly for Wales gave legislative consent but the Scottish Parliament continued to refuse it, with only the Scottish Conservatives dissenting.

This still left the issue of what kind of UK-wide frameworks might be necessary to replace the overarching European regulations. For the UK Government, this was a technical, rather than political, matter. It drew up lists of specific items for each of the devolved territories, divided them into matters where no action was needed, where legislative frameworks might be required, where non-legislative frameworks would suffice and where responsibility was uncertain. If legislative frameworks were required, these would be subject to the non-binding legislative consent (Sewel) convention. An intense process was undertaken at official level to identify which precise powers would need to be addressed.

The Welsh Government (2017a, b) argued that UK-wide frameworks were acceptable but should be negotiated on a basis of equality among the four nations rather than imposed from above. The Scottish Government accepted a need for some (negotiated) 'cross-border frameworks' (Russell 2017), but otherwise emphasized its scope for autonomous policy-making, with limited, voluntary cooperation. The Northern Ireland parties showed a rare unity in resisting any loss of competences. The issue had a particular relevance there, given the extensive cooperation in European programmes with the Republic of Ireland, notably in relation to agriculture, tourism and economic development.

After the initial clash over taking back powers, UK frameworks could be reduced to technical matters, negotiated in detail at official level, with the constitutional implications in abeyance. The transposition into the UK of the broader concept of the internal market was altogether more politicized and difficult. The EU internal market is not a precise set of competences but a broad, transversal principle implying not just free trade but regulatory harmonization, and limiting government interventions that might distort market competition. Its ramifications are discussed more fully in Chapter 8. The very concept of an internal market is a highly charged and politicized matter, posing the question of the proper scope of market principles, as opposed to social or environmental norms, and of the boundaries between the state and the private sector. The EU internal market is subject to the complex European system of multilevel policy-making involving the Commission, member states, the European Parliament and the Court of Justice. Measures are subject to the principles of subsidiarity and proportionality. In the absence of these features, a UK internal market principle could mean substantial recentralization of powers. The UK Government's position was stated by the Advocate General, Lord Keen (2018): '[I]f we are to have a single market for the United Kingdom, we require a body to have jurisdiction over that single market…that ultimately has to be the Parliament of the United Kingdom.' This is, in effect, how it was done, resulting in a significant recentralization (Chapter 8).

While many of these large issues could be fudged or 'muddled through', the question of international trade deals, whether with the EU or third countries, was more urgent. Trade agreements in the modern world go beyond trade in the narrow sense of exchange of goods and cover services as well as ancillary matters including standards, environmental provisions and labour regulation. Agricultural trade is particularly difficult, touching, as it does, subsidies to farmers, food standards and environmental matters. In the devolution statutes, international trade is reserved but many of these related issues are not. The UK Government was given powers to secure compliance with international agreements in the devolved territories, but these were not exercised much because trade agreements were an EU competence and EU provisions clearly do apply across the nations. Depending on the scope of trade agreements, it was likely therefore that they would lead to the UK increasingly encroaching on devolved competences. This provoked demands in the devolved bodies that their competences needed protection and, at the same time, that they should have an input to trade negotiations. The UK Government promised only consultation.

Underlying these arguments are fundamental questions about the nature of the UK constitutional settlement and the way it works. In contrast to those in other countries, it lays down a fairly clear division of responsibilities. There are few concurrent competences and no category of framework laws as in Spain and Italy and, in the past, in Germany. Instead, each government looks after its own responsibilities, with some memoranda of understanding and sporadic forums like the Joint Ministerial Council where necessary for coordination. Only in relation to European matters was there a consistent need to coordinate policy positions in order to agree a negotiating line; the Joint Ministerial Council (Europe) was the only one that worked regularly throughout the period prior to the UK's departure from the EU.

The European Union, by contrast, operates according to the 'community method'. This involves an intricate pattern of negotiations at EU and member-state level. Policy initiation is reserved for the European Commission, which is independent of member states. Proposals are then subject to extensive consultation with member states and stakeholders before going to the Council of the EU (representing the member states), where they are mostly decided by qualified majority voting. They also need the agreement of the European Parliament. Some provisions take the form of law, directly applicable across the EU and enforceable in the courts and, ultimately, the Court of Justice of the European Union. Others are directives, instructions to member states to implement the policy, often by transposing the directive into domestic law. The Commission then has the role of monitoring compliance and the Court of Justice of the European Union rules on infringements. If the matter was devolved within the UK, then it was usually the devolved legislature that did the transposition, although the UK Government was responsible for any failure. The overarching principles of subsidiarity and proportionality are intended to guarantee that action will be taken at European level only if it cannot be done at a lower one, and that it will not exceed the level of detail that is necessary, allowing discretion in implementation.

It was therefore disingenuous of the UK Government to argue that it could replace the EU as the maker of policies, while the devolved administrations would continue to administer them. The UK devolution settlement includes nothing like the EU guarantees for member states, there is nothing equivalent to the Commission as a body independent of the states, the courts are not able to restrain central interventions, and there are no principles of subsidiarity and proportionality. Transferring EU competences back to Westminster rather than the devolved level would therefore, mean centralization. On the other hand, allowing them to revert to the devolved nations would create a gap in coordination mechanisms and frameworks.

While the Scottish Government saw the whole episode as a pretext for recentralization, the Welsh Government (2017a, b) saw an opportunity to transfer ideas from how the EU works into the UK context, consistent with its vision of union and cooperative federalism. This would include a UK Council of Ministers to operate on similar lines to the Council of the European Union. The difference between Scottish and Welsh reactions is largely political. The ruling Scottish National Party was intent on Scottish independence in the longer term. Yet it also reflects distinct understandings of union and devolution in the two nations. Scotland's size, its capacity for policy-making and its extensive legislative competences mean that any government there is likely to stress autonomy. Wales, more tightly bound into England, has tended to stress interdependence. Both visions, however, saw EU membership as underpinning their visions of union.

Reconfiguration

A third possibility is that the nations of the UK could be differentially engaged with Europe in a radical reconfiguration of the union. While in principle, the

EU is an association of states, some member states have opt-outs from some provisions and some non-member states opt in to some programmes. Even some regions of member states have opt-outs. Greenland, a self-governing part of Denmark, withdrew from the European Communities (now EU) in 1979. The Faroe Islands, also part of Denmark, never joined. The Canaries and Azores have special fiscal and customs arrangements. Yet there is no provision for part of a non-member state to opt in. There were suggestions in the aftermath of the referendum, that Scotland and Northern Ireland could remain in the EU. One was that England and Wales could withdraw, allowing Scotland and Northern Ireland to take over the UK's membership (O'Leary 2016). Yet this would require Scotland and Northern Ireland to acquire all the competences necessary to act as an EU member state, which would look a lot like independence and undermine the very foundations of the UK union. The concept of a 'reverse Greenland' was floated, but this would meet the same objection.

Without abandoning its preferred policy of independence in the EU, the Scottish Government (2016) made a concrete proposal for selective participation in Europe. Scotland would remain in the Single Market for goods and services, associated with the European Economic Area, in which Norway, Iceland and Liechtenstein (the EFTA countries) have full access to the Single Market but must accept its rules without having a say in how they are made. Agriculture and fisheries are excluded and the EFTA countries are not part of the Customs Union. In the Scottish proposals, Scotland would remain in the UK customs area.[7] There would be free movement of workers between Scotland and the thirty EU-EEA countries, and Scotland would participate in European social provisions, academic exchange and research and aspects of EU Justice and Home Affairs policies.

While the aim was to keep open access to both EU and UK markets, there would nevertheless be new borders and barriers. With Scotland within the UK customs area, there could be tariffs and controls on trade with the EU, unless the UK had a free trade agreement with the EU. If the UK and EU were to diverge over regulations on goods and services, then Scotland, retaining EU rules, could face restrictions of trade with England. Although these might be limited by double compliance rules to ensure that Scottish services were compliant with both UK and EU regulations, this would not ensure goods coming from the rest of the UK into Scotland were compliant. While the

[7] If the UK remained within the EU Customs Union (as then seemed possible), Scotland would also be within it.

EFTA countries are in the Single Market and outside the Customs Union, the only example of a state in the Single Market and in a customs union with a non-member state is Liechtenstein, a micro-state dependent on Switzerland. Free movement of workers between Scotland and the EU would be easier to manage and has been suggested regularly to meet the cross-party consensus in Scotland, which favours free movement; it could be monitored at the place of work rather than at the border. Allowing Scottish workers reciprocal rights in other EEA states, however, would require provisions to define a Scottish worker. Perhaps the biggest difficulty in the proposals was that, for Scotland to remain compliant with Single Market regulations, the Scottish Parliament and Government would require new competences across a wide range of Single Market matters that are currently reserved to Westminster. In that case, it might be argued, independence would be an easier solution.

In the event, the UK Government refused to discuss the provisions, seeing them as incompatible with the Union. They remain of interest, however, not merely for historical reasons, but because some of these very provisions were later incorporated into the Northern Ireland deal. Unable to advance this kind of formal link with Europe, the Scottish Government sought instead to remain in dynamic alignment with EU regulations in areas under its control, posing a challenge to whatever UK frameworks might be imposed on them. After an early bill had fallen on technical grounds (UK Supreme Court 2018), a European Union (Continuity) (Scotland) Bill was introduced in 2020 to give Scottish ministers powers to align Scotland with EU regulations in devolved matters.

Northern Ireland presented some of the same difficulties about borders but in a more acute, urgent and politically sensitive form. A combination of the Common Travel Area, the Good Friday Agreement and the European Single Market had emptied the border of much of its functional substance and removed it as a physical presence, while leaving it intact as a jurisdictional boundary. With the UK outside the Single Market and Customs Union and the Republic of Ireland within, there would be an economic border between the two parts of Ireland. This would hinder the operation of all-Ireland institutions and markets and represent a symbolic return to a very visible manifestation of partition after years in abeyance.

Both the SDLP (2017) and Sinn Féin (2017) pressed for a differentiated settlement but they could do little on their own. The real leverage arose from the fact that the Northern Ireland settlement had been agreed in partnership with the Republic of Ireland, with key parts secured in an international treaty. Ireland was doubly affected by Brexit (Murphy 2018). One concern was bilateral trade across the Irish Sea with Great Britain, which still represented a large part of Irish imports and exports. The other was the impact on the Northern Ireland settlement. The Irish Government took an early decision for Ireland not to rely on bilateral deals with the United Kingdom, where it would be the weaker party, but to play as an integral part of the EU side (Connelly 2017). The strategy was rewarded when the EU agreed that the Northern Ireland border should be one of the three issues[8] to be addressed before substantive Brexit negotiations could begin. As the Northern Ireland Assembly and Executive were not operational during the crucial time (2017–20), there was no local political input.

While all sides agreed that the Good Friday Agreement should be safeguarded in any Brexit deal, there was little agreement on what this entailed. The UK Government took a narrow interpretation, relying on the wording of the Agreement, which indeed says little about Europe. The Irish Government took a more expansive view, including everything that that the combination of the GFA and the single market had achieved. The UK Government defined the border in a restrictive way, referring to 'physical infrastructures' such as customs posts; if these could be avoided by electronic processing or putting the structures away from the border, that would meet the requirement. Others pointed out that a 'virtual border' was still a border and that controls away from the border were still controls, which posed obstacles to trade and movement. For its part, the EU was concerned to maintain the integrity of its Single Market, meaning that the Irish border could not be used as a back door into or out of it. Yet, if the border between two parts of Ireland were to be kept open, then, to preserve the integrity of the EU internal market and prevent any circumvention of it, there would have to be controls between Northern Ireland and Great Britain, a 'border in the Irish Sea'.

The issue was played out at two levels. On the one hand was a transactional and technical approach focused on practical difficulties. This was the strategy adopted by the UK side, along with a tendency to minimize the problems.[9] It was not only the UK side that took this line. At one point, EU negotiator Michel Barnier argued that border controls in the Irish Sea would be only 'technical' (Randerson, 2018). Both ignored the larger significance of the Irish border, which goes to the heart of larger questions of the historic partition of the island and the competing territorial imaginations of the two communities. A border, whether on the island or in the Irish Sea could represent not

[8] The others were the rights of citizens and the financial settlement.

[9] Some pro-Brexit politicians insisted that they would not put up a border in Ireland at all and that if any border were imposed, this would be the fault of the Europeans and the Irish (Redwood 2017), which seems to sit ill with the promise to 'take back control of our borders'.

only an obstacle to trade but a fracturing of the territorial imagination of one or other of Northern Ireland's communities.

In the first agreement between the UK Government and the EU, Northern Ireland was to be given special status, remaining within the EU Customs Union and largely in regulatory alignment with the EU. This was blocked by the Democratic Unionist Party, on which the UK Government was dependent for parliamentary support. In the next version, the whole of the UK was to remain in a single customs territory with the EU. There would be as much regulatory alignment between Northern Ireland and the EU as was required to satisfy the Good Friday Agreement; the lack of agreement of what this entailed was glossed over. These arrangements would remain in place until a substitute could be found in the future long-term agreement between the EU and the UK, hence the name of 'Irish Backstop' (Connelly 2018). This satisfied neither the DUP, who complained that there would be a border in the Irish Sea, nor the hard-line Brexiters in the Conservative Party, who objected to the UK remaining effectively in the Customs Union. While in principle the backstop was to be superseded by the long-term arrangement, it is difficult to see how this could work unless it incorporated exactly those elements of the backstop to which the unionists had objected.

Following the Conservative victory at the General Election of 2019, the UK reverted to a version of the original proposal, so that Northern Ireland alone would be effectively within both the EU and UK customs territories and largely in regulatory alignment with the EU. This was to be achieved by a complex set of arrangements that bear some resemblance to those proposed by the Scottish Government in 2016. Goods going to Northern Ireland from Great Britain would face customs and regulatory checks but could claim a rebate on any tariffs if it could be proved that they were not going to enter the EU. This did put a border in the Irish Sea as the price for keeping open the land border with the Republic. There was provision for the Northern Ireland Assembly to withdraw from these arrangements later.

The example provides more evidence that Northern Ireland is not seen in Westminster as part of the union in the same way that Scotland and Wales are. The border in the Irish Sea represents a shift in the meaning of union, although such a border had existed during and for a while after the Second World War. For a time it appeared as though at least a section of the Conservative Party had such a principled objection to it and, in alliance with the DUP was taking its unionism seriously. In the event, the matter was merely a pawn in the Brexit game, which the Conservative Government privileged over their unionism.

It took a three and a half years and two general elections to get a Brexit deal though the UK Parliament but finally, with a pro-Brexit Conservative majority following the General Election of 2019, it went ahead. It did not carry the devolved legislatures, all of which denied the EU Withdrawal Agreement Bill legislative consent, including nationalists and unionists in Northern Ireland, Scottish and Welsh nationalists and the Labour, Liberal Democrat and Green parties. In the meantime, Brexit had undermined the devolution settlement and caused a serious fissure in the Union.

7
Union and Unionisms in the United Kingdom

Nationalism and Unionism

Two ideologies or worldviews have dominated constitutional debate across the United Kingdom: nationalism and unionism. At times of heightened political tension, such as the Irish Home Rule debates of the 1880s and early twentieth century, or the Scottish independence arguments in the twenty-first century, these are presented as diametrical opposites, the one favouring a radical division of the territory into separate units, the other supporting continued territorial integrity. John Lloyd (2020: 60) claims that 'the opposition of nationalism and unionism is fundamental', In Northern Ireland, they define two distinct political communities while in Scotland the division has become the principal political cleavage. Yet neither is easy to define: the two traditions have a lot in common and they overlap at numerous points.

Nationalism, as noted earlier, is a twofold claim: an ontological claim that the nation exists (*demos*) and a teleological and normative claim that it should be self-determining. Yet the national identities do not have to be exclusive, and self-determination may take many forms. The challenge from the periphery emerged as we have seen, as a demand for Home Rule or federalism and not, except among a minority in Ireland, for separation. Separatism became hegemonic in nationalist Ireland only in the aftermath of the 1916 Rising and was hardly broached in Scotland until the 1920s. Even schemes for effective independence were often placed within the Empire, by analogy with the British Dominions, whose independence developed incrementally. Some expressions of 'nationalism', indeed took the form of insisting that the UK be recognized as a union, as opposed to a unitary state; as we will see, some unionisms made exactly the same claim. In the Scottish independence referendum campaign of 2014, fought over a 'clear' binary question after middle-ground proposals had been kept off the ballot paper, both sides converged towards the centre ground. The nationalist side promised to remain in five of the six current

State and Nation in the United Kingdom: The Fractured Union. Michael Keating, Oxford University Press (2021).
 DOI: 10.1093/oso/9780198841371.003.0007

unions (monarchical, currency, social, European, defence) and to withdraw only from the 'political' one (Keating and McEwen 2017).

Unionism is even more complex. Unionists in some plurinational states, such as Canada or Spain, have refused to recognize the component territories as nations in their own right, since they fear that conceding the ontological claim would mean conceding the teleological and normative claims as well. Some forms of assimilative unionism in the United Kingdom have taken the same line, but for the most part union has been seen as compatible with a plurality of national realities. Union*ism* as a political movement can, however, carry a heavy historical charge, especially in Northern Ireland. While rival state and sub-state nationalisms in other plurinational states have articulated fully fledged doctrines spanning all three elements, unionisms in the United Kingdom are often weakly articulated. So, in Canada or Spain, it is common to talk about the 'national unity' question, neither the expression nor an equivalent are to be found much in the UK. Unionism has developed more as a political practice than as a doctrine, and is articulated more at the periphery than at the centre. For most of its history, it remained 'banal', an unstated assumption about the state rather than a fully articulated ideology (Kidd 2008). While British pride and identity could be projected outwards against external others, its inward articulation as *demos*, *telos* and *ethos* was less pronounced.

Because the United Kingdom had been created by successive unions, each taking its own form, unionism was always differentiated. It was most clearly specified in Ireland in reaction to Home Rule proposals from the 1880s. After the independence of most of the island, it retreated to the six counties of Northern Ireland, where it took on its own qualities, at once stridently British and particularist. Scottish unionism can be traced back before the union itself (Kidd 2008), but was defined during the twentieth century by opposition to Irish and then Scottish Home Rule and, later, to independence.[1] It was more difficult to talk of Welsh unionism in the nineteenth and early twentieth centuries, given the weakness of the nationalist challenge, but there has always been a strand in the labour movement that saw nation as a distraction from class politics. English unionism was understated as union was not challenged there, and English political culture had no problem in assimilating English and British political identities. Devolution at the end of the twentieth century forced unionism to define itself again, incorporating devolution into its

[1] 'Unionism' in Scotland long referred to the Irish union, as did the name of the Scottish Unionist Party after 1912.

concept of union and searching for an overarching message that could encompass the whole state.

The inchoate nature of unionism makes it difficult to define it as an 'ism' (ideology) at all, although the same question has often been posed of nationalism (Freeden 1998). There is a substantial body of thought and beliefs, linked at different times to particular political movements, but not a definable core. Nor is it helpful to elaborate a taxonomy of unionisms, as though each had an internal consistency and was distinct from the others. Instead, there are a number of threads which unionists weave together in varied ways to defend the political order in different political circumstances.

Integration

One strand of unionism has taken the form of British nation-building, placing the unity of the United Kingdom into a modernist *telos* or historical narrative of progress and integration into a single *demos* with a progressive *ethos*. The influential 'Whig' historiography (Butterfield 1968), which presented the story of the islands as a steady and largely peaceful path to liberalism and social and economic betterment, is the British counterpart of a modernist narrative of progress as territorial integration and functional differentiation (Chapter 1). Critical events, such as the Glorious Revolution of 1688, feature in the narrative both as progress and as moments of restoration and rebalancing of the constitutional order, while the unions of England with the peripheral nations are an integral part of the story.

Colley (1992) has emphasized the role of the Protestant religion in forging this common British (if not UK) identity. Certainly, the Whig narrative links Protestantism both to liberalism and to union. Yet divisions within Protestantism worked against integration and sustained differentiation in Scotland, Northern Ireland and Wales. Nor was the Protestant and Whig tradition consistently liberal in *ethos*; indeed, it is strikingly sectarian. The Scottish Claim of Right (1689) prohibited the printing or distributing of 'popish books' and the public saying of Mass as well as the employment of Catholics in any public office whatever. The greatest flaw in the progressive Whig account is in Ireland, whose relationship with the state was characterized by quasi-colonial domination, and where the 'Glorious Revolution' ushered in the Penal Laws against the Catholic majority. The Irish union was fatally flawed by the refusal of the King and Parliament to agree to Catholic emancipation as a condition for its enactment. Unionism in twentieth-century Ireland was marked by sectarian hegemony under the Stormont regime.

Another problem with integrationist narratives is that it was never clear what the nations were to be integrated into. The term 'North Britain' was first deployed in Scotland after the union of the crowns and again after 1707. Although it lingered until the late nineteenth century, it never came into general use and, as long as England refused to become 'South Britain', the term lacked meaning. The term 'West Briton', by contrast, was a derogatory term used by Irish nationalists. The concept of Briton in Wales has a distinct lineage, applying to the original inhabitants of the island and their retreat in the face of the Anglo-Saxons, but that is different from the idea of post-union Britain, and jars with English myths based on Anglo-Saxon memes. If it sounds pedantic to point out that the term 'British' does not correspond to the United Kingdom of Great Britain and (Northern) Ireland, it does highlight the ambiguity about the essence of the nation.

In the absence of a strong common British reference point, integrationism can easily become Anglocentric, presenting the United Kingdom as an extension of England into the peripheral and more backward parts of the archipelago. Until the late twentieth century, it was common for histories of the United Kingdom to be called histories of England, with the peripheral nations entering side stage at various points, without altering the course of the progression. J. R. Seeley's (1883) influential book, *The Expansion of England*, expounded the idea that the political community of England had spread liberty to the world by overseas settlement. Dicey, in his various writings, often used 'England' and 'Great Britain' interchangeably, or referred to 'England or Great Britain', as though remembering to add the longer form but without dropping the shorter. Pre-union Scotland is presented as backward, and subsequent progress, including industrialization and commerce and what came to be known in retrospect as the Scottish Enlightenment, are credited to union. Seeley has just one paragraph on the union with Scotland, extolling the way in which Scotland was able to share in the profit and glory.

The Anglocentric strand could at times take on tones of cultural superiority, recalling the colonialist stereotypes employed elsewhere in the Empire, together with sectarian assumptions about the superiority of Protestantism. As Colls (2002) notes, integration was seen as inherently benevolent as it spread the benefits of English progress to the backward periphery. Constitutionalist A. V. Dicey lamented the unfitness of the Irish for self-government, saying, 'That the people of England should have been ripe for Protestantism at a time when the people of Ireland has hardly risen to the level of Roman Catholicism was to each country a grave misfortune' (Dicey 1973: 90). Reginald Coupland (1954) in an otherwise balanced book on Scottish and Welsh nationalism, gave vent to some quite similarly prejudiced remarks about the Irish in Scotland.[2] John Stuart Mill (1972) starkly contrasted the backward condition of the Welshman or the Scottish Highlander with their future as members of the British nation. Whig historian Trevelyan (1926) credited England with giving commerce and culture to 'poor and isolated' Scotland.

During the twentieth century, a different strand of integrationist unionism emerged in the labour movement, resting on two pillars. The first was the primacy of social class as the basis for group identity, with national divisions being at best a distraction and at worst a ploy by capitalists to divide the proletariat. This sentiment was particularly strong in Wales, where the sense of territorial identity has historically been less institutionalized than in Scotland or Ireland. Aneurin Bevan, a Welsh Labour minister and founder of the National Health Service, firmly believed that Welsh problems could only be approached as part of wider British issues (Davies 2017; Johnes 2012). As future leader of the Labour Party, Neil Kinnock (1975), declared: 'I am not in favour of the representation of particular difficulties as being characteristic of membership of a nation rather than membership of a class.' He went on to emphasize the utilitarian benefits of union: 'I do not have a Unionist's interest in unity. For me it has been profitable for the people of the valleys that I represent. I differ to that extent from Unionists in other parts of the House.' While class politics trumped nation in Scotland and Wales, it fought a losing battle with nationalism and sectarianism in Ireland. The British Labour Party originally organized in the industrial north of Ireland and even held its 1907 conference in Belfast. This fell victim to the nationalist polarization and Labour sat out the crucial election of 1918 in Ireland. A Northern Ireland Labour Party continued throughout the Stormont period to promote a cross-community politics of class (Patterson 2006, 2013) but, while it occasionally threatened the hegemony of Ulster unionism, it did not win over the Catholic working class.

This is not to say that class politics was consistently inimical to all forms of nationalism. Class rhetoric in the labour movement was couched, implicitly or explicitly, within a British national frame, and solidarity drew heavily on

[2] 'For the miserable conditions of the Irish countryside had not qualified those who had fled from it for civilized civic life. Ignorant and filthy, they were largely responsible for the epidemics of dirt-born disease which decimated Scottish town-dwellers until the nineteenth century was far advanced' (Coupland 1954: 259).

themes of nationality. Cosmopolitan visions of solidarity were rarer, and both the trades unions and the Labour Party harboured elements opposed both to peripheral Home Rule demands and to European integration.

The second pillar of labour unionism was the use of the centralized state as an instrument to achieve social progress (Jones and Keating 1985). Nationalization of the means of production, distribution and exchange referred to the British nation. The weakness of the peripheral economies after the First World War produced a reliance on redistribution of resources from the centre. The welfare state was built on UK lines, and the National Health Service, while devolved in Northern Ireland and administratively decentralized in Scotland, also referred to the British nation as the natural unit of solidarity. After the Second World War, there was strong resistance from within Welsh Labour even to the extension of the kind of administrative devolution that had proved largely uncontroversial in Scotland; it was not until 1965 that a Welsh Office was established.

'Integration' has sporadically been advanced in Northern Ireland as an alternative to Irish unity, devolution and direct rule. Enoch Powell, an English Conservative turned Ulster Unionist because of disagreement with his old party's pro-Europeanism, consistently interpreted unionism as integration into a single British nation (Corthorn 2012).[3] Apart from some sections of Conservativism, however, the integration option met with little favour in London, where the political class was content to take the vexatious politics of Northern Ireland out of British politics. It was never, in any case, clear what integration meant, whether Northern Ireland would be governed like an English county, or like Scotland and Wales.

While the integrationist narrative tended to Anglo-centrism, this does not imply that it was always imposed on the smaller nations in a colonial manner. As in France and other European countries, peripheral populations were often attracted by the prospects of advancement through integration. Scottish intellectuals often adopted English historiography as their own (Devine 2008; Finlay 1998; Kidd 1993). Middle-class and liberal Irish unionism drew inspiration from the (idealized) English model from the late nineteenth century (Todd 1987).

Yet progressive/integrative unionism has always faced alternative narratives from the periphery. While Scottish historiography could be assimilated to an Anglo-centric British narrative, there was always a counter-current in Irish historiography (Jackson 2012). Home Rule and nationalist movements

[3] A UK Unionist Party was committed to integration but made little electoral headway.

of the periphery have been informed by myths of the common people and the supposedly natural egalitarianism of their societies. Agrarian protests in Ireland, Scotland and Wales were infused with national ideas, especially where landlords could be presented as alien to the nation. Sections of the emerging labour movement in Scotland and Wales were tempted to nationalism, and Home rule movements were imbued with progressive ideas, which linked social and economic with national advance. Assimilative unionism, moreover, has always competed with a different strand, which seeks to incorporate the nations on different terms while retaining political unity.

The Patriot Tradition

The 'patriot' strand is consciously anti-assimilationist, insisting on the ontological claim of nationality for the smaller nations while simultaneously stressing the *telos* of union. Morton (1999), in the Scottish context, coined the term 'unionist nationalism',[4] a deliberate paradox that points to the ways in which local patriotisms could co-exist with commitment to the greater union. The patriot tendency is well captured in Ward's (2005) portraits of seven Scottish, Welsh and Northern Irish figures who made a conscious effort to insert their nations into union without abandoning local interests or sensibilities. Such local and regional patriotisms were common in consolidating European states of the eighteenth and nineteenth centuries (Applegate 1999; Núñez Seixas 2001), where they sometimes represented distinct ways of belonging to the larger nation and at other times formed the basis for alternative national projects. Typically, they were conservative and suspicious of the modern, centralizing state and would often emphasize historic provincial and local rights. This did not mean they were always reactionary or opposed to all change. Often, indeed, they used tradition as a way of coping with change and modernity, codifying memory at a time when oral tradition was being lost (Nora 1984).

An Irish 'patriot' tradition goes back to the late seventeenth century, aiming to give Protestant Irishmen the same rights as Englishmen (Kelly 2014). In the late eighteenth century, the Irish Parliament under the leadership of Henry Grattan, asserted a degree of independence, but in loyalty to the Crown. Largely confined to the Protestant minority, this form of patriotism could never become dominant in Ireland and, following the parliamentary

[4] Torrance (2017) reverses it to 'nationalist unionism'.

union, found little political space. From the mid-nineteenth century, politics was increasingly polarized between Home Rule nationalism and uncompromising unionism, largely corresponding to the religious cleavage. By the First World War, unionism itself had begun to retreat to a defence of Protestant Ulster. The sentiment, however, did linger to some extent in Northern Ireland in what Todd (1987) calls the Ulster British tradition, as opposed to the Loyalist tradition based on conditional loyalty.

Scottish patriot unionism was careful to dissociate itself from assimilative ideas and to cherish Scottish traditions and institutions. In the nineteenth century, it even sought to appropriate Robert Bruce and William Wallace, heroes of the medieval independence struggle, on the grounds that they had kept Scotland intact until it was able to enter into a union of equals. Scottish cultural practices, lampooned by Trevor Roper (2008) and others as 'invention of tradition', were, as elsewhere in Europe, a response to modernization and assimilation while emptying them of political content. Once Jacobitism had ceased to be a military threat after 1746, it could be romanticized along with the old hierarchical Highland social system, with due encouragement from Queen Victoria. Walter Scott, once dismissed as a nostalgic opponent of modernity, is now seen as a key figure in legitimizing union by showing how it provided necessary progress while retaining Scottish nationality.[5]

Another strand of patriot unionism was a product of the urban bourgeoisie, interested in the practicalities of government and modernization while retaining the traditions and institutions of the nations. An early example is the National Association for the Vindication of Scottish Rights founded in 1853. A campaign for a Secretary (of State) for Scotland succeeded in 1885 and administrative devolution steadily expanded thereafter. During the twentieth century, Scotland organized a territorial lobby, working to secure advantages within the union state but without raising divisive constitutional questions.

Patriot unionism was a strong element in the Scottish Unionist Party[6] formed in 1912 from the merger of the Conservatives and Liberal Unionists, and which did not change its name to Conservative until 1965. During the mid-twentieth century, it retained a distinct Scottish *ethos* and message which fed into the 'one-nation' Conservatism and paternalist social attitudes and allowed the right to reconcile itself with the welfare state (Torrance 2017, 2020a). Although patriot unionism was, with a few exceptions, strongly against Scottish Home Rule (Mitchell 1990), it provided a weapon against centralizing left-wing governments. In the 1940s, Unionists could claim that the Labour

[5] Scott's friend Maria Edgeworth undertook a similar task in Ireland but without such lasting effects.
[6] Although 'Unionist' referred to the Irish union, it was also against Scottish Home Rule.

Government's nationalization policies meant denationalization in Scotland as power was taken down south. As the party declined electorally after 1959, it retreated to its rural heartlands, where these messages still resonated and its MPs still reflected its traditional agricultural and military leadership (Keating 1975). It also gained in some regions by the effective absorption of the old Liberal Party, with some of its candidates presenting themselves as National Liberals or Liberal Unionists. Margaret Thatcher was the first Conservative leader who appeared totally unfamiliar with the distinctive Scottish brand, although not for want of trying (Torrance 2009). During her time, the old patriotic unionism went into decline, depriving Conservatism of what would have been a useful resource in the post-devolution period (Convery 2015). A patriot tradition also existed on the left, personified by William Ross, a Labour Secretary of State (1964–70 and 1974–6) a cultural 'nationalist' and fierce defender of Scottish interests but, until a late stage in his career, vigorous opponent of devolution.

Welsh patriot unionism had less of a historical or institutional base to build upon, given that the Principality had been absorbed juridically into England without an Act of Union recognizing a preceding jurisdiction. From the national revival of the nineteenth century, however, Wales began to follow Scotland's demands for recognition as a constituent nation of the United Kingdom. This incipient Welsh nationality was almost entirely free of separatist elements. On the contrary, it was Britain or the United Kingdom that made Wales as a political community possible (Williams 1979); the alternative was absorption into Greater England. There were successful moves for a national university (1893), a national museum (1912), and national sporting teams. It was not until 1967 that the jurisdiction was formally named 'England and Wales' and it was made clear that laws passed only for England did not include Wales. As in Scotland, there was a focus on practical issues related to government and development. A longstanding demand that Wales should have its own Secretary of State was finally realized in 1965.

Language and Nonconformist religion had provided the basis for the Welsh national revival from the nineteenth century but by the 1970s they were widely seen as in decline. Yet a new form of patriot unionism was emerging around the needs of economic modernization, treating Wales as a unit. Administrative devolution was extended, a process that continued under the Conservative governments of the 1980s and 1990s. A resolution of the language issue was found by making wide provision for it without imposing it on non-Welsh speakers.

An English patriotism has long subsisted within an 'Anglo-British' consciousness (Kidd 1993). The idea of England has been around for centuries although there are endless debates about when, why and how an English political consciousness emerged. Some scholars date English national consciousness to long before union (Hastings 1997; Greenfeld (1992), while Kumar (2003) and Stapleton (2009) see it emerging in the late nineteenth century. Some observers have praised English restraint or even humility (Stapleton 2009) in subordinating their claims for the wider good. Others have lamented it; Orwell (2018) famously claimed that England is the only country whose intellectuals are ashamed of their own nationality. Kumar (2003) argues, rather, that the English have practised an imperial or missionary nationality beyond their own frontiers, imbuing both the union and the Empire with English ideas and dominating their historiography. During the twentieth century, politicians in England learned not to use the term England to refer to the United Kingdom, but often seemed to forget that England was one of the components.

It was devolution which crystalized a sense of English political identity, not in the form of separatist or even devolutionary demands, but as an ontological claim for recognition. England and Englishness, moreover, are constructed in rather different ways. There is a nostalgic, conservative vision of England as the lost 'green and pleasant land', hostile to immigration and suspicious of multiculturalism, found both in right-wing populism and communitarian visions such as Blue Labour. A movement on the liberal left aims at rescuing Englishness from the far right (Denham 2018; Kenny 2014; English Labour Network 2017). George Orwell, cited by unionists as a British icon, more properly falls within the English patriot tradition.

In some ways, such patriotic stirrings can be seen as the precursors of Home Rule and nationalism and many individuals did make that journey. Yet the distinction is useful since many patriots remained committed to the Crown and State and the principle of parliamentary sovereignty and supremacy. The patriot tradition is an ontological or reflexive rather than a teleological nationalism, more concerned with preserving and promoting the nation than constitutional transformation. This instinctive loyalty distinguishes them from another strand, in which local rights are supreme and loyalty is conditional.

Contractualism

Contractual unionism takes the idea of union even more seriously, defending the existence of distinct political communities or *demoi* within the state, united by pacts, with loyalty conditional on their being respected. Pactism may be rooted in contested interpretations of legal norms, including union treaties and devolution statutes. It may also draw on looser ideas of nation or community and interpretation of history.

Scottish contractualism has a number of historical roots. Some point to the 1320 Declaration of Arbroath, expanding it into a claim that Scotland has a native constitutional tradition of conditional loyalty and even of popular sovereignty. Historians disagree about its significance (Smith 2020). The popular sovereignty reading of the Declaration has generally been discounted, but the contractual element, provides a reference point for arguments about sovereignty, counterposed to Westminster claims of supremacy. Contractualism is also rooted in the political conflicts of the seventeenth century, when the opponents of the Stuart monarchs insisted on the idea of a 'covenanted king', to whom only conditional loyalty was owed. The idea has biblical origins and the claim, secured finally in the settlement of 1689, referred to the balance between Church and State. It was then incorporated into the Acts of Union, which founded the United Kingdom. Questions about the independent sphere of ecclesiastical government were at the heart of disputes about the union for the first century and a half of its existence.

Contractual unionism also draws sustenance from the circumstances and nature of the Union itself. Scotland, it is argued, did not surrender sovereignty because the old Scots Parliament was not fully sovereign, and there is nothing in the Acts of Union to suggest that the new Parliament was. Instead, there is a distinct tradition of sovereignty in Scotland, which must be regarded as part of our unwritten constitution (MacCormick 1999). Like so many others, this argument is available both to nationalists and unionists. The former claim that it really means that Scotland is, at the end of the day, sovereign. Unionists argue that it is at the heart of what the union, properly understood, is about. Arch-unionists Dicey and Rait (1920: 100), known for their defence of parliamentary sovereignty and denial of pre-union legal rights, conceded that there was something in that argument.

The most celebrated moment in Scottish contractual unionism was the case of *MacCormick v Lord Advocate*, decided in 1953. The issue at stake was whether Queen Elizabeth should be known as Elizabeth II in Scotland when neither Scotland nor the United Kingdom had had an Elizabeth I. The court dismissed the case, but it became more famous for an *obiter dictum* delivered by Lord Cooper, himself a former Scottish Unionist MP and Lord Advocate, which has become a standard point of reference in Scottish constitutional debates (see Chapter 4).

Contractual unionism has come and gone in Scottish political consciousness but remained sufficiently alive to animate the debates around devolution from the late twentieth century. John MacCormick's Home Rule campaign in the 1940s was called the Scottish Covenant. In the late 1980s, the Scottish Constitutional Convention issued a *Claim of Right* (1988) echoing the practice and language of seventeenth-century dissenters and nineteenth-century radicals and insisting on Scotland's right to determine its own future. Some supporters of devolution might have balked at the use of the 1689 precedent, which had been highly sectarian, but accepted that: 'We acknowledge the sovereign right of the Scottish people to determine the form of Government best suited to their needs'. An extended version (Dudley Edwards 1988) deliberately used the expression 'English constitution' to criticize the application of English doctrines to Scotland, and argued that the preservation of Scottish institutions implies a 'right to some degree of self-determination'. All but one of Scotland's Labour MPs signed up, reassured by the fact that the Convention was a devolutionary body, which the SNP had boycotted because independence was not on the agenda. Since devolution, Scottish politicians of all parties have claimed ownership of the Claim of Right, but have interpreted it in very different ways (Chapter 4).

Contractualism has sometimes been used for partisan ends by unlikely people. In 1950, Winston Churchill argued that Scotland (which at that time leaned more to the Conservatives) should not be obliged to accept socialism imposed from England (Mitchell, 1990). The argument resurfaced in the 1980s and 1990s as to whether the Conservative governments of the time had a mandate in Scotland, given their failure to win anything like a majority of seats. This was an easy argument for nationalists to make. For the Labour Party (by then the dominant party in Scotland), it was more dangerous, since it could feed nationalism, and might raise questions about the English mandate for any future Labour government relying on Scottish or Welsh seats for its majority.[7] It did, however, expose the fact that union had worked for almost the entire era of mass democracy with concurrent parliamentary majorities in England and Scotland. Their absence after 1979 was clearly a factor in powering the new movement for devolution.

A contractual element mixed with the patriot tradition in Irish conservative unionism, based on the 'ancient constitution' and Ireland's status as a kingdom (Jackson 2014b). Some Conservative opponents of the disestablishment of the Church of Ireland in 1869 argued that the bill was unconstitutional because the Union was a pact between two nations, which could not be amended unilaterally (O'Day 2001). No such recourse was open to Catholics, who had never been party to a contract, so that the failure to grant Catholic Emancipation

[7] Donald Dewar, Labour's leader in Scotland, was particularly insistent on this point.

after the union of 1800, a clear a breach of faith, could not be argued to violate the terms of union.

As Irish unionism retreated to the north in the late nineteenth century and became more militant, it drew sustenance from the old Scots Covenanting tradition brought there in the seventeenth century. Drawing on biblical imagery, Ulster (or Protestant Ulster), was presented as a self-referential community that had defended its own rights over centuries. The victory of William of Orange at the Battle of the Boyne and the siege of Derry were deployed to underpin the slogan of No Surrender. In 1912, unionists gathered in Belfast to sign 'Ulster's Solemn League and Covenant', which pledged to resist Irish Home Rule by all means. There followed gun-running to militants and open resistance to the authority of Parliament. Preparations were made for a coup in Ulster and the takeover of government. Again in the 1970s, sections of unionism radicalized, toyed with a unilateral declaration of independence and defied the British state to bring down the power-sharing institutions set up under the Sunningdale agreement. 'Loyalism', paradoxically, came to be the term used for Protestant paramilitaries prepared to defend the union forcibly against the British state itself.

In a less militant mode, contractualism returned as a unionist argument against the Anglo-Irish Agreement of 1985. This, they complained, was reached without the consent of the Northern Ireland parties, a legislature or the people, and was negotiated with a 'foreign' government, breaching conventions about the province's place in the Union. As Aughey (2001b: 310) put it: 'In the unionist case it implies that meddling with the status of Northern Ireland without consent of the people there is not a prerogative of Westminster.'

Although the vocabulary is not used, contractualism is at the heart of the Good Friday Agreement, with its multiple requirements for consent among the parties within Northern Ireland and the two sovereign governments. In that case, there is an explicit mechanism for withdrawing consent to the union by reunification with the south. More generally, it is argued that consent must be read into any interpretation of the agreement, meaning that the constitutional settlement cannot be seen purely as the product of the sovereign UK Parliament, revisable by it alone (McCrudden and Halberstam 2018).

The Home Rule Tradition

While it is obvious that unionists are opposed to secession, the key dividing line for much of the nineteenth and twentieth centuries was at a different place, between proponents of the unitary constitution and supporters of Home Rule or devolution. This raises another paradox when we consider that Home Rule was usually proposed as a way of reconstructing, not destroying the union. The failure of Irish Home rule in the early twentieth century encouraged teleological arguments (from both nationalist and unionist quarters) about the inevitability of Home Rule leading to independence. This allowed them to draw a clear line though the constitutional middle ground; even contractual unionists could advance this argument. Yet historians have argued that Irish Home Rule was a distinct project, which remained viable until a late stage (Bew 1994; Jackson 2004). The Home Rule traditions in Scotland and Wales, while not bearing fruit until the end of the twentieth century, resurfaced regularly from the late nineteenth century (Butt Philip 1975; Kane 2015; Keating and Bleiman 1979; Mitchell 1996, 2014). Home Rule features, then, in both nationalist and unionist traditions.

The case for Home Rule has been argued on three broad grounds. One was that of nationality, with the premise that this did not entail a separatist destiny but a return to older understandings of union. A conservative version drew on the patriot tradition, proceeding from ontological to teleological understandings of nationality. A progressive version tapped into radical traditions and myths that contrasted the peripheral nations with the centre, seen as the protector of vested interests. The second argument concerned efficiency and good government. In the early twentieth century, there were frequent references to the need to relieve congestion in the 'Imperial Parliament'. The efficiency and modernization argument emerged again in the 1960s, articulated by Mackintosh (1968) and by some members of the divided Kilbrandon Commission (Royal Commission on the Constitution 1973). The third argument was that devolution was the best way to keep the union together; in this sense Home Rule was the true form of unionism (Bryce 1887; O'Brien 1887).

For Daniel O'Connell as for eighteenth-century Scots Jacobites, the key was 'repeal' of the union legislation, so reverting to the monarchical union and remaining within the Empire. Later this evolved into the Home Rule formula of subordinate legislatures under Westminster, also known as devolution, the preferred term from the 1970s. It is here that the lines between unionism and nationalism become most blurred, especially over the final point of development or *telos*. Isaac Butt (1874) was clear that Home Rule was not independence and has been characterized as a constructive unionist (Reid 2014). Charles Stewart Parnell (1886) was capable of describing Home Rule as a final settlement of the Irish question, while elsewhere asserting that no man could set bounds to the march of a nation. Gladstone (1886) made it clear in the same debate that the Home Rule Bill would leave Westminster supremacy intact and was a means of preserving union.

In an effort to bring some intellectual consistency to the debate and find a stable solution, one strand in unionism has regularly toyed with the idea of federalism. Indeed, the idea has appeared so often that Jackson (2018) has called it the 'constitutional wonder drug'. It would not entail asymmetry or special treatment for any nation, and could eliminate many of the anomalies of partial devolution but, unfortunately, it has never been defined. The problem is that federalism itself may be based on either nationalist or unionist premises. Rokkan and Urwin's (1983) mechanical federalism is not the same as their organic federalism. A large body of literature has contrasted mononational federalism, based on the US model, with plurinational federalism, resting on the basis of distinct national communities with their own inherent rights and a negotiated order (Burgess 2006; Gagnon and Seymour 2012; McGarry and O'Leary 2007).

Joseph Chamberlain (1887: 35), who split the Liberal Party over opposition to Gladstone's Home Rule proposals, had himself earlier proposed Irish local councils, which could in turn elect an all-Ireland central council to take charge of administration and 'sweep away all the network of boards appointed by the English Government, carrying with them the seal of English authority'. Later he even came, reluctantly, to accept a federal system, but one in which Westminster would retain the last word on everything. Pacificus (1910), a pseudonym for Scottish unionist Frederick Scott Oliver, advocated federalism to preserve the union while admitting that his scheme, by preserving Westminster supremacy, was not actually federal in the strict sense. Around the First World War and its aftermath, there was a flurry of federalist proposals, culminating in a Speaker's Conference. Conservative opponents of devolution in the 1970s talked of federalism as an alternative, and the question has been revived in the context of devolution (Torrance 2014). Unionist federal proposals, however, rarely breach the sacrosanct principle of parliamentary sovereignty and supremacy.

By the time devolution happened as the end of the twentieth century, it had garnered very wide support, as shown in the results of the Scottish and Northern Ireland referendums of 1997 and 1998. Even Wales, previously overwhelmingly opposed, voted in favour. Yet the very width of support disguised a lack of depth or conviction. Devolution appealed to a wide swathe of opinion, from unionists for whom it as a reluctant concession to those for whom it was a precursor to independence. Unionism proved intellectually ill-equipped to deal with devolution when it actually happened.

Neo-Unionism

One point at which the various strands of unionism came together was on the principle of the sovereignty of the monarch-in-parliament. This might be stretched a long way, as in the case of Ulster 'loyalists' defying the government of the day in the name of the higher values of union. Ideas of mechanical federalism could be entertained. Yet traditional unionism could not countenance the establishment of national legislatures for the component parts, drawing their authority from their own constituent *demoi*. Whatever Gladstonian Home Rulers might say, such parliaments, it was feared, would inevitably assume unlimited authority (Dalyell 1977; Wilson 1970); the fact that it was supported by people with precisely such ambitions further tainted it in unionist eyes. Sometimes it is difficult to discern the principle at stake here. Home Rule and devolution debates in Parliament between the 1880s and the First World War, and again between the 1970s and the 2000s, are replete with technical objections and anomalies, from fiscal arrangements to the West Lothian Question, but these are hardly decisive. The underlying principle, however, to avoid combining national recognition with institutionalized political power, was consistent. Ontological and teleological nationalism had to be kept quite separate.

This being so, it is remarkable how easily the spell was broken at the end of the twentieth century. The old Gladstonian Home Rule programme of asymmetrical and partial devolution had been realized, without any traumatic consequences. Apart from a short-lived rearguard action in Wales, unionism accepted the new dispensation almost immediately. It appeared that new lines of division had now been drawn as unionism was redefined to include supporters of devolution and deployed in opposition to secession. Thus stated, unionism appeared dominant across the United Kingdom, as supporters of secession in its various forms were clearly in the minority. In practice, matters were not so simple and a new middle ground opened up for 'third way' ideas like devolution-max or post-sovereignty. Yet these have rarely been articulated as a distinct or intellectually coherent option. Instead, the main dividing line remained that between nationalism and unionism, with unionists now defending the new status quo of devolution in the context in which secession, especially in Scotland and Northern Ireland, was a more realistic prospect than ever.

McLean and McMillan (2003: 241) proclaimed that unionism was dead outside Northern Ireland but that union might survive. Certainly, the old understated unionism had to give way to a more robust defence of union in theory and in practice. For the first time, it sought consistent principles, which would work across all three unions and appeal to distinct ideas of union's history and purpose. Banal unionism, in Kidd's (2008) formulation, had to give way to analytic unionism. Old unionist formulas, with their multiple and sometimes discordant strands had to give way to a new unionism for new times, a neo-unionism.[8] Unionism is seeking now to refound itself in its own *demos*, *telos* and *ethos* and distinguish itself from nationalism. The ironical outcome is that in doing so it has not only made itself into a form of nationalism but has claimed exactly the same normative foundations as its 'nationalist' opponents.

The central thrust of this can be described as a 'civic unionism', seen as the realization of equal citizenship stripped of 'nationalism', where nationalism is defined as ethnic particularism and exclusivity. Instead, there is a shared *ethos* of civic values. This is an old theme in the study of nationalism, bearing a resemblance to the civic ideologies that formed the basis of the American and French revolutions at the end of the eighteenth century.[9] A more recent version is Habermas' (1998) post-national or constitutional patriotism, in which adherence to the institutions of the state replaces blood and belonging. It is not necessary that the shared *ethos* be particular to the state or union; usually it is based on universal values, with the claim that this is the best place for their realization. Critics of minority nationalism such as Hobsbawm (1992) and Dahrendorf (2000) have argued that the shared identity of the wider state is necessarily more inclusive than, and ethically superior, to that of the component parts, which are depicted as ethnic.[10] Civic unionism in the United Kingdom accepts that the component nations can retain their culture, history, differentiated identity and national diversity, but draws this same essential difference between identities at the two levels. Without denying the plurality of the United Kingdom, David Miller (1995) defends the essentially progressive nature of British national identity, into which Scots should be socialized.[11] So the higher, union level is presented as the location of *ethos*, the higher moral values that legitimate the polity and substantive matters of citizenship and rights.

The search for a common *ethos* finds its most striking expression, under both Labour and Conservative governments, in campaigns to promote

[8] For reasons I do not understand, some self-defined unionists have objected to this term, but it is not intended to be pejorative.

[9] There are affinities here with the much-contested concept of 'civic nationalism', but civic unionism presents itself as the antidote to nationalism.

[10] For a criticism, see Keating (2001).

[11] It is not clear how Ireland fits in.

'British values' against both internal and external challenges. They feature in the UK citizenship test and the Prevent counter-terrorism strategy. Schools are required to promote 'the basic British values of democracy, the rule of law, individual liberty, and mutual respect and tolerance for those of different faiths and beliefs' (Ofsted 2014)—ironically, this applies only in England. The Constitution Reform Group (2018) lists the values of the rule of law and equality before the law; the protection of fundamental rights and freedoms; defence of the realm and the conduct of foreign relations; the promotion of tolerance and respect; equality of opportunity; provision of a safe and secure society; provision of a strong economy; protection of social and economic rights, including provision of access to education and health and other social services (including the National Health Service); and the benefits of shared history and culture.[12]

The problem is not merely that these are universal values and not particularly British; that is common to many unions and civic nationalisms. It is rather that these same values also animate the rival nationalisms of the periphery, which have sought to stress their 'civic' credentials (Keating 2001). So, to make the unionist case, the rival nationalisms have to be portrayed as inward-looking, backward and exclusive. Michael Gove (2018) defines unionism as being about liberty, institutions and the rule of law, and based on individuals, in contrast to 'identity politics' of both left and right in the peripheral nationalisms.

It is not only the periphery that is treated this way. The same arguments extend to the emerging English nationalism, a purportedly reactionary form of identity based upon a supposed working-class white culture, challenged by multiculturalism, immigration and European integration. In these images, Englishness is ethnicized in ways that become difficult to reconcile with the multicultural pluralism that underpins other re-imaginings of Britishness. The stereotypical vision of Englishness as insular reaction has been criticized by intellectuals on the centre-left, who have sought to recuperate older ideas of Englishness, rooted in popular culture, suspicion of authority, and progress, as a counterpoint to the appropriation of Englishness by exclusive nationalism tinged with xenophobia. That Englishness would be civic in nature, so that Britishness and union would not have to bear the whole burden of civic identity (Kenny 2014).

[12] A wag might note that these provide an ironic instance of the tendency that George Orwell (2018) detected as an English characteristic, the drawing up of lists.

The overarching narrative of Britishness is part of a broader strategy that also embraces multiculturalism, a challenge arising from the experience of immigration (e.g. Katwala 2005). Gordon Brown (2014) has suggested that the British *demos* differs from that of the component nations in being inclusive and multicultural, and that it is the only one that can be hyphenated, as in Black-British or Muslim-British. In fact, these ethnic identities have been hyphenated with both Scottishness and British; hyphenating them with English is more difficult. In any case, while both are about pluralism, the multicultural challenge, concerning the co-existence of different cultures, values and ways of life, is not the same as the challenge of plurinationalism, which is about the boundaries of political community or *demos* and the scope of the polity in which universal values will be developed. The constituent nations of the United Kingdom are themselves sites of multiculturalism and have adapted in various ways. The new vision of Britishness recalls the efforts of Pierre Elliot Trudeau to contain Quebec nationalism by reducing it to another expression of multiculturalism beneath a stronger pan-Canadian carapace. Critics have long argued that Canada should rather be understood as a complex state of nations, not organized hierarchically (McRoberts 2019; Romney 1999).

Like the old Whig accounts, civic unionism faces its most serious challenge in Ireland, although it has periodically been deployed there. Dicey (1973), while opposed to self-government, was critical of the special measures known as 'coercion' in Ireland. Liberal unionists supported Catholic Emancipation as a necessary concomitant of union with Ireland.[13] A civic unionism has been identified in nineteenth-century Belfast before giving way in the face of sectarian politics (Bew 2009). In the 1960s, opponents of the Stormont regime were able to turn unionism against itself by challenging the regime to give them their rights as British citizens. The challenge soon mutated into the old nationalist lines but it did (along with the breakdown of public order) force the UK Government to abandon its previous policy of giving Stormont a free rein. Meanwhile, the civic tradition re-emerged among unionist reformers (English and Walker 1996), sometimes expressed as 'constructive unionism' (Gailey 2001). This has aimed to take unionism out of its ethnic redoubt as unionists sought to adapt to new conditions and move away from ideas of Protestant supremacy. A new generation of intellectuals aimed to show that unionism was not to be equated with nationalism, since it appeals not to

[13] They also opposed the imposition of the English Test Acts on Scottish Members of Parliament, who were not members of the Church of England.

particularism but to citizenship (English 1996; Farrington 2006). One product of this was the Alliance Party of Northern Ireland, but the theme was adopted in some unexpected quarters. In the 1980s, some creative ideas came from Loyalist paramilitaries previously mired in sectarianism (Walker 2004) although, unlike Republicanism, Loyalism did not manage the transition to elective politics. By the second decade of the 2000s, even the Democratic Unionist Party (DUP) was laying claim to civic and liberal ideas (Tonge et al. 2014). Arlene Foster's (2018) appeal to British values reached back to the old British unionism (Todd 1987) and Belfast liberalism, but this sat uneasily with the DUP's distancing itself from British social liberalizing measures or from the social liberalism of the Republic of Ireland. Same-sex marriage and abortion were eventually imposed by Westminster against DUP opposition.

Along with broad, ethical arguments, neo-unionism has deployed teleological and concrete, instrumentalist defences of union focused on economics and welfare. The economic case, which hinges on large home markets and economies of scale, is addressed more fully in Chapter 8. It is a difficult argument for unionist supporters of Brexit, which shrunk the internal market. Indeed, there is an argument that small states may do well within free trading regimes if they make the right institutional and policy choices (Keating and Harvey 2014; Baldersheim and Keating 2015).

Instrumental arguments also draw on welfare unionism, stressing the need for a wider area and population to sustain a full welfare system, pool risks widely and cope with asymmetrical shocks. Yet this argument is more easily available to social democrats than to neoliberals and supporters of the minimal state. In any case, it is not axiomatically true that larger unions are more inclined to sharing than are small states. If social solidarity has been under threat in the United Kingdom, it has been at the centre and not the periphery. Neo-unionists have sought to harness the National Health Service in the cause of union, although this is already devolved to the nations and organized on different principles, reflecting distinct ideas of public service. This matter is discussed in Chapter 9, which explores the extent to which the United Kingdom is a welfare and social union.

Instrumental defences of union are thus inadequate on their own, since the link between these policy goals and a particular geographical polity is elusive. As always, there needs to be a historical back-story. Whig teleological history never quite recovered from its evisceration back in the 1930s by Herbert Butterfield (1968) but Whiggism never disappeared. Neo-unionist intellectuals have heeded Butterfield's (1944) later argument that, while much of Whig history may have been bad science it is good politics or, as Ansari (2018) puts it, they should not throw the baby out with the old Whig bathwater. Neo-unionists have revisited the Union of 1707 in the context of the Glorious Revolution of 1688–90 as part of the progressive narrative but stripped of sectarianism. Yet, whatever the history of the Scottish union, it is difficult to invest the Irish union with the higher ethical status given its origins in a colonial project (O'Leary, 2019a), and the experience of Unionist hegemony under the Stormont regime.

Neo-unionists have devoted much effort to debunking the nationalist myths of Scotland, Ireland and Wales (Trevor Roper 2008; Ansari 2018). These efforts, however, risk falling through an open door, as Scottish, Irish and Welsh historians have already done that job themselves in successive rounds of revisionism. *Pace* Whatley (2012) or Ansari (2018) few Scots intellectuals believe that the Jacobites were Scottish nationalists or take *Braveheart* or *Outlander* as anything other than escapist entertainment. Unionist intellectuals (Lloyd 2020; Kidd 2018) have identified Scottish cultural nationalism with the eccentric Anglophobe Hugh McDiarmid, whose political influence was, at most, marginal.[14] In fact, the cultural revival since the 1970s has produced a large corpus of work critical of contemporary Scotland and of complacent assumptions about its nature. There have been debates about the role of Scots in imperial exploitation and slavery and about sectarianism (Bruce et al. 2004; Devine 2000; 2015; Fry, 2002). Revisionist critiques of the nationalist account of Ireland had started early in the 1930s, followed by further reassessments in the 1980s and after the Good Friday Agreement (Jackson 2014a). Anglocentrism has also returned, as some unionists have co-opted the figure of George Orwell, who might properly be considered an English nationalist (and who used the terms England and Britain indiscriminately) for the Union (Ansari 2018).

There is a recurrent Anglocentrism also in the wider debate about constitutional reform. Aughey's (2007) balanced analysis still puts English constitutionalism in the central position, incorporating the United Kingdom in a progressive and liberating manner so that the choice between England and Britain does not need to be made. Less cautious thinkers have simply ignored the question. Jack Straw (2008), then Lord Chancellor, listed all the key milestones in English constitutional development but failed to mention the unions with Wales, Scotland and Ireland. Lord Goldsmith's (2008) report on citizenship, commissioned by Gordon Brown as Prime Minister, devoted a long

[14] Craig (2018: 20) argues that 'no nationalist party in the world... has been less focused on mobilizing culture as part of its political strategy than the SNP'.

section to citizenship education, linking this to the inculcation of Britishness; but the account refers exclusively to the English education system (Hassan and Shaw, 2019). He recommended an Oath of Allegiance to the monarch and a Pledge of Allegiance to the United Kingdom by young people coming of age, with only a passing acknowledgement of how this might go down in Scotland or Northern Ireland.

The same issue arises in relation to proposals for a British Bill of Rights, an idea that was inspired by two motives. One was Eurosceptic, aiming to liberate the UK from 'foreign' judges. The other was neo-unionist, seeking to cement the Union around an *ethos* of common values, rights and duties. The problem with this is not so much the substantive content of the basic rights but the way in which these were to be linked to citizenship, *demos* and national identity. In the initial formulations, no attention was given to the way in which this would go down in Northern Ireland, where a substantial section of the population does not share a British identity and where the Good Friday Agreement explicitly tells them that they do not have to. In a less acute form, the issue arises in Scotland, with its substantial non-British identifying population. The House of Lords and House of Commons Joint Committee on Human Rights (2008) preferred the title 'UK Bill' rather than 'British Bill' on the grounds that some people do not consider themselves British, but English, Scottish, Irish or Welsh. This merely begs the question of what 'UK' used as an adjective covers, if it is to be more than a geographical expression. Indeed, they go on to say that

> there is an inevitable and entirely appropriate link with national identity. A national bill of rights is an expression of national identity and the process of drawing one up deliberately invites reflection on what it is that 'binds us together as a nation', what we regard as of fundamental importance, and which values we consider to guide us. It is potentially a moment of national definition.
>
> (House of Lords and House of Commons Joint Committee on Human Rights, 2008: 96)

JUSTICE (2007) explicitly excluded Northern Ireland from its proposed bill, which is defined as British, but it says nothing about the implications in Scotland and addresses only the English legal system. The Constitution Reform Group (2015), similarly proposes a 'charter of the union', as does the Bingham Centre's (2015) Charter of Union.

Gordon Brown (2014: 37), by contrast, seeks a synthesis of English and Scottish values, making for a distinctive British *ethos*, arguing that 'it was Scottish ideas of solidarity that combined with English ideas of toleration and liberty to create a union that remains greater than the sum of its parts'. Quoting the Irish patriot Henry Grattan, Brown (2006) sees England as the source of liberty, while Scotland contributes solidarity. Yet, while avoiding Anglocentrism, this risks falling into stereotypical and essentialist representations of the two nations. In a neat inversion, Lee (2011) criticizes Brown for appropriating for Britishness what are actually English progressive values, so 'negating' England.

In its concern with Britishness, neo-unionism often fails to place the union in broader geo-political frameworks, now that Empire is no longer available. Already in the 1970s, the new 'islands history' (Pocock 1975; Jackson 2014b) challenged insular, teleological and Anglocentric accounts of the formation of the Union, postulating new ways of understanding the complex relations of 'these islands' and their interlinked histories. The concept of 'the totality of relationships among the peoples of these islands', used in the Northern Ireland agreement,[15] offers a break with Anglocentric understandings. The most striking absence is of a link to the European project. While Europe provided other nations the opportunity to redefine and orient their national imaginations, in different ways, it had very little impact on the UK national project. Rather than Britishness being expanded and adapted to the new order, it was almost always presented as something in tension with it. As Chapter 6 has shown, the European Union, together with the European Charter on Human Rights, have underpinned the Millennium settlement in important ways, providing an external support system for the reformed union. They have also transformed the politics of nationalism in the peripheral nations. Britishness and unionism, however, had largely failed to incorporate this dimension, until the European referendum in 2016, which divided unionists among themselves and posed serious questions about the nature of the post-Brexit polity. For supporters of Brexit, Europe provided the 'other' against a new Britishness which could be defined in a stridently nationalist mode. For Remainer unionists, Brexit posed an existential threat to the Union itself.

Neo-unionism, less reliant on mystical or tradition-bound attachment to union, has relied heavily on *telos* and *ethos* as justificatory themes. Yet these

[15] The expression goes back to 1980 and Brian Lenihan, Irish foreign minister, claimed to have invented it (O'Leary 2019c).

can never, by themselves, determine the geographical or social boundaries of the state or nation as they can be realized at various levels. The argument must therefore be closed by appeal to *demos*, the unitary fount of authority. The Brexit referendum provided a new opportunity for this, as Conservatives, notably Prime Minister Theresa May, constantly repeated that 'the British people' had decided to leave the European Union. Indeed, this assertion in itself seemed largely to displace *telos* and *ethos* in making the argument for Brexit itself. Yet, in making this argument, they had to ignore the fact that both Scotland and Northern Ireland had voted to remain.

The Crisis of Unionism

It is a paradox of unionism that it comes in so many guises. Its various strands overlap or are pursued at different times and places. Local patriotism sometimes develops into contractual unionism when implicit understandings are challenged and political interests feel threatened. Solidarity unionism and contractual unionism can co-exist (Aughey 2018). Contractual unionism in turn can morph into nationalism if it appears that the contract is being broken. The various strands are intertwined (Todd 2019; Walker 2004), and the same party might draw on different ones depending on the circumstances. It is at times of crisis that the differences are exposed, as in the Home Rule arguments of the late nineteenth and early twentieth centuries and the devolution debates of the 1970s and 1990s, which pitched devolution against the unitary state; or the secessionist questions posed in 1921–1 and 2014, when Home Rule was measured against independence.

The genius of unionism in the past was precisely that it was not uniform or unitary. It wove together chords appealing to different audiences, who were often not listening to each other. The symbols of state provided a focus for unity, while the doctrine of parliamentary sovereignty appeared to solve the question of where ultimate authority lay (Rose 1982). Contractual unionism may have pushed this to its limits but even that was usually advanced in the name of monarch and union and the maintenance of the established order. Critics have pointed out that the new, relentless search for *demos*, *telos* and *ethos* is essentially un-British and a departure from older ideas of union, as is the constant evocation of citizen duties. The result is a unionism which, more than ever, serves itself as a form of nationalism. Indeed, some unionists have been strong defenders of the nation-state mode of political organization (for example Lloyd 2020). Aughey (2001a, 2018) is exceptional among unionist thinkers in seeing the dangers of 'high unionist' rhetoric and teleological unity, calling instead for an understanding that balances contractualism and solidarity and calls for allegiance to institutions rather than shared foundations.

One answer to the question of why unionism accepted devolution is that nothing did really change. The new settlement is bolted onto the old constitution, rather than changing its fundamentals. Unionists have almost all come to accept devolution but without accepting its implications for the nature of the polity. They may recognize national pluralism but never allowed this as a basis for legal order. The Constitution Reform Group (2018), for example, presents what appears at first as a radical reconstitution of the Union on the basis of four self-determining nations, but then ends up insisting that none of this should alter the sovereignty and supremacy of the Westminster Parliament. Neo-unionism has accepted a devolutionary arrangement that was anathema to previous generations of unionists, but only by encompassing it within a polished-up unionist narrative. It has yet to come to terms with post-sovereign perspectives or constitutional pluralism (MacCormick 1999; Keating 2001; Chapter 4 in this book) breaking with the assumption that sovereignty is monist and must all be located in one place.

While Scottish neo-unionism has incorporated much of the old Home Rule agenda about decentralization, it has not always accepted the deeper implications of self-determination and union. Erstwhile devolutionists, for their part, are now part of a neo-unionist coalition that defines itself against nationalism, when previously they were part of a national-leaning coalition. The old patriot tradition, with its fierce defence of local traditions and rights, survives in Wales, where the independence challenge is weaker and devolution settlement less complete, giving Welsh Labour the opportunity to present itself as a patriotic contender, defending both the Union and Wales's position within it, within a *telos* of federalism. Northern Irish unionism, for its part, has largely retreated into a defensive mode under the influence of the DUP, as its shrinking electoral base reinforces its reluctance to compromise. Faced with the tricky case of the Northern Irish union, the unionist think tank *These Islands*, setting out its vision of the whole, delphically proclaims that 'more unites the three nations of Great Britain than divides them, and that good relations between the various communities of Northern Ireland, Great Britain, and Ireland are all the more important to work for in the wake of Brexit' (http://www.these-islands.co.uk/values/d2/0).

Scottish, Irish and Welsh nationalism, now identified as the clear separatist opponent, in the meantime, have engaged in debates about moving beyond traditional models of statehood, crystallized in their support for remaining in the European Union. Ireland has long sustained a debate on post-nationalism (Kearney 1997), although post-sovereignty might be a more appropriate term.

Parties in Northern Ireland accepted a settlement that fell short of the aspirations of both sides, while in the Republic the new talk about unity after Brexit raised questions about the way the state itself would have to change its *ethos*, institutions and national story. Scottish nationalists during the 2014 referendum campaign offered 'independence-lite' and Welsh nationalism has, after many hesitations, embraced independence; this is also an independence-lite within the European Union. As for *ethos*, unionism faces the problem that the substantive values on which it stakes its claim are precisely those being claimed by its nationalist adversaries in the periphery.[16] Neo-unionism and civic unionism have been largely stripped of the sectarian baggage of the past and have striven to be more than greater England but have never quite captured the old patriotic traditions. Nationalism and unionism have each constructed images of the other to suit their own purposes but actually have a good deal in common, as neo-unionism has transmuted into a more muscular form of British nationalism. While agreeing broadly on ethos, nationalism and unionism still differ on the foundations of authority and constitutional *telos*. Civic unionism, however liberal, is still unionism, just as civic nationalism is still nationalism. Chapter 10 will show how voters respond to these perplexing political offerings.

[16] Ansari (2020) writes of these values having been 'appropriated' by Scottish nationalists, as though they were the rightful property only of unionists.

8

Economic Union

The Principle of Economic Union

The United Kingdom was created as, and remains, an economic union. Yet defining what economic union entails has proved difficult, as have assessments of the benefits and costs to the constituent nations. One is negative integration, the removal of barriers to the free movements of goods, services, capital and workers. Another is the single or internal market, which goes beyond free trade to cover a wide range of market and governmental activities that might, in a modern, regulatory state, affect competitive conditions. The third is that of territorial cohesion or balanced development, which implies positive policies to correct spatial disparities. These are all contested concepts and have posed recurrent problems in the history both of the United Kingdom and of the European Union.

The convergence theory of economic union tells us that, when different territories are brought together, levels of production and living standards will even out, based on the free movement of factors of production. Capital will flow to regions where there is plentiful and cheap labour, while labour will move to the prosperous places where well-paid jobs are available. Technical knowledge and innovations will be adopted quickly across the union. Backward regions will experience a 'catch-up' with the advanced ones. According to the principle of comparative advantage, each region will then specialize in those sectors in which it excels, so maximizing overall national output. All areas will benefit from access to a larger home market, and economies of scale will enhance productivity, requiring only a laissez-faire or non-interventionist economic regime.

Theories of uneven development point in the opposite direction. The creation of states itself may create disparities, enclosing territories within politically determined boundaries, which may benefit some of them and disadvantage others. As European states formed and consolidated in the nineteenth century, coastal trading cities, central in transnational trade links, became peripheral parts of national economies, while inland capitals benefited.

State and Nation in the United Kingdom: The Fractured Union. Michael Keating, Oxford University Press (2021).
© Michael Keating. DOI: 10.1093/oso/9780198841371.003.0008

Territorial tensions were provoked by arguments over free trade vs. protection, each of which would benefit some regions and harm others. In such a situation, wealthier regions, possessing a stronger infrastructure and knowledge base, are systematically advantaged in attracting capital. Peripheral territories, not in control of their own production, serve as sources of raw materials or cheap assembly for the dominant centres. Where political and administrative power is centralized, the pattern is reinforced as transport infrastructure is focused on capital cities, further increasing disparities (Keating 2013). At the extreme, there is even an 'internal colonialism', (Lafont 1967; Hechter 1975). Similarly, as the European Union developed from a free trade area into a single market, a debate ensued about whether this would reduce or exacerbate territorial disparities.

In the post-war years, interventionist European states addressed the issue in successive phases of regional policy. The aim was to modernize underdeveloped and declining regions and integrate them into national economies prior to insertion into European economic space. As the territorial equivalent of national development policies, this was sometimes known as 'spatial Keynesianism' intended to address 'market imperfections', which were preventing the declining regions from taking their place in the national division of labour. Politically, they had the advantage of appealing to all. Declining regions would gain additional investment and employment. Booming regions would benefit from relief from congestion and pressure on housing markets and services. The national economy would benefit from mobilizing otherwise idle labour and infrastructure. There was also a strong political rationale as spatial policies are used to secure loyalty to the political order in territories with autonomist or secessionist movements.

This phase came to a peak before the economic crisis of the 1970s, after which regional policies were run down. One factor was that diversionary policies were less effective in an open European and global economy where investors, discouraged from expanding in one part of the country, could just leave and go elsewhere. Interventionist policies had also become expensive at a time of fiscal constraint following the oil crises of the 1970s. From the 1970s, the European Union stepped into the breach, with its own regional or cohesion funds. Initially, the UK benefited substantially, but later funding was diverted towards the new members states of southern and then central Europe. A commitment to territorial cohesion was, moreover, inscribed into the treaties as part of the European conception of union.

At the same time, there was a shift in intellectual thinking away from centralized, diversionary policy towards 'endogenous development' focused on the capacity of regions themselves. Post-war thinking had assumed that territories were more or less interchangeable, so that investments would have the same effect everywhere; now more emphasis was put on the characteristics of regions themselves, including their institutional capacity, entrepreneurial potential and even culture. Attention thus shifted from integrating regions into national economic space and towards regional competitiveness in European and global markets. The new emphasis on competition tends to subordinate social to economic imperatives but the idea that territories as such compete for markets, investment and innovation has in turn been widely criticized (Bristow 2005, 2010). By definition, it is impossible for all regions to become more 'competitive' as competition entails winners and losers. Competitive regionalism may just provide a pretext for states to disengage from responsibility for their spatial economies. It has, however, become a powerful theme in the rhetoric of territorial politicians and of states and international agencies. This exposes an ambivalence at the heart of the concept of territorial cohesion, as to whether it is an integral part of economic policy, aimed at improving markets, or a 'social' corrective to the market itself. The concerns of this chapter thus overlap with those of the next.

The United Kingdom as an Economic Union

In many respects, the United Kingdom formed by the unions of 1707 and 1801 followed the standard pattern. There was negative integration, abolishing tariffs and harmonizing duties in order to create a common market, rapid in the case of Scotland and phased in Ireland, where protectionist tariffs were retained until 1824. Taxation took longer to unify, with differential provision in response to production and consumption patterns and to political pressures in Scotland and Ireland. Ireland was not brought into income tax until 1853 (Hoppit 2018). Subsidies were kept for the Scottish woollen industry, on the grounds that Scotland had lost out from the unification of customs and excise. These were later eliminated but provision was long made for supporting fisheries in Ireland and Scotland. From the 1860s, taxes were largely harmonized in accordance with Treasury doctrine, with the exception of municipal rates, which were brought effectively under central control in the 1980s.

The external context for union in the United Kingdom, however, differed from the continental model. While other countries alternated between free trade and protectionism, the UK became a beacon of free trade and its constituent nations were embedded in an international division of labour. In the late nineteenth century, as the UK's competitive advantage waned, there were increasing calls for protectionism, but this took the form of 'imperial preference' in which the Empire rather than the United Kingdom would constitute the protected home market (Edgerton 2018). It was not until after the Second World War that the United Kingdom became a clearly bounded economic space. The debate around 'global' Britain versus a nationally oriented strategy returned in the twenty-first century with the Brexit debate.

Industrial development in the nineteenth century was disproportionately concentred in the periphery of the United Kingdom, notably central Scotland, south Wales, the north-east of Ireland and the north of England. South Wales sucked workers from the rural areas and coastal towns into its raw materials production, in turn exported across the world. Mining and quarrying accounted for 52 per cent of all Welsh employment in 1911 (McCrone 2017) while Welsh mines accounted for almost a third of all world coal exports (Morgan 1981).

Scotland did not have the same dependence on raw materials as Wales; indeed, its economic structure was close to the British average (McCrone 2017) although there was a concentration of heavy industries in west-central Scotland, geared to imperial markets. On the eve of the First World War, the Clyde was responsible for a fifth of the world's shipbuilding (Clyde Valley Regional Planning Committee 1946).

Ireland was drawn selectively into imperial and global markets. Already in 1800, England took 85 per cent of Irish exports and supplied 80 per cent of its imports, although some of this was accounted for by colonial trade, which had to pass through British ports, Ireland being excluded before union from direct trade (Bartlett 2004). With the end of protectionist tariffs, nascent Irish industries like cotton were killed off (MacDonagh 89; O'Rourke 2016). A tripartite economy developed, with commercial agriculture in the east dependent on British markets; small-scale subsistence agriculture in the west; and industrialization in the north-east (Girvin 1989). Ireland was the only UK nation in which employment in agriculture exceeded that in industry in the late nineteenth century (Geary and Stark 2002).

It is impossible to give a straight answer to the question of whether the smaller nations gained or lost from the Union. We would need a counter-factual account of how they would have done without union, which in turn depends on the policy choices that would have been made. A full assessment, moreover, would need to look at which sectors, social classes and regions within the nations benefitted or lost.

The very choice of units of analysis is a politically charged matter. The UK nations are essentially the product of history and politics and do not correspond to economic units in the sense that economists understand that term. The regions of England are purely statistical units and have been changed regularly over time. Until the 1960s, Wales was often bundled statistically with England. It remains highly interdependent with England, and a significant proportion of its population works there, with many English-based workers coming the other way. Northern Ireland became a statistical unit only after the partition of Ireland in 1922. The figures for England are weighted by London, which boomed in the nineteenth century, while the old agricultural regions such as East Anglia, stagnated. The industrialized north-east of Ireland resembled western Scotland or south Wales. Taking all this into account, however, we now have a considerable amount of data both on current balances across the UK and on historic patterns, although difficulties remain in attributing economic activities to specific locations.

The nationalist perspective is that Ireland did poorly from the Union. The Famine in the 1840s cost the country 40 per cent of its output and resulted in a massive fall in living standards, which has cast a massive shadow over understandings of the Union. The British response may have owed more to laissez-faire dogmatism than to anti-Irish prejudice, but it showed a lack of solidarity and provided an enduring motif for nationalists. Recent scholarship has showed that per capita growth in the post-Famine period compared well with the UK and some European countries although Ireland's overall GDP was dragged down by large-scale emigration (Geary and Stark 2002; McLoughlin 2017; Lennard and Andersson, 2016). Even some of the productivity catch-up with Great Britain may have been due to emigration (Geary and Stark 2002). In any case, uneven development on the island makes it difficult to treat it as a unit (Girvin 1989). The most common view is that Scotland suffered in the early years of the Union but, took off from the time the Industrial Revolution (Lee 1995; Lenman 1977). During the nineteenth century, it gained from access to imperial markets and capital.

As industrialization progressed in the late nineteenth century, there was some territorial convergence. Overall, economic disparities across the UK declined from the 1860s until the First World War (McCann 2016). Crafts' (2005b) calculations suggest that Scotland and Wales did relatively well out of the industrial revolution of the late nineteenth century. Between 1871 and 1911 Wales' per capital GDP progressed from 86.8 per cent of the UK average to 90.1 per cent. Scotland's increased from 90.4 per cent to 102.1. According to Geary and Stark's (2002) calculations,[1] Ireland went from 58 to 62 per cent. London's advantage, however, was spectacular, going from 141.9 to 165.6 per cent of the average. Statistics available for the beginning of the twentieth century suggest that industrial output in Ireland stood at £78; Scotland at £98; and England (with Wales) at £104 (Gribbon 1989).

Not surprisingly, interpretations of gains and losses have been politically articulated within national frameworks. Irish nationalism consistently portrayed the country as a colony of England, which imposed a division of labour in which it exported agricultural products and manpower and imported industrial products. This inclined nationalists to protectionism and, in some versions, a vision of a pre-industrial Ireland of farms and small manufacturers. Unionists in the North were eager to attribute the success of industrialization there to the Union and Empire, together with stereotypical portrayals of Ulster Presbyterians as more commercially and industrially minded than their Catholic compatriots (Patterson 2013).

In Scotland, a dominant unionist narrative credited the Union for the nation's industrialization and prosperity. There were periodic complaints that Scotland's special conditions had not been recognized but it was not until the rise of Scottish nationalism during the twentieth century that a consistent economic critique of the Union emerged. It was not couched, as in Ireland, in anti-colonial rhetoric, but rather as a complaint that UK Governments pursued restrictive macro-economic policies attuned to the overheated economy of southern England. Economic conditions were not usually interpreted within a national frame in Wales but, from the nineteenth century, there were complaints that Wales's massive contribution to the Industrial Revolution was not appreciated at the centre.

Economic Union in the Twentieth Century

Up to the First World War, the component parts of the United Kingdom were part of a UK market that was itself inserted into a free-trading *laissez faire*, global order sustained by the British Empire. The late nineteenth century saw increasing demands for protectionism to face competition from countries like Germany and the United States, which had themselves industrialized behind tariff barriers. There was a related stress on British 'national efficiency'. The

[1] Using the same methodology.

initial focus was on the Empire as a trading block with the United Kingdom relying on its overseas possessions for raw materials and markets. This 'imperial preference' made little headway, but the collapse of the international trading system during the 1930s finally put an end to the free trade regime and in 1932 tariffs were introduced, with preferential reciprocal treatment for the Empire.

Economic crisis and protectionism did not affect all areas equally. After the First World War the industrial regions of west-central Scotland, south Wales, Northern Ireland and northern England, reliant on declining sectors and imperial markets, went into long-term relative decline; the downturn in coastal and the rise of road transport has also been cited (Crafts 2005a). The trend to overall territorial convergence reversed (McCann 2016). While the south of England recovered quickly from the 1930s' recession, attracting new, light industries and services, the heavy industrial areas did not recuperate until rearmament during the Second World War and continued their decline again from the 1950s (Campbell 1955).

From the Second World War, the idea of a bounded British (or UK) national economy and a developmental state (Edgerton 2018), took hold as the Empire faded into memory. Under governments of both major parties, the state committed to intervention to secure growth, full employment—and regional balance. The first responses came in the 1930s with the Special Areas (Development and Improvement) Act (1934), widely regarded as a 'political palliative' (Levitt 2014: 26). Following the Second World War, there was a Distribution of Industry Act (1945) and more ambitious measures for regional development, including new towns. More extensive programmes for territorial cohesion were launched in the 1960s, along with national planning and growth strategies, started under the Conservative Government of the early 1960s but taken to fruition by the succeeding Labour Governments (1964–70 and 1974–9). Labour's ill-fated National Plan (1965) was complemented by regional plans, including for Scotland and Wales and similar, but hesitant, initiatives in Northern Ireland. Public investment was focused on infrastructure in development areas. In 'diversionary policy', controls were placed on industrial expansion in booming areas, while investment grants, and, for a time, Selective Employment Tax benefits were given in development areas. Economic (Development) Councils, assisted by civil service Boards in Scotland, Wales and the English regions, aimed to harness local initiative. The apotheosis of the regional development phase came in 1974, when the whole of Scotland and Wales became eligible for industrial investment assistance. Under the Stormont government, industrial assistance was brought in after the Second World War, at rather higher levels than in the rest of the UK and in the 1960s' regional development policies followed similar lines to those in Great Britain (Bew et al. 1996). An Economic Council was established in Northern Ireland under direct rule in 1976.

This all transformed the politics of union. In the past, it offered the peripheral territories opportunities for trade, investment and careers across a free-trading UK and Empire. This was now replaced by dependency, as central government provided investment and protection within a national development strategy. Although nationalism started to grow in Scotland and (to a lesser extent) Wales and there were some regionalist stirrings in England, the assumption was that grievances were economic and not political and could be addressed by central government attention. There was similarly belief that development could reduce tensions in Northern Ireland. Yet regional policy itself served to frame economic development territorially and defined the nations and regions as economic units. Improvements in the quantity and quality of regional data also focused attention on territorial performance. Regional policy was accompanied by a strengthening of administrative devolution, and in 1975 Development Agencies were set up for Scotland and Wales. While regional policy had a strong technical rationale, politics was ever present. Faced with a decision on whether a major steel plant should go to Scotland or Wales, the Conservative Government of Harold Macmillan, in a Solomonic compromise, split it in two. Investment priorities in Northern Ireland were coloured by considerations of the community division. Nationalists regularly complained of a bias against the western counties, while unionists argued that investment was more effectively made in Belfast and eastern counties. While the idea of a Scottish Development Agency had a long history, it was the nationalist threat that ensured its place in Labour's 1974 manifesto.

During the post-war era, there was a resumption of territorial convergence (McCann 2016). Between the 1960s and the1990s, Scotland improved its relative economic position and fluctuated around 92–3 per cent of the UK average per capital GDP (Boyle 2018). Wales more or less maintained its ranking (Lee 1995) until the end of the 1990s and then grew more slowly than the UK, both absolutely and per capita (Dorsett 2013). Northern Ireland experienced a time of catching up between the 1960s and mid-1990s but thereafter dropped behind again (Nguyen 2019). There were also variations among the English regions. With a caveat for the methodological difficulties, this suggests that regional policy maight have worked for the peripheral nations.

The arrival in 1979 of a Conservative Government committed to non-intervention and reducing the scope of the state marked a sharp shift from diversionary regional policy and spatial planning (Wood 1994). The regional economic development councils in England were abolished. Spending on regional grants of all sorts fell by over 90 per cent (in constant prices) between its peak in the mid-1970s and the beginning of the 2000s, taking support for the poorest areas[2] well below the EU average (Wren 2005). This was accompanied by talk from Conservatives of the peripheral nations suffering from a 'dependency culture', too reliant on state support and public employment,[3] matching similar arguments about the welfare state. Intervention did not completely disappear. After some struggles within the Government after 1979, the Scottish and Welsh Development agencies were retained, stripped of some of their more interventionist competences. Later the Scottish Development Agency was transformed into Scottish Enterprise with a more private-sector orientation (Halkier 2006). From the early 1980s intervention shifted to the local and urban level.

UK or GB-wide regional policy finally came to an end in 1999 as the relevant powers were devolved to the nations. This contrasts with the devolution proposals of the 1970s, which would have retained a GB-wide anti-disparity regime, but is consistent with the move towards competitive regionalism and decentralized development policies. The continued economic responsibilities of the UK meant that economic policy was in practice shared between the UK and devolved governments. A concordat was negotiated on financial industry in order to avoid excessive competitive bidding.

Traditional regional policy survived in the form of the EU's expanding structural and cohesion policies, which required that the UK (or the devolved governments) provide matching funding. The UK had been a proponent of European regional policies in the 1970s as it would be a beneficiary and, after a big expansion of funding in 1988, they took on an enhanced political salience as evidence for Europe's positive effect in the nations and regions in the context of reduced UK support. From the 2000s, as funding shifted to the newer member states, the UK became less enthusiastic, and after 2010 argued for the renationalization of the policy except for the poorest states. In the last spending round before Brexit, European funding was particularly important for Wales and Northern Ireland (Table 8.1) although the figures should be treated with caution. There is a longstanding and bewildering debate about 'additionality', that is, how far the European moneys simply replace UK funding.

[2] What were then known in EU parlance as 'Objective One' areas.

[3] The theme was reprised as late as 2012 by Alan Massie, *The Telegraph*, 08-10-2012.

Table 8.1 Structural funds 2014–20

	% Funds	% Population
England	63.8	84
Scotland	8.2	8.2
Wales	22.2	4.7
N. Ireland	5.6	2.7

Alan Greer, *The European Referendum, Agriculture, Food and Rural Policy Issues*, Royal Society of Edinburgh, 2016; SPERI Political Economy Research Brief, 24, *UK Regions and European Structural and Investment Funds*, University of Sheffield, 2016.

Table 8.2 Ownership of business by GVA, 2017, percentage

	Scotland	N. Ireland	Wales	England	London
All Foreign-owned	28	21	28	26	29
EU	11	11	12	9	9

Source: Office for National Statistics, Annual Business Survey, 2019.

The move to competitive development from the 1980s was accompanied by a renewed emphasis on attracting foreign direct investment (FDI). After a struggle within government, Scotland kept its own inward investment agency, Locate in Scotland. Support for inward investment was then devolved in 1999, subject to the intergovernmental concordat. As Table 8.2 shows, Scotland and Wales have shared fully in the internationalization of business and particularly (with Northern Ireland) European investment.

There is another side to the FDI strategy, however, that it weakens economic centres in the UK periphery. In the late nineteenth century, there were indigenous local business classes in the old industrial areas. Scottish businesses were in interlinked shareholdings (Scott and Hughes 1980; McCrone 2017). Coal owners in Wales were mostly Welsh by birth, although distant in class from the workers (Morgan 1981; Johnes 2019). Northern Ireland had a dense network of local business leaders (Bew et al. 1996). The local bourgeoisies were influential actors locally and could articulate a territorial interest in national politics. In the south of Ireland, the old Anglo-Irish Ascendancy class were losing sway, and small farmers gained ownership of their land thanks to British legislation. After the First World War, there was a steep decline in local ownership of business in Scotland, Wales, Northern Ireland

and the regions of England. This was seen as a threat from the 1930s, and the early 1980s saw a debate about the dangers of dependence on external control (Ashcroft and Love 1993). There was a celebrated battle over whether Scotland's remaining banks would be protected from takeover by rivals in the south. That only changed when the Royal Bank of Scotland went on an aggressive quest to acquire banks in England and then overseas. External ownership (the direct consequence of inward investment) could, it was feared, expose fragile economies to decisions taken elsewhere and undermine local networks. As the Monopolies and Mergers Commission (1982) put it in the Royal Bank case: 'We accept that in certain cases, the comparative difficulties of regions like Scotland have been accentuated by the acquisition of locally managed and controlled businesses by companies from outside, whether from elsewhere in the United Kingdom or overseas.' External ownership was particularly important in manufacturing and high technology sectors. Scottish ownership of Scottish businesses fell steadily between the 1970s and the 2000s, while the interlinked structures of businesses had largely disappeared (Baird et al. 2007).

Politically, the loss of ownership undermined the basis of the Scottish and Ulster Unionist Parties, dependent, as they were, on a local bourgeoisie for leadership, organization and finance. Indeed, the lack of local financial supporters was one factor behind the folding of the Scottish Unionist Party into the Conservative Party in 1965. Yet the extensive privatization programme of the Thatcher and Major governments was not used as an opportunity to rebuild local business ownership or a business class in the nations and regions and so to recreate the old unionist elite. Instead, there was a reliance on a small number of business people close to government. Neo-liberal unionism, ironically, may have helped to undermine the Union itself.

The Internal Market

In the late twentieth century, the UK economy became more internationalized. Trade represented 65 per cent of GDP in 2018, compared with 55 per cent in 1951 (Ward 2018). Forty-seven per cent of the total was represented by trade with the EU (Ward 2020). Wales, Northern Ireland and northern English regions are the most export-oriented territories and are most dependent on EU markets (McCann 2016; Ward, 2020). We lack comprehensive figures on trade among UK nations and regions to compare with external trade but some data are available for Scotland and Northern Ireland. Scottish

Table 8.3 Destination of external sales, Scotland and Northern Ireland 2017, percentage

	Scotland	Northern Ireland
Rest of UK	60	48
EU	18	10 (excluding Ireland)
Rest of World	22	22
Ireland		20

Source: National Statistics; Northern Ireland Statistics and Research Agency.

'external' sales in 2017 were equivalent to 54 per cent of GDP; in Northern Ireland the figure was around 60 per cent. As Table 8.3 shows, these sales are mostly to the rest of the UK, but there is a strong dependence on overseas markets.

In contrast, Ireland has moved further out of the UK economic zone. In 1924, 99 per cent of exports of the new Irish Free State were destined for the UK. This was still 75 per cent in 1960 and 60 per cent in 1970, but by 2018 was just 22 per cent (Bradley 1999; WITS, 2017; Ask About Ireland, nd).

The UK clearly remains an important internal trading zone. Whether it constitutes a 'single market' in the technical sense is another matter. It has been argued by unionists that the Acts of Unions of 1707 and 1800 created not only a free trading zone but a UK 'single market' (Commission on Scottish Devolution 2008; Taylor 2019). This is misleading and anachronistic. The concept of a single or internal market only makes sense in the context of a modern, interventionist, regulatory state where the aim is to harmonize (or provide for mutual recognition of) rules on matters such as product standards, public procurement, professional qualifications and other matters that might violate its principles. None of these issues troubled the framers of the union statutes. The Scottish one was restricted to trade in the traditional sense:

> That all parts of the United Kingdom for ever from and after the Union shall have the same Allowances Encouragements and Drawbacks and be under the same Prohibitions Restrictions and Regulations of Trade and lyable to the same Customs and Duties on Import and Export And that the Allowances Encouragements and Drawbacks Prohibitions Restrictions and Regulations of Trade and the Customs and Duties on Import and Export settled in England when the Union commences shall from and after the Union take place throughout the whole United Kingdom.

The Irish Act is even briefer:

> his Majesty's subjects of Great Britain and Ireland shall, from and after the first day of January one thousand eight hundred and one, be entitled to the same privileges, and be on the same footing as to encouragements and bounties on the like articles, being the growth, produce, or manufacture of either country respectively.

In any case, the two acts of union entailed the abolition of the local parliaments, not the establishment-devolved legislatures which might endanger common provisions. The various Home Rule proposals for Ireland and Scotland in the late nineteenth and early twentieth centuries included free trade provisions but were equally silent on modern regulatory and welfare issues.

The Millennium settlement largely followed federal theory in assigning macro-economic stabilization and monetary policy to the central level. This also coincided with the division of competences between Whitehall and the Scottish and Welsh Offices; Northern Ireland inherited somewhat broader competences from the old Stormont system. There is no single/internal market provision, apart from a vague reference in the Northern Ireland Act. Lord Hope (2012a), in *Imperial Tobacco* suggested that there is:

> a common theme. It is that matters in which the United Kingdom as a whole has an interest should continue to be the responsibility of the United Kingdom Parliament at Westminster. They include matters which are affected by its treaty obligations and matters that are designed to ensure that there is a single market within the United Kingdom for the free movement of goods and services.

The judgment did not, however, extend this principle to allow the appeal in question, which concerned the regulation of tobacco advertising. Regulatory challenges under the Acts of Union have fared no better. The Court of Session (2013) in the case of Minimum Pricing for Alcohol gave short shrift to such an argument, noting that the Acts of Union did not overrule the Scotland Act. Lord Kerr (2018) in the House of Lords argued that '[w]e do not have a single market in the UK now; it is variegated, as are the views on the extent to which it needs to be further harmonised or advanced'. The internal market of the UK was, rather, guaranteed by the European Union. It is a highly contested concept (Weatherill 2017) and even the terminology is confusing. The EU has sequentially used 'common market', 'single market' and 'internal market', but now has aligned references in the treaties to 'internal market'. The basic question is how far, in any advanced regulatory welfare state or union with two orders of government, there needs to be uniformity of market conditions across the whole territory beyond the old negative integration by free trade and movement provisions.

The very concept is a contested one. Modern states based on the mixed economy and welfare state recognize that certain matters (like the production and distribution of consumer goods) should be left to the competitive market, private production and consumer choice. Others (like the police and military) should be a government monopoly. There is less consensus on exactly where the market ends and social, cultural or environmental considerations should take over. Should health and education be left to the market or be a governmental responsibility? If they are offered as public services, should private operators be allowed to tender to provide them? Should islands ferries be seen as an economic sector or a vital public service?

A second question concerns the territorial extension of the market and how much variation should be allowed across the component parts of a union. Should the devolved governments be able to impose more severe restrictions on the sale of alcohol or tobacco than in England on public health grounds? Should crofters in the Highlands be entitled to special support on social and cultural grounds? Can devolved governments impose stronger environmental regulations on developments?

The European Single Market programme from the 1980s aimed to take the EU beyond a free trade area and 'complete' the internal market. At the same time, it recognizes that public services should be largely exempt from market competition, and that social and environmental regulations should sometimes trump the market. It is not a fixed set of regulations but a living principle and decisions can be politically contentious. Going beyond the old 'conferral' principle whereby the EU was give specific powers, it operates transversally, across many fields in a way that can be expanded over time (Weatherill 2017). Measures are brought forward by the European Commission and adopted by the Council of the European Union (representing member states) and the European Parliament. They are implemented by laws directly applicable across the Union or transposed into national law by member states (or sub-state governments where appropriate). The whole process is governed by the principles of subsidiarity and proportionality. Subsidiarity means that action should be taken at the lowest level possible. Proportionality means that measures should only be as detailed as necessary, allowing for flexibility in their application. Infringement of the rules is dealt with by national courts and, ultimately, the Court of Justice of the European Union. There is no equivalent in the UK devolution settlement.

Nor is there anything corresponding to the elaborate, multilevel process found in the EU for making internal market rules. There is no equivalent to the Commission to make proposals and monitor compliance. The UK courts do not have the same role and expertise as the Court of Justice of the EU in enforcing market rules. There are no principles of subsidiarity and proportionality. This meant that the UK Government's Internal Market Bill, introduced in 2020, created a constitutional storm. It provided for non-discrimination against goods and services traded between parts of the United Kingdom and for mutual recognition of product and production standards and professional qualifications. This mirrors the European provisions but without the EU's constitutional safeguards. While the devolved governments would be able to make their own regulations, these would apply only to their own producers and could be undercut by goods and services coming from, or imported into, other parts of the United Kingdom with lower standards. There is a series of exemptions from mutual recognition, including existing measures (as long as they are not substantially modified), health, social services and the legal and teaching professions. The scope, however, remained wide.

These questions of where market competition ends and social, environmental, community, public health and other considerations begin have long been in the background of devolution debates. In England, market-type mechanisms and competition have been introduced into public services in health and education, allowing private operators to bid for contracts and provide services. This is much less extensive in Scotland and Wales where an older ethos of public provision has survived. Ferry services in Scotland, seen as essential to the maintenance of fragile communities in the islands, are subsidized on social grounds. Agricultural policy in post-Brexit England is predicated on market principles and the withdrawal of direct support. In Scotland, Wales and Northern Ireland, agriculture plays a broader role, maintaining population in fragile and remote areas and sustaining traditional cultures, languages and ways of life. Measures to control alcohol and tobacco in the interests of public health (a devolved matter) have been challenged under EU internal market rules and might be under a UK internal market regime. Stricter environmental regulations might also be considered to interfere with the market and discriminate against some producers of goods and services.

This issue goes to the heart of the union and its meaning. A broad interpretation of the internal market could undermine devolution and curb the regulatory freedom of devolved governments. If it were accompanied by a tighter specification of the 'social union' (Chapter 8), this might mitigate some of the effects but lead to recentralization as Westminster laid down the rules. Alternatively, there could be an intergovernmental mechanism for working out the rules, which would imply the UK Government (in respect of England) submitting to common frameworks, something it has shown no inclination to do. The only concession made during the parliamentary passage of the Bill, however, was another (non-binding) consent mechanism for any alterations to the list of items exempted from mutual recognition.

The internal market, formerly defined by European rules, will also be subject to external influences through trade and other agreements with the EU and with third countries. Trade deals in modern time have expanded beyond narrow considerations of tariffs and quotas, to include regulatory equivalence, environmental questions and labour standards. International trade is clearly a reserved matter but these issues cover devolved competences. It may be that harmonization within the UK will continue therefore to be driven by external pressures. These are likely to be more contentious than those arising from European regulations since, hitherto, there have been broad understandings about the European social market economy and environmental issues that are not necessarily shared by potential trade partners.

The Disconnected Union

There has been a series of debates about the effects of successive policy turns on economic disparities across the UK. The argument, and particularly international comparison, is bedevilled by technical difficulties, including the choice of unit of analysis. Generally speaking, the smaller the unit that is used, the larger the disparities are likely to be, whereas over large units they have a greater tendency to even out. There is another problem in taking GDP generated in a place as the measure, since this may reflect the concentration of employment, with people commuting in from elsewhere; again, that is more of a problem with smaller units. Scotland, Wales, and Northern Ireland are not economically defined units, but they are the constituent parts of the union and so differences among them do matter for our purposes. Taking all this into account there has been a growth of regional disparities since the 1980s, making the UK one of the most territorially unequal of advanced economies. This holds generally true even using a battery of different measures and definitions (McCann, 2016, 2019). The OECD (2018) ranks the UK as having among the highest territorial disparities amongst its member states, with the most pronounced differences at the local level. The general picture is that the south of England has come up relatively, while Wales, Northern Ireland and the old industrial regions of England have come down.

Devolution certainly focused attention on economic disparities across the Union. There was a debate in the early years of the Scottish Parliament, centred on the contention that Scotland was in dire economic straits, suffering from long-term decline (Alexander 2003). It is true, as the alarmists claimed, that Scottish GDP had been declining as a proportion of the UK total, but that is because population was not growing as it was in England. GDP per capita, the real measure of welfare, had grown at the same rate as the average for the rest of the UK since the early 1960s (Boyle 2018). It is Wales and the northern regions of England that have lagged behind (Table 8.4). The real story, however, is the massive advantage of London and the South East, already visible in the late nineteenth century and growing since then. In the seventeen years from 1999 to 2016, Northern Ireland grew faster than the UK average in five years, Wales in eight, Scotland in seven and London in thirteen (Office for National Statistics 2017). Uneven development is not just a phenomenon affecting the peripheral nations of the United Kingdom but something deeply entrenched at the centre. What McCann (2016) calls 'the UK's internal economic disconnection, dislocation and decoupling' is also a product of differentiated integration into global trading and investment regimes. While London and south-east England generate the largest absolute amounts of external trade, it is the poorer peripheral regions that are the most trade-dependent (McCann 2016). By this time, the issue was thoroughly politicized in the peripheral parts of the UK, even if it was slow to make it onto the agenda at the centre. To use the European language, there was a serious question of territorial cohesion in the UK internal market (Table 8.4).

Table 8.4 Gross Value Added per capita, 2017. UK = 100

UK	100
Scotland	92
Wales	72
Northern Ireland	76
London	178

Source: Office for National Statistics.

Rebalancing Economic Union?

The concept of economic union within the UK has thus experienced several phases and redefinitions. Initially, it took the form of negative integration, the removal of barriers to trade. Subsequently, the question was how the nations fitted into the global and imperial free-trading orders under British hegemony. The rise of a British developmental state in the twentieth century implied more positive measures for integration and a new territorial division of labour within it. This coincided with economic decline across large parts of the periphery and a response in the form of active, diversionary regional policies, tying in the nations in relations of dependency on England and on the British state. That in turn made way for a strategy of competitive development and external investment attraction, implying less dependence on central state resources, but raising the prospect of greater economic disparities. In the 1999 legislation, regional development policy was largely devolved. This contrasts with the devolution proposals of the 1970s when regional policy was seen as essentially a central competence aimed, as it was, at reducing disparities between the nations and regions. At that time, items like the development agencies and assistance to industry were to be retained at the centre, under the control of the territorial offices. The 1999 settlement also followed modern regional development theory, with its emphasis on local efforts and endogenous development. This was combined with a continued emphasis on the competitive attraction of foreign direct investment. There were some limits on competition in inducements to invest. The designation of assisted areas, in which investment subsidies are permitted, is reserved to the UK Parliament; these were also governed by EU rules. A Concordat was agreed on aid to industry to discourage wasteful competition and subsidy.

The transfer of responsibilities to the devolved governments has led to substantial divergence in economic development spending. HM Treasury (2019) figures suggest per capita spending on enterprise and economic development in Scotland, Wales and Northern Ireland was some two and a half times the level of England or any of its regions.

Following the Global Financial Crisis and then the referendum on leaving the EU, there was a certain return to intervention and industrial policy.[4] There was also a renewed sensibility to territorial inequalities in the face of evidence of increasing disparities. Yet by this point, the UK lacked competence in the

[4] Which the Conservative Government now called 'industrial strategy' to distinguish it from the 'industrial policy' explicitly repudiated by the Conservative Government of the 1980s.

field, which was largely devolved. Initiatives for territorial development were thus focused on England. The thrust was a return to active spatial policy but, given the current state of thinking, there was no question of reverting to the diversionary measures of the 1960. Rather, the emphasis was on competitive regionalism and 'levelling up, focused on the city–regional level. As the Conservative Party sought to recover in the cities of northern England, a Northern Powerhouse initiative was unveiled. Metropolitan regions (established by the Conservatives in 1974 and abolished by the same party in 1986) were reinvented under a new system of mayors, who would govern with associations of local councils. City Deals were introduced as a vehicle for central government to gain leverage over local spending (by providing matching funds) and prioritize economic and infrastructure projects. A Shared Prosperity Fund was introduced to replace European cohesion funding. None of this, however, matched the scale and scope of regional policies of the 1960s and 1970s.

After the arrival of the SNP Government and the 2014 referendum in Scotland, the UK Government, increasingly concerned about its lack of visibility in Scotland, rolled out some of the English initiatives across the devolved nations. City deals allowed it to spend in projects that mixed reserved and devolved matters and leveraged funding from devolved and local governments. This must be seen more as a political strategy than a cohesion policy as the amounts of money involved are very small and there is the danger that these ad hoc projects may cut across local priorities. Money going into the deals is 'additional' to what the devolved governments get through the block grant and, at local level, to what local authorities receive from the devolved administrations. There is something disingenuous about this claim, though. If all parts of the UK benefit, it is merely a different way of distributing available resources. Headline figures can look generous, especially if expressed as the total over periods of up to ten years. In practice, the amounts of money involved are very small compared with the existing spending of the devolved administration. By 2019, the UK Government had committed £1.4 billion to Scottish deals over ten years, which represents less than 0.02 per cent of public spending in Scotland over ten years at current rates.[5] They require the devolved and local governments to contribute a share, so potentially distorting their own spending priorities. While initially, the UK Government share was tied to reserved competences, this was gradually relaxed. Most seriously of all, spatial policy, unlike in the 1960s, does not seem to include London,

[5] 75.3 billion a year.

which is the real outlier in development and growth. As with the political constitution, attention to the periphery has left the centre largely untouched.

Whatever rebalancing policies emerge from Brexit must be set against the effect of Brexit itself, which appears to be territorially uneven, with some of the areas that voted to leave losing out most (Chen et al. 2017). London is likely to be less hard hit than Wales and the Midlands and North of England, which have already been falling behind. The United Kingdom remains, in the conventional sense, an economic union, but territorial cohesion appears ever more elusive.

9
Social Union

Defining the Social Union

The United Kingdom has often been described as a 'social union' but the meaning and implications of the term are multiple. One sense is purely sociological. In the run-up to the Scottish independence referendum, SNP First Minister Alex Salmond (2012) used it to refer to family and friendships across the border. Prime Minister Theresa May (2019b), deploying the metaphor of the family, presented a conservative vision of social union as underpinning shared institutions, including the armed forces, the BBC and the NHS. Another meaning is about sharing burdens and allocating resources according to need (McLean et al. 2013), what former Labour Prime Minister Gordon Brown (2012, 2014, 2019) calls the 'sharing union'.

This idea has its roots in the concept of social citizenship, advanced by T. H. Marshall (1992) in the post-war years as a third stage in the development of citizenship and rights, beyond the civil and the political. The core principle is of equal entitlement to at least a minimum of social provision, drawing on two further ideas. One is that of mutual insurance, that it makes sense for us to insure against social risks like illness, or unemployment and against old age. The bounded nation-state is seen as the best unit for doing this in so far as all social groups are contained within it, with no possibility of opting out. The other is affective solidarity, that we are prepared to help others with whom we feel a natural affinity, hence our co-nationals (Miller 1995).

Marshall made no reference to territory and treated the United Kingdom as a unitary nation-state. In a plurinational union, it is not obvious what the 'national' unit is and therefore where affective solidarity might lie (McEwen 2006). In a federal or devolved state, the question is whether governments should be able to offer different benefits or whether people in the same circumstances should get the same treatment wherever they live. Governments in wealthy areas could afford to provide more. There is also a risk that, if one region levies higher taxes in order to provide better services, wealthy individuals and businesses might move out and (less likely in practice) poor people might

State and Nation in the United Kingdom: The Fractured Union. Michael Keating, Oxford University Press (2021).
 DOI: 10.1093/oso/9780198841371.003.0009

move in. The consequence may be a 'race to the bottom' in the form of low taxes and less generous services.

For this reason, theories of federalism have long argued that redistributive services such as cash benefits should be located at the higher level. It is also widely considered appropriate that business taxation should be collected at the central level so as to avoid market distortions that might arise from different tax regimes.[1] A case is also made for fiscal equalization, transferring resources so that all regions can afford to provide the same level of services. Yet fiscal equalization is not easy to define, let alone apply. It can be applied on the basis of need, so giving more to areas that are judged to have greater requirements for spending, because there are more severe social problems or because the cost of providing services is greater (for example in remote areas). Equalisation can apply also to resources, giving more to poorer areas or those with less taxable capacity (where the product of the same tax would produce less revenue per head). All of these are fraught with methodological problems and may be politically contentious. For example, providing Welsh or Gaelic language education may be seen as an objective criterion of need in certain areas, or a policy choice of the respective governments.

Fiscal equalization might ensure that all territories can afford the same services; it does not ensure that individuals will be treated the same way as long as governments can choose how to spend their money. One place might favour spending on old people while another one prioritizes education for the young. So, the principles of territorial equity and interpersonal equity will always be in tension. Some states have sought to resolve this issue by laying down state-wide frameworks or minimal levels of provision, while allowing the regions to decide on the details.

Issues about the distribution of taxation and spending marked the UK union settlements from the start, bedevilled Home Rule schemes and set much of the political left against devolution during the twentieth century. When it finally occurred at the end of the century, it was in the context of a complex welfare state that was itself undergoing radical adjustments.

Taxing and Spending

The distribution of burdens featured in the negotiation of both unions but the sophisticated data or modelling tools needed to underpin an equitable

[1] In practice, business taxes in federal systems are often allocated to the lower tier, leading to fierce competition for investment. In the European Union, member states have resisted such tax harmonization, but differences in business taxes within those states are regulated.

settlement did not exist. Arguments in Scotland revolved around the 'equivalent', a term that was to feature a great deal in subsequent debate. In 1707 it was set as the amount Scotland would have to receive for the adjustment of customs and excise, assumption of a share of the English national debt, and compensation for the shareholders in the failed Darien colonization scheme. The Irish Act contained long and complex provisions for financial contributions and debt.

In both cases, the idea was that eventually there should be a unified tax system across the United Kingdom so that individuals in the same circumstances would pay the same wherever they lived. The Scottish Act set out detailed provisions for balancing out taxes and liabilities in the meantime. The Irish Act set a contribution for Ireland to pay (2/17 of Imperial expenditure) but left it to a future Parliament to harmonize rates; this was achieved in 1817 and the Irish Exchequer was then abolished. Power was, however, retained to set exemptions and abatements in Ireland and 'in that part of the United Kingdom called Scotland.'

If the project of unifying taxation across the United Kingdom were to have come to fruition, the very idea of measuring the contributions of the component nations could have become irrelevant (Royal Commission on the Financial Relations between Great Britain and Ireland 1896). In practice, this was never achieved. The principle of personal equality consistently collided with that of territorial equity, and arguments about the relative burdens and gains of the territories have persisted ever since. There was a series of inquiries in the nineteenth century to assess the burden on Ireland, and between 1885 and 1921 the UK Government published estimates for England (including Wales), Ireland and Scotland. Inquiries were established for Scotland after the Second World War in response to political pressures. Since the 1970s, there have been regular calculations of taxation and spending across the nations and regions, becoming more methodologically advanced and politically salient over time.

Even as taxes were harmonized, they fell unequally in different territories. During the mid-nineteenth century, the UK moved to free trade, abolishing tariffs on most products while maintaining excise duties on some, including alcohol. It was claimed that this discriminated against Scotland and, to a lesser extent, Ireland, because of the tendency of their populations to consume more spirits and less beer. The abolition of the Corn Laws, allowing the free import of wheat, was more valuable to English consumers than to Ireland, where subsistence agriculture was more common. A wider argument concerned taxable 'capacity', another contested term referring to the surplus of production, which was larger in England than in Ireland. Attributing revenues for consumption taxes was difficult on imported items like tea, which tended to be landed in England and then distributed through the United Kingdom. In more recent times, there has been dispute about attributing revenues from North Sea Oil. If offshore production in Scottish waters were attributed to Scotland, it would seriously distort calculations of Scotland's GDP,[2] but if they are omitted it looks as though Scotland is more dependent on transfers than is the case. So, the North Sea is treated as a separate region (Extra-Regio) but its tax revenues can be added to Scotland's or not, depending on the purpose of the calculation.

Taking all this into account, it appears that Scotland was relatively lightly taxed after the Union. Efforts to extend the malt tax there were rebuffed on the grounds that barley was a staple and later it was charged at half the rate of England (Hoppit 2019). From the late eighteenth century, with the wars in America and France, the burden increased but was still lower per capita than England. Estimates for Wales suggest it was lower still there. Ireland also got off quite lightly in the early years of union but there was a sharp shift in the 1850s, as income tax was extended there, which attracted criticism later from the Royal Commission on the Financial Relations between Great Britain and Ireland (1896), especially as it had occurred in the aftermath of the Famine. By the end of the nineteenth century, per capita tax burdens had largely converged, with Scotland somewhat above and Ireland somewhat below the average (Hoppit 2018).

Had the UK been a unitary state, then the distribution of expenditure by territory (as opposed to social groups) might become irrelevant, but this was never to happen. Yet allocating expenditure to the nations is also fraught. Until the end of the nineteenth century, this consisted largely of military spending and service on the national debt (36 and 27 per cent respectively in 1890). A distinction was drawn between Imperial expenditure (such as the military), of benefit to all, and domestic spending, which could be attributed to the nations, but this was by no means simple. It was argued, for example, that Ireland benefited less than Great Britain from the Royal Navy, whose main task was to keep open the trading routes from which Ireland drew less benefit.

As the state expanded its domestic role in the late nineteenth and early twentieth centuries, there were regular arguments about who benefited from the additional expenditure and how it should be calculated. Instead of elaborating a coherent territorial framework, the Treasury, whose consistent

[2] This would not help Scotland as it would undermine its claim to be a deserving case for support.

concern was to control expenditure, sought to fight off bids from the territories as it did from departments. As Scotland acquired its own spending department in 1885 in the Scottish Office, these pressures were institutionalized and focused; an Irish administration had been in existence since the union of 1801. In 1888, faced with the need to allocate spending on rates relief among the nations, Chancellor of the Exchequer George Goschen opted to use the ratio of probate duties in England, Ireland and Scotland. This expanded into the Goschen Formula, which lingered on for some seventy years and allocated increases in expenditure among England and Wales, Scotland and Ireland in the ratio of 80:11:0, a rough proxy for populations. The Treasury always detested the formula because it allowed the territorial lobbies to game the system.[3] For any given programme, they would claim their existing allocation, plus a Goschen share of whatever extra England was getting. Using, this as a floor, they would then argue for extra where their circumstances were distinct.

By the 1950s, the Treasury had largely succeeded in eliminating Goschen in an effort to control expenditure. The effort, however, was counter-productive as now the Scottish Office was able to make ad hoc arguments on specific matters, while still claiming a population share of everything else on grounds of equity. Moreover, it had gained a certain amount of leeway in using its population-based allocations rather flexibly. The system was summed up in an exchange between John Mackintosh MP and the Permanent Secretary of the Scottish Office.

> Mackintosh: There is something slightly peculiar, though, that you build up a total of Scottish expenditure by a set of ad hoc arguments and bargains, but you then establish a total to which you have some sort of claim, within which you have a certain flexibility?
>
> Sir Douglas Haddow: I find it a very rewarding system, sir.
>
> (Select Committee on Scottish Affairs 1969)

There does seem to have been some rough idea of justice, as advantages in one field were offset in another, but there was no systematic calculation of the overall effect. For UK ministers, any advantage for the peripheral nations was a small price to pay for peace and quiet, since it made little difference to the overall totals.

[3] This is clear from the correspondence reported in Levitt (2014).

The issue came to a head again in the 1970s, when a squeeze on public expenditure coincided with plans for devolution to Scotland and Wales. The Treasury realized now that controlling the overall totals would be more effective than trying to manage the detail. There was no conscious decision to put in place a new system of territorial finance but, as with Goschen, a short-term expedient turned into a long-lasting formula. This is the Barnett Formula,[4] after the Chief Secretary of the Treasury, although Joel Barnett (2011) himself never acknowledged it and spoke out against it regularly for the rest of his life, urging that it be replaced by a needs-based system. It provides that any increase or decrease in expenditure for England should be applied to Scotland, Wales and (later) Northern Ireland in proportion to their population. Under the 'block' allocation principle, the respective Secretaries of State were then allowed to spend the money across their range of responsibilities, not necessarily making the same choices as were made for England. The formula long remained shrouded in mystery and it took years of parliamentary questions and freedom of information requests to extract the details.

When the devolved institutions in Scotland, Wales and Northern Ireland were set up twenty years later, the Barnett Formula was simply rolled over to them.[5] It is not an equalization mechanism and takes no account of either needs or resources. It is, however, quite easy to apply and saves the Treasury from having to intervene in detail and face the kind of bargaining and special pleading that happened in the past. The formula is not even statutory: the three devolution acts merely stipulated that the Secretary of State could make payments to the devolved institutions.

Winners and Losers

In theory, Barnett should have led to a convergence of per capita expenditure levels over time as the element distributed according to population increased while the old base became a smaller part. It is not clear that this was intended (Bristow, 2008) and convergence would not necessarily have made the system any more, or any less, fair: it is merely a statistical property of the formula. In practice, convergence did not happen for many years. As Figure 9.1 shows, the spending relativities of the nations have remained very stable since 1999.

[4] The term was coined by academic David Heald.

[5] The initial draft of the Northern Ireland Bill also included the old Stormont tax powers, but these were removed at the behest of all the Northern Ireland parties, who feared having to pay for their own costs in the future.

London has consistently high levels, as does Scotland. Wales comes in rather lower. Northern Ireland's relative spending has decreased because of the lower cost of security since the Good Friday Agreement.

These figures, however, cover all expenditure, not just that within the block. Expenditure on social protection, including pensions and welfare benefits, is largely reserved and allocated according to individual need. As Figure 9.2 shows, this also allocates most to Northern Ireland, followed by Wales, Scotland and England. As this accounts for around a third of all identifiable expenditure, it does amount to a substantial form of equalization.

Even expenditure levels within the block, however, did not converge as anticipated, for a number of reasons. Until 1992, the population relativities were not adjusted to take account of change. This benefited Scotland, which

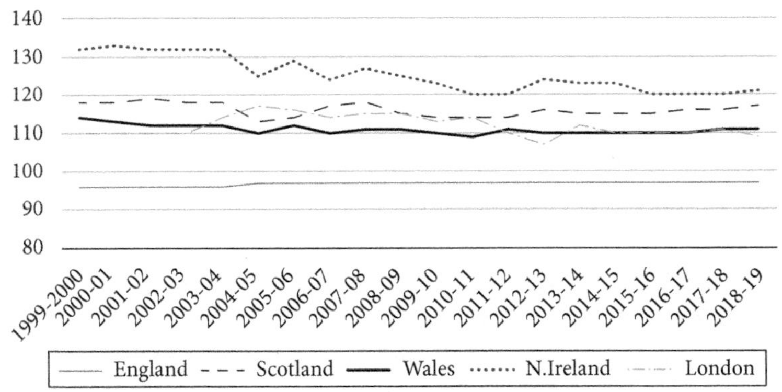

Figure 9.1 Public expenditure per head, UK = 100
Source: HM Treasury Public Expenditure Statistical Analysis.

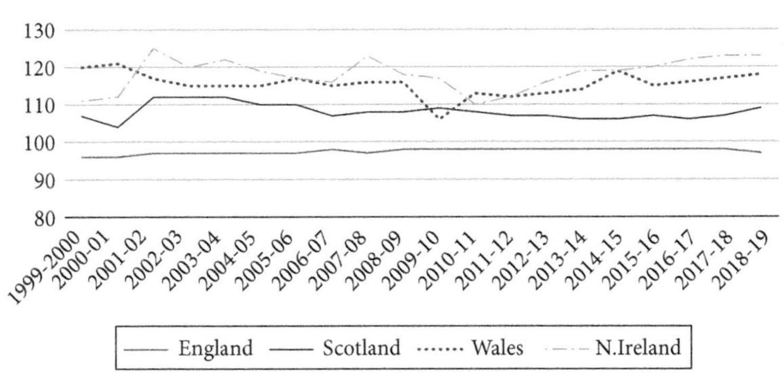

Figure 9.2 Expenditure on social protection per head, UK = 100
Source: HM Treasury Public Expenditure Statistical Analysis.

had a declining population. Even after this, the updated population figures applied only to the changes, not to the base. There were various initiatives which by-passed the formula, and political considerations.

There has, nevertheless, been something of a 'Barnett squeeze', particularly on Wales. Gallagher and Hinze (2005) found it in the early years of devolution, taking expenditure on agriculture and social protection out of the totals. The Holtham Commission (2009) similarly found a squeeze, in which Barnett-funded spending in Wales had fallen from 125 per cent of the English per capita in the years before devolution to 112 in 2010 and threatened eventually to erode away all Wales' advantage. Poole et al. (2016) came to the same conclusion, up to 2016. The squeeze was particularly severe during times of rapid expenditure growth in the early 2000s, as would be expected from the operation of Barnett; it was arrested and slightly reversed in the years of austerity after the financial crisis, but this only meant that Wales enjoyed a small share of cuts. Hague (2017) comes to similar conclusions.

Whether this is 'fair' or not can be judged by two quite different criteria: whether each nation gets to spend what it earns; and whether it gets what it needs. The UK Treasury makes estimates of the 'fiscal balance' of each nation and region, the difference between taxes raised there and government spending. The Scottish Government also calculates Government Revenue and Expenditure in Scotland (GERS), and Northern Ireland has a Net Fiscal Balance Report. The calculations all show that London and south-east England (and sometimes eastern England) have a fiscal surplus, while everyone else is in nominal deficit. So, London's consistently high expenditure is more than covered by revenue raised there. Wales and Northern Ireland (along with north-east England) have the lowest revenues per capita and are in consistent deficit (Keep 2019). Scotland's case is complicated by the way North Sea Oil revenues are calculated and it is now normal to make two calculations, one with a geographical share of the oil revenues and one without. Including the oil revenues still shows Scotland in deficit in most years but, if we take a long perspective to include the massive oil revenues of the 1980s, then the totals are closer to balance.

Calculating need is even more fraught, as it depends on applying contested criteria and it has hardly ever been attempted. In anticipation of devolution in the 1970s, a Needs Assessment Exercise suggested that Scotland received more spending than would be justified by the need criteria it applied, but Wales received less. The methodology was rather crude and the findings were widely disputed. The Holtham (2009) Commission on Funding and Finance for Wales set up by the Welsh Government did another exercise, applying the various criteria used to allocate local and regional spending in England, also finding that Wales was under-funded.

The Politics of Barnett

The Barnett Formula has come under attack from several sides and for very different reasons. In England, it is widely seen as an unfair subsidy for the devolved territories at the expense of English taxpayers. Such criticisms are largely aimed at Scotland, fuelled by the publication of the GERS figures and come from the political left as well as the right. This is usually linked with complaints about Scotland's more extensive universal services, with the implication that these are financed by England. Barnett was a target of opposition on the part of the UK Independence Party and the Conservative right, seeking to tap into the latent English nationalism.

Scottish nationalists argue, to the contrary, that, taking into account oil revenues, Scotland pays its own way. The argument really hinges on which base years are used for the calculation, given the volatility of oil prices. They also argue that an independent Scotland would pursue different economic policies, so that its own-source revenues would be higher. By definition, this argument cannot be tested. In the meantime, Scottish politicians of all parties have defended Barnett against English criticisms but not always in full understanding of what it entails. When it was suggested that agricultural and regional development spending after Brexit should be subject to Barnett, there was massive opposition on the part of some devolved ministers and civil servants, who insisted that this would mean Scotland getting only its population share of total spending. In fact, applying Barnett would have meant that Scotland, Wales and Northern Ireland would keep their existing high levels and only the changes from one spending round to another would be allocated by population. Barnett also featured in the famous Vow issued by the unionist parties during the referendum campaign, when they pledged to retain it, and in the Conservative leadership campaign of 2019 when candidates promised in Scotland (but not in Wales) to keep it indefinitely.

In Wales, there is general opposition to Barnett since it delivers lower levels of spending than in Scotland and does not take account of Wales' relative needs. All parties have argued for a new needs-based system, from which Wales could expect to benefit (Holtham 2010).

Defenders of Barnett have relied on two arguments. One is that the system is simple and works automatically, taking the politics out of the vexed issue of territorial finance (Gallagher 2020). This certainly explains the formula's remarkable longevity, although the point about simplicity can be exaggerated. In practice, a lot of judgements have to be made about the appropriate comparators and there have been multiple adjustments and refinements over the years. The second argument is less well founded. That is that Barnett actually equalizes on the basis of need. The Labour-Liberal Democrat-run Scottish Executive (2003) claimed that '[w]ithin the United Kingdom the levels of expenditure vary from one constituent part to another, reflecting the needs rather than the tax capacity of an area'. Gordon Brown (2019), defended 'the Barnett formula—which allocates resources by taking account of differing needs and changing demography across the four nations of the UK.' As Prime Minister, Theresa May (2019) stated that '[t]he Barnett formula delivers spending per head significantly higher in Northern Ireland, Scotland and Wales than the UK average, to reflect particular needs'. Boyce (2018: 11) claims that 'the Goschen Formula was ultimately replaced by the Barnett Formula in 1979, which was designed to acknowledge that public spending needs in Scotland were higher due to a relatively poor health record, greater dependence on local authority housing, a higher proportion of young people in education and the increased cost of providing public services in sparsely populated areas.'[6] Yet, if need criteria had been the key factors, Wales should have benefited more. Brown (2014: 219) stated that 'it made sense for each nation to pool its resources across the whole country so that if there were a higher incidence of disease and greater health needs in one part of the country their risks could be shared across the whole country'. There has never been a UK-wide budget for the NHS. It is notable that all the analysis papers by Treasury officials during the independence referendum campaign of 2014 carefully avoided making claims about Barnett being based on need.

Devolution of substantial taxation powers to the devolved legislatures, in principle, makes them more reliant on their own resources. This would increase inequality unless, as happens in most countries, there is some fiscal equalization to allow poorer places to afford the same level of services as wealthier ones. Under legislation in 2016, income tax was devolved to Scotland (the whole tax) and Wales (the first 10 per cent), along with some smaller taxes. Half of Value Added Tax receipts were to be assigned to Scotland, without the power to vary the rate; this was postponed because of technical difficulties. Northern Ireland was promised powers to vary

[6] This appears to be a misinterpretation of a sentence in Peden (2005: 235) referring to the 1978 Needs Assessment Exercise, which was never applied; Peten makes it clear that Barnett was the *alternative*.

corporation tax, in order to compete for investment with the Republic of Ireland, although that, too, was postponed. Under the EU rules prevailing at the time, it would have to be clear that the resultant shortfall in revenue fell upon the Northern Ireland Assembly's budget. Yet no general system of equalization was introduced. The Barnett Formula was retained, with a deduction to allow for the lower taxes raised by the UK Government in Scotland and Wales. There were some safeguards in this Block Grant Adjustment such that, if an economic shock caused a fall in tax revenues across the UK, the devolved governments would be protected. Any shortfall in taxes affecting only a devolved territory would be for that government to deal with. In addition, an ad hoc equalization mechanism was introduced for Wales, which ensured that its spending remains at around 115 per cent of the UK average per head. This is to be renegotiated periodically. The 115 per cent figure was calculated drawing on the work of the Holtham (2010) report, commissioned by the Welsh Government. This is the only needs-based element in the entire system.

These provisions are incorporated in Fiscal Frameworks negotiated between each devolved government and the Treasury. The outcome is a differentiated set of arrangements, which have in common only the residual Barnett formula based on the historical base and population relativities. Far from moving to a consistent set of principles based on needs and resources, the UK has continued its traditional mode of bargaining between centre and periphery, using some simple rules of thumb and accommodating political pressures.

The Welfare State

The earliest measures for relieving the poor were taken separately across Ireland, Scotland and England & Wales, and there was no provision in the union settlements to unify them. The English Poor Law dated back to Elizabethan times and stipulated that local communities were responsible for helping the indigent. This was overhauled by the Poor Law Amendment Act of 1834. In Scotland, the pre-union law survived until the Poor Law Scotland Act of 1845, which retained significant differences from the English system. By contrast, the English Poor Law was extended to Ireland in 1834 as a measure of modernization but also with the intention of preventing the Irish destitute ending up in Great Britain (MacDonagh 1989). The first pan-UK measures were not taken until the Liberal Government of the early twentieth century, when old age pensions, unemployment insurance and other benefits were introduced on a uniform basis, supported by employer and employee contributions. There was no territorial differentiation, but the effect was to redistribute resources depending on the demographics of the component nations and their contributions to revenue. Old age pensions in 1909 turned a surplus in Irish revenues into a deficit (Vaughan 1989). The same appears to have happened in Scotland; at the start of the twentieth century, it was contributing its population share to 'imperial' expenditure, but by 1910–11 this had fallen (Crammond 1912).

The separate poor law systems lasted until after the Second World War when the Labour Government laid the foundations of the modern welfare state. The National Assistance Act of 1948 created a single system for Great Britain, removing its administration from the Scottish Office. The National Health Service was introduced by a separate Act in Scotland but the principles were essentially the same. The main parliamentary debate was on the England and Wales bill, with Scottish MPs making a full contribution. The debate on the Scottish bill provoked less controversy, partly because the basic principles built on precedents there. Administration was in the hands of the Scottish Office although, playing the Scottish card, the Conservatives accused the Government of not paying enough attention to Scottish conditions (Stewart 2003).

Although all these matters were devolved in Northern Ireland, the Stormont Government chose largely to match the emerging welfare regime in Great Britain with the Health Services Act (Northern Ireland) 1948, the National Assistance (Northern Ireland) Act 1948 and the National Insurance Act (Northern Ireland) 1946. Although the Ulster Unionist Party was ideologically suspicious of the welfare state, it saw it as an important tool to steer the Protestant working class away from socialism and the Northern Ireland Labour Party and even to make partition less intolerable for Catholics. Crucially, the UK Government agreed to pick up the bill, effectively abandoning the financial provisions of the Government of Ireland Act (Boyce 2006). This was enshrined in the 'parity principle', dating from the early days of Stormont, under which citizens of Northern Ireland were entitled to the same level of services as those in Great Britain.

Labour's network of welfare provision across the United Kingdom played consciously into its self-promotion as a patriotic party with a sense of British national identity; the *National* Health Service was to be a long-lasting motif of Britishness, with a prominent place in the patriotic display put on for the 2012 Olympic Games in London. The welfare state also reconciled the working classes to the state and constitutional order. Yet, while it was quite advanced for its time, whether it amounted to a full regime of social citizenship on Marshallian lines is more debatable. Welfare and public service development in the 1940s and early 1950s was subordinated to spending on rearmament and the commitment to maintaining a global political and military role. Unlike the emerging Nordic models, there was a weak universalistic ethos in which all classes shared the same civic experiences. The basis of welfare was largely selective and reliant on means testing. Publicly-owned housing, intended as a mechanism for social mixing, was soon residualized as accommodation for those who could not afford to buy. Private schools educated only a small proportion of the population but they were grossly overrepresented among political, social and economic elites, especially in England.

Home Rule Bills in the late nineteenth and early twentieth century had almost nothing to say about these issues, as nothing like the modern welfare state existed. The 1999 devolution settlement for Scotland and Wales largely followed three convergent logics: the standard prescription of federal theory; the division between the responsibilities of the territorial offices and Whitehall; and the division between the Barnett-financed block transfer and cash welfare benefits. Overtly redistributive policies, including almost all taxation and cash benefits, were reserved to Westminster. Other domestic services were devolved. Northern Ireland inherited the old Stormont powers but also the parity principle with the UK meeting the costs although, like other principles, it has remained rather vague in its application (Northern Ireland Assembly, 2011). It was put to the test with the welfare reforms of the Conservative–Liberal Democrat coalition (2005–10) which entailed substantial cuts in welfare. The nationalists in Northern Ireland vetoed the reform under a Petition of Concern. In response, the UK Government stopped the relevant payments so that Northern Ireland would have been obliged to make the cuts or find the money from its own budget. Eventually, the Assembly agreed to Westminster taking back the powers temporarily, in order to make the changes. All that remained were some powers used by the Northern Ireland Assembly and the Scottish Parliament to mitigate some of the effects, such as the 'bedroom' tax, payment of housing benefit and the timing of Universal Credit payments.

If the core of the social union consists of payments to individuals under the heading of 'social protection', then it remains intact. Basic welfare benefits and pensions are paid to individuals according to their circumstances irrespective of where they live. As Figure 9.2 shows, per capita payments have consistently been higher in the devolved territories than in England.

Northern Ireland and Wales have been the main beneficiaries but Scotland has also gained more than England. Within England, of course, there are also significant differences.

Public Services

Reserving welfare and redistributive competences to Westminster, however, does not exhaust the question of distribution and fairness. The Beveridgian welfare state was based on assumptions about the economy, the labour market and family structures from the mid-twentieth century. There was provision for families, for the aged and for what were assumed to be temporary periods of unemployment. Assistance mostly took the form of 'passive' support in cash payments to those in need—which potentially could be anybody. By the 1990s, attention had shifted to 'new social risks' based on access to labour markets, age, gender and location. With the return of long-term unemployment, there was a focus on 'activation', aimed at getting people into work. There was also a political sea change, from the old idea of social security (for everyone) to 'welfare' (for the most needy only). With the return of a Conservative-led government in 2010, older rhetoric about the deserving and undeserving poor returned, as politicians divided the population into 'strivers and skivers' or 'workers and shirkers'.[7]

Under the Scotland Act (2016) a range of welfare benefits were devolved to Scotland. These did not cover the major social risks or insurance against cyclical economic shocks, but permitted some variation in personal payments. Scotland was also allowed to top-up reserved UK benefits using its own resources. While the scope for using these powers is limited, it did give the Scottish Government the opportunity to reintroduce the language of 'social security' instead of the more derogatory 'welfare'.

In the modern state, however, redistribution is not confined to cash payments. All public services have a distributive effect, benefitting some individuals or sections of the population more than others as governments choose to favour old people, young people, ill people or whatever. Services can be supplied to everyone (the universal principle) or only on the basis of need (selectivity). These are political choices, often made by inertia or for electoral

[7] Chancellor George Osborne (2012) declared at the Conservative Party Conference: 'Where is the fairness, we ask, for the shift-worker, leaving home in the dark hours of the early morning, who looks up at the closed blinds of their next-door neighbour sleeping off a life on benefits.' Labour Shadow Cabinet Member Liam Byrne (2011) had claimed that 'many people on the doorstep at the last election felt that too often we were for shirkers, not workers.'

considerations, but they also reflect broader philosophies. Universalist approaches draw on the idea of social citizenship to bind everyone into the community of solidarity and gain middle-class support for the welfare state. Selective approaches seek to target resources to those who really need them. The devolved governments in the UK have considerable latitude in the provision of health care, education, social care, concessionary fares on public transport or winter heating allowances. They can also choose whether to introduce competition and market mechanisms into public services, such as has occurred in England with the internal market in the National Health Service and academy schools (taken out of local government control) and free schools (privately run but publicly funded). Broadly, Scotland and Wales have, given the choice, opted for universality and against private provision and marketization.

While Conservatives have often been critical of these decisions on ideological grounds, they have not generally condemned the idea of divergence. That has been more of a problem on the centre-left, for whom the welfare union has been a central pillar of the political union itself. In the early years of devolution, this provoked a lot of concern in New Labour circles in England, which were themselves inclined towards market competition in public services and selectivity. From one perspective, universalism is a legitimate exercise of autonomy by the devolved governments. From another, it violates the principle of equal treatment of individuals since people are treated differently according to where they live. Welfare innovations in the devolved nations also put pressure on the UK Government to follow suit. There was an early confrontation when Scottish First Minister Henry McLeish decided to accept the recommendations of a British Royal Commission and to pay for personal care for elderly people whose medical costs were covered by the NHS (McLeish 2004). While England increased university fees massively, Scotland abolished them and Wales introduced selective measures of support. Both Scotland and Wales abolished prescription charges. In Wales, the Labour administration of Rhodri Morgan boasted about the divergence, putting 'clear red water' between themselves and London. Scottish Labour was much more discreet, but the SNP Government after 2007, continuing on the same lines, made more of the differences.

Several arguments became confused in the criticism of divergence in social policy and public services. One concerns the merits of universalist policies themselves, which may not actually be socially progressive: there is an argument that providing free higher education is a subsidy to the better off. So, Gordon Brown (2014) criticizes the SNP on these grounds, citing free school meals and prescriptions.[8] They cannot, however, be criticized for undermining public provision.

The second is the old idea of a race to the bottom. Scotland and Wales, it was suggested, were undermining UK-wide standards and should be restrained. In some cases (as in Trench 2010) the argument seems to be that divergence in social policy itself threatens the union. Yet, in every case, it was not Scotland and Wales, but the UK acting for England that was moving away from the old universalist model. If there was a race to the bottom, it was led by England, while the devolved territories were racing to the top. That was certainly the fear of the UK Labour Government in its efforts to stop the Scottish Labour-led Executive reforming the finances of care for the elderly.

A third argument concerns inter-territorial equity and why Scotland and Wales should get better services. The implication is that they can do this only because they are subsidized by England. That, however, is about the workings of the Barnett Formula and whether it is fair, not about how Scotland and Wales choose to spend their own budgets, bearing the opportunity costs of some choices as against others.

A fourth argument seems to be based on interpersonal equity, comparing people in identical circumstances in the different nations. McLean et al. (2013) question whether it is fair that Scottish citizens should get 'free' personal care when those in England do not.[9]

There has been a stream of proposals over the years aimed at preventing devolution undermining welfare and public service standards. The (Calman) Commission on Scottish Devolution (2008, 2009) was preoccupied with the issue, noting that 'devolution, as it currently exists, would in principle allow for a fundamentally different welfare state in Scotland or in England, at least in relation to health or education'. Their recommendation was that '[t]he Scottish Parliament and UK Parliament should confirm that each agrees to the elements of the common social rights that make up the social Union and also the responsibilities that go with them'. Gordon Brown (2014) suggests that there should be a core of 'covenanted services' finances from UK taxation to ensure equal provision. This would entail removing the block element of the transfer to the devolved territories, so that part of it was earmarked for specific services. It would also imply framework laws to make sure that the devolved governments spent the money in the right way.

[8] Ironically, Brown himself had introduced winter heating allowances for over-60s and free television licences for the over-75s, irrespective of means.

[9] The reality is much more complicated than this.

It is indicative of neo-unionist thinking that these are all addressed at preventing the undermining of standards where it is not happening—among the devolved governments, when the real challenge has been at the centre and in England. Neither Labour nor Conservative governments have been open to the idea that the devolved bodies should be able to restrain Westminster or bind it to higher standards of universal services. Whatever the substantive merits of the case, the issue of university fees in England proved the point. When the Labour Government raised fees in England, it refused to accept that this had implications for Scotland, Wales and Northern Ireland. Indeed, while the SNP on that occasion broke their rule of not voting on English matters at Westminster, the Government whipped its own Scottish MPs to support the measure.

A Sharing Union?

The United Kingdom was not established as a social or welfare union, and it is difficult to put welfare among its foundational myths. That idea is, rather, a product of the twentieth century, particularly its middle years, when the concept of a British nation coincided with the emergence of the welfare state. The nature of that welfare state, however, left the notion of social citizenship underdeveloped. Reserved services and benefits continue to be allocated on an individual basis, which in effect amounts to a territorial transfer mechanism, corresponding to differing economic and political circumstances. While the welfare state has resisted efforts in the 1980s and 2000s to roll it back, the expansion of universal services effectively stopped in the 1970s, and from the 1980s, welfare was increasingly stigmatized. Nobody seems to have thought of using Universal Credit, for example, as an icon of national unity and citizenship. The National Health Service (NHS) remained a symbol of shared interests and values much cited by welfare unionists but it has developed along different lines across the nations.

The effect of devolution has not been to undermine welfare but to permit the development of differentiated ideas of social citizenship, a trend found also in other European countries. The *ethos* of social solidarity and sharing does not inherently belong to either nationalists or unionists, but both have used it in order to shape their appeal, to postulate alternative conceptions of the *demos* and to give a teleological rationale to their constructions of community.

10

The Public and the Union

Constituting the Nation

The United Kingdom is a contested political object. Competing frames for understanding it are the unitary nation-state or a plurinational union, but these are mere ideal types, modes of understanding derived from historical, legal and political theory. Citizens' own ways of understanding are always more complex, making multiple connections among *demos*, *telos* and *ethos* and linking them to competing political projects. We have seen, for example, how political competition has at times polarized between 'nationalists' and 'unionists', but also how difficult it is to translate this distinction into meaningful political choices, let alone stark alternatives. This chapter explores public attitudes to show how citizens locate themselves across this complex field, sometimes exerting 'bottom-up' pressure on political leaders and at other times responding to political cues and events.

A distinction was made earlier between the ontological claim that the nation exists (expressed as national identity) and the teleological and normative claim that it should be self-governing. There is a relationship between the two but it is not always straightforward. Few scholars nowadays believe that national identities are fixed or primordial or that they directly predict political choices. Rather, social identity theory (as applied to the study of nationalism by Reicher et al. 2009) shows how identities serve to constitute communities which are more than the sum of individuals. In this way, they help define the 'we' who are affected by social and economic forces and opportunities, the *demos*. As Ernest Renan (1882) showed in the late nineteenth century, such identities are not based on objective criteria, which can be determined beyond argument. Nor, on the other hand, are they purely subjective, just the way individuals feel. Rather, they are inter-subjective, a set of meanings shared among members of the group. They thus represent not a set of attributes but rather a network of relationships. As well as constituting groups, they are lenses through which we understand the world and our place in it and sometimes assign values or *ethos*. The nation may then be credited with a *telos*, or shared destiny and constitutional future, but this may take various forms, including

State and Nation in the United Kingdom: The Fractured Union. Michael Keating, Oxford University Press (2021).
 DOI: 10.1093/oso/9780198841371.003.0010

an independent state or self-government within a wider imperial or union framework.

National identities are by definition both inclusive (of co-nationals) and exclusive (of others), but these social boundaries vary in their rigidity and permeability. They may be pervasive but hardly noticed, as in the banal nationalism of Billig (1995). At other times, national identities are highly contested and hence visible. They may be fixed over long periods and deeply felt, or malleable and flexible, even negotiated by individuals on a daily basis according to the context (Todd 2018, 2019). They may be singular so that one identity excludes others, or multiple and complementary. They may require a strict set of necessary and sufficient criteria to qualify, or the criteria may be mixed and matched in all manner of ways to assess individual cases (Bechhofer and McCrone 2009). National identity and constitutional preferences are not fixed entities or attitudes but fields on which a variety of themes can be played. The connections can change over time and the political implications can sometimes shift rather quickly before settling down in a new constellation.

Measuring Identity and Constitutional Preferences

There is now a mass of survey data on these matters, especially in Scotland and Northern Ireland.[1] The data do not 'speak for themselves' and must be interpreted with care. A survey is an individualized instrument, focusing on one person at a time, while national identities and their consequences are collective phenomena, experienced in specific contexts. The categories which

[1] The *Census* in England and Wales, Scotland and Northern Ireland since 2011 asks about national identity, referring to the nations of the United Kingdom. It also asks about 'ethnicity', which includes hyphenated identities such as Chinese-, Indian- or Caribbean-British. In the Scottish census these can be hyphenated with Scottish but in England and Wales only with British. The *Scottish Social Attitudes Survey* and the *British Social Attitudes Survey*, ask questions about identity and constitutional preferences. The *British Election Study* has an expanded sample in Scotland and questions tailored to the Scottish context. There is a *Scottish Election Study* and a *Scottish Referendum Study* but their results are less easily available for secondary analysis. There are regular academic and commercial surveys, most of them reported on the *What Scotland Thinks* site (http://whatscotlandthinks.org), which also contains valuable analysis. Its sibling, *What the UK Thinks* (https://whatukthinks.org/eu/, reports on attitudes to Brexit. The *Northern Ireland Life and Times survey* (https://www.ark.ac.uk/nilt/) regularly reports on attitudes in the province and is complemented by various other academic surveys on individual issues including Brexit. There is a *Welsh Election Study*, which also covers the referendum of 2011 (https://github.com/WelshElectionStudy). A regular *Future of England* survey reports attitudes in England and also, more generally. The *Labour Force Survey* has been used to assess identities in England (Owen 2015).

Where I have referenced a survey here (for example British Election Study), it means that we have conducted a secondary analysis of the data. Where authors are cited, it refers to publications.

social scientists use may not be the same as those with which citizens work, especially contested concepts such as nationality and ethnicity. These may at one time be related to culture, history, sport or landscape and at other times take on political significance. As we have seen, the meaning and implications of being 'British' can vary from one context to another. If people do not feel strongly European, it does not mean that this is not a background element in their political orientations. People will respond at particular times to political cues, and identities may be shaped by their choice of political party as well as the other way around.

The alternative to the survey is an ethnographic approach, which involves examining the responses and feelings of people in specific social contexts without using pre-formed categories. This can yield rich results but without the comparative and quantitative rigour of surveys. Focus groups are also used to see how people respond to cues. The most fruitful approaches of all are those that combine survey research with ethnographic work (Bechhofer and McCrone 2015) but they are rather rare. They do remind us to pay careful attention to the working and context of any piece of survey research.

The 'Linz/Moreno Question'[2] asks people whether they feel Scottish and British on a five-point scale: only Scottish; more Scottish than British; equally Scottish and British; more British than Scottish; only British. The same question is used, *mutatis mutandi*, in England, in Wales and in Northern Ireland. The 'forced identity question', simply asks respondents to choose between being either British or English/Scottish/Welsh. Matters are more complicated in Northern Ireland, where the choice of Irish or British may be supplemented by the categories of Ulster or Northern Irish. Northern Irish surveys also ask people whether they identify as nationalist or unionist, the official designations in the Northern Ireland Assembly. These questions have generated important findings but they assume a spectrum with British and sub-state identities at opposite ends, so that more of one implies less of the other. Yet it is logically possible that one person could feel both more Scottish and more British than another person. For another, national identities might be irrelevant. Surveys have adapted to this by asking the strength of each identity on a scale.[3]

[2] Pioneered by Juan Linz in Spain, and imported into Scotland by Luis Moreno.

[3] The approach used in the Census is less satisfactory. In England and Wales, it allows respondents to choose as many identities as they like from a list. As some respondents opt only for one, this can give a misleading figure for exclusive identities in England and Wales, especially as it is the English or Welsh identities that come first in the list. The Scottish Census gets at strong identities more directly by asking respondents specifically whether they are 'only Scottish' or 'only British', but this means that the results cannot be compared with those in England and Wales.

While the ontological dimension of nationality is explored by questions on identity, the teleological dimension is probed by questions about constitutional preferences. This also poses difficulties in wording and interpretation. Political demand is not independent of supply (the options on offer) and these may change over time. The most straightforward pose the choice between union and independence (in Scotland and Wales) or between union and Irish reunification (in Northern Ireland). Yet even questions about independence may take a hard or soft form. Only since the question was agreed for the 2014 Scottish referendum has a standard question been available there. Not surprisingly, softer questions attract more support than harder ones. Another approach asks about preferences on a five-point scale, ranging from the UK controls everything to Scotland/Wales/Northern Ireland controls everything. The intermediate points are that the UK Government controls everything except foreign affairs and defence (the best interpretation of 'devolution max'); and devolved Government controls everything except foreign affairs, defence, taxation and welfare (the 1999 settlement). Although the first option is effectively equivalent to independence, it has consistently gained more support than when the term 'independence' is used. Similar effects have been found in other plurinational states including Canada and Spain (Keating 2001). Other intermediate choices have included a Parliament or an Assembly in Wales at the time when the Assembly lacked legislative powers; and devolution with and without tax powers.

A further complication is that the status quo, with which constitutional change is compared, is constantly changing. Now that Scotland and Wales have tax competences, the option of devolution without them would represent a loss of power. Constitutional options risk becoming too complicated and outstripping the understanding of citizens.[4] Accordingly, surveys in Scotland and Wales often merge some of the options to create, as far as possible, a choice among independence, devolution and recentralization.[5] In Northern Ireland, the choices have historically been between remaining in the UK and a united Ireland, but since the establishment of devolved government, that has been available as a third option.

Key events may also alter the supply of realistic options and shift attitudes quite suddenly in what are called 'critical junctures'. The Irish Rising of 1916 was one such event, precipitating the demise of Home Rule and the victory of

[4] This is not to suggest that citizens are ignorant. The options themselves are surrounded by uncertainties.

[5] This can be done in the survey questionnaire or subsequently by merging responses. Sometimes, a 'devolution-max' category is included.

secession. Referendums, with their stark choices, may be critical junctures, shaping identities and attitudes which then persist over time. So, in Scotland, the 2014 referendum entailed a prolonged debate about independence as a realistic prospect and consolidated opinion into two camps. The Brexit referendum had similar effects. In Northern Ireland, by contrast, the Good Friday settlement, and its final endorsement in the St Andrews Agreement, presented a viable middle-ground solution, which rapidly gained wide support, something that became apparent when the Northern Ireland Life and Times Survey changed the questions to reflect the new option.

The same applies to Europe. For some years, a seven-point scale was used, going from withdrawal from the EU to the creation of a European government, with intermediate options including staying and reducing the EU's powers, and remaining and increasing its powers. The 2016 Brexit referendum changed the political agenda so that being Eurosceptic, which in the past may have meant resisting more integration and rolling back some of the existing provisions, now meant leaving the EU altogether. This has changed the political supply and moved the entire spectrum in a Eurosceptic direction as citizens who previously supported reducing EU powers moved to the Leave camp. Another, less expected, effect was a rise in the proportion of people identifying as strongly European as those voters were mobilized.

We have seen how Europe is understood in different way and plays into the constitutional question, and how it served to underpin the complex, asymmetrical devolution settlement. Political leaders have woven the European dimension into their messages and strategies, also in multiple forms. Just as with national identity, we cannot assume, as is often done, that European identity is in competition with other levels of belonging. On the contrary, it can be complementary, competing or in a different bracket altogether. It is certainly not something that most people think about most of the time and may be invoked only when challenged. At the same time, it may be latent and unstated but nevertheless present. Again, as with national identity, what matters is not just its existence but its strength and the uses to which it is put. It has long been observed that UK citizens feel less European than most of their continental counterparts and that membership of the EU has been a constant source of political conflict since the 1960s (Carl 2017; Clarke et al. 2017).

What is largely missing in the UK surveys is anything about *ethos*, the values that people attach to specific national identities and projects. This is surprising, given the stress that unionists have placed on the virtues of Britishness and the similar appropriation of the higher values by nationalists. There are, however, some data on welfare and sharing, tapping appreciations of the social and economic dimensions of union.

When all this is done, there remain some apparent contradictions in people's attitudes. Citizens may be cross-pressured, expressing multiple identities and supporting elements of both union and independence. At critical moments, there may be more polarization and individuals are forced to choose. Sometimes they opt for elements of both union and secession (Keating 2001) or support local control over wide policy fields but oppose policy differentiation among the nations (Henderson et al. 2013). Citizens do not, in other words, always fit into the categories devised by academic analysts. There may also be a high degree of uncertainty, which is why, in the following charts and tables, I have chosen to report the 'don't knows' as well as the definite answers.

Scotland

At one level, Scottish identity is pervasive and almost banal. Almost everyone in Scotland thinks of themselves as in some way Scottish, far exceeding the numbers who were born in Scotland. Research has shown that people have multiple ways of defining who belongs to the nation, including birth, parentage, residence and commitment; these can be mixed and matched in different ways (McCrone and Bechhofer 2008, 2015). The most significant survey finding has been the persistent attachment to a dual identity as Scottish and British. Within this broad heading, there has been a movement towards the more Scottish options. On the forced choice question, between 1974 and 2005, the proportion opting for Scottish increased from 65 to 74 per cent and those opting for British decreased from 31 to 15 per cent (Bechhofer and McCrone 2007). This change took place almost entirely during the 1980s and 1990s (Bond 2003: Bechhofer and McCrone 2007) and so is not a response to devolution. A more plausible explanation is alienation from the UK Government of the time, which had never received even a plurality of support in Scotland. After devolution, Scottish identity stabilized and then started to decline somewhat from 2007, just when the SNP came into government, which may have been a sign that devolution had reduced alienation (Figure 10.1).

Examining strength of identity reveals a similar picture. More than half of Scots consistently express a Scottish identity at the strongest point on the seven-point scale; the strongest British identity receives only around 30 per cent support (Scottish Social Attitudes Survey, 2014-18). Deeper probing, however, reveals that these identities are not necessarily in competition, except perhaps at times of stress. Many Scots see themselves as both strongly Scottish and strongly British. Our secondary analysis of the British Election Study data

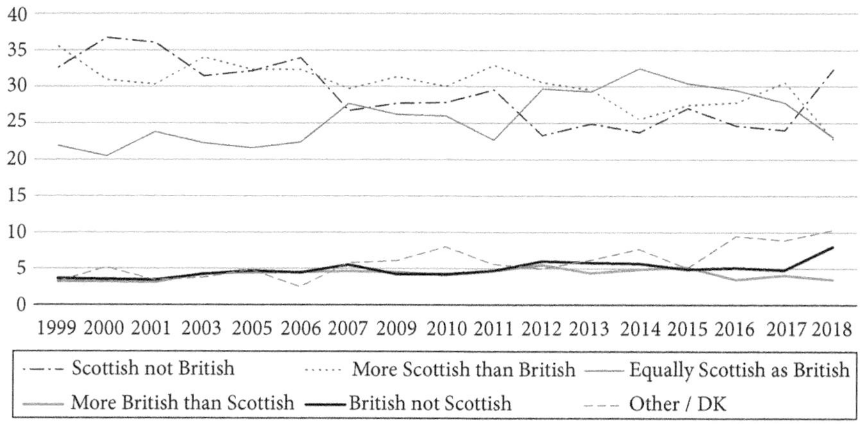

Figure 10.1 National identity, Scotland 1999–2018, percentage
Source: Scottish Social Attitudes Survey.

shows that, in 2018, 67 per cent of those with a weak Scottish identity had a strong British identity but so did 44 per cent of those with a strong Scottish identity.[6] It may not be a surprise that in 2007 more than half SNP voters feel only Scottish—but almost half of them also retain a British attachment. A fifth of Conservatives felt only Scottish, a sign that the old patriot tradition was not entirely extinct (Bechhofer and McCrone 2007). Bechhofer and McCrone (2015) divided Scottish identifiers into 'dualists' (strongly Scottish and British) and 'nationalists' (strongly Scottish and weakly British). The latter group accounted for just 25 per cent of voters. Research in Spain has similarly teased out the distinct dimensions of identity to show how the numbers of unconditional nationalists and unionists, consistent across all dimensions, are rather small (Moral 1998).

As to broader dimensions of community, the feeling that Scots and English share a common British past, including that of the Empire, also survived, encompassing over half of SNP voters, not far below the proportion of other parties (Bechhofer and McCrone 2007). All this confirms that Scotland is not a 'divided society', that is one that is split into separate communities or pillars according to national identity or ethnic markers. Scots have since the 1970s become more likely to identify with a fellow Scot of a different class than and English person of the same social class (Paterson et al. 2001) but that may be more to do with the decline of class than the rise of nation. If unionism is in trouble, it is not because exclusive Scottish has displaced a broader identity with the union.

[6] To facilitate the analysis, the eleven-point scale was collapsed to a three-point scale.

Surveys since the late 1960s have consistently shown support for at least some degree of self-government.[7] Until the arrival of devolution, they also showed something between 20 and 30 per cent preferring to keep direct rule from Westminster. Following the establishment of the Scottish Parliament, this opposition faded away rapidly and has rarely risen into double figures. There has, instead, been a constant demand for more powers in general, and powers over taxation and welfare (the main non-devolved domestic policies) in particular. The Scottish Social Attitudes Survey (SSA) asks a rather general question on 'Which institution ought to have most influence over how Scotland is run?' Over the years, between two-thirds and four-fifths have answered that it should be the Scottish Parliament.

Independence, however, is a different matter and support has historically depended partly on how the question is worded. Surveys in the 1970s suggested that support fluctuated around 20 per cent (Brand 1978; Royal Commission on the Constitution 1973; Macartney 1980). During the 1990s, this rose to around 30 per cent. Devolution did not seem to make a difference (Curtice and Ormston 2013), contrary to the predictions of those (both nationalists and unionists) who had predicted that it would be a stepping stone to independence. Neither the election of the SNP Government in 2007 nor its absolute majority in 2011 can be attributed to a surge in support for independence; in 2007 it was actually going down. Matters only changed with the Edinburgh Agreement of 2012, which presented independence as a viable prospect. The referendum posed the question of independence in binary form, with no option for a 'third way', and this change in the political supply may have changed the pattern of demand. The experience may also have normalized the question of independence. The referendum campaign saw a further rise in support to around 45 per cent (Figure 10.2).

This became a new plateau as the polls showed support for independence flat-lining in the following years. Even this may have represented less of a step change than appears at first sight. While support for independence increased markedly during the referendum campaign of 2014, surveys showed that, offered a five-point scale from no parliament to independence, voter preferences remained more stable (Liñeira et al. 2017). It appears that many had decided that a Yes vote was the most effective way to progress their journey to more powers without representing a fixed destination. That in turn may reflect the strategies of the two sides in the referendum campaign, as the Yes side moved

[7] As did some tests of opinion in the 1940s and 1950s (Torrance 2020a).

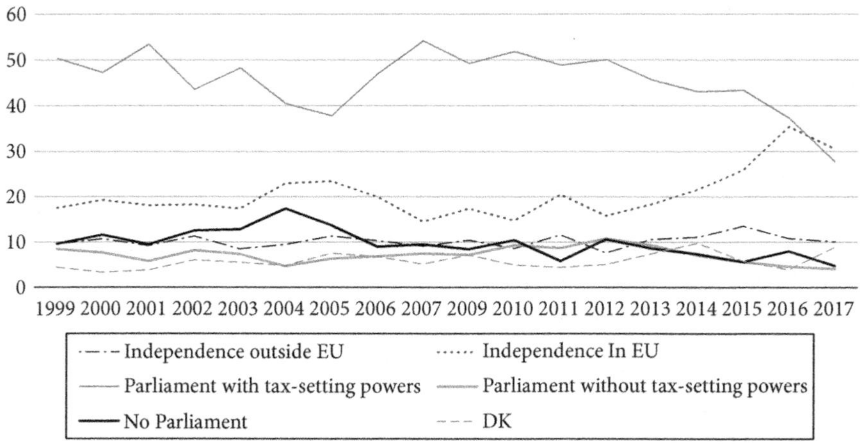

Figure 10.2 Constitutional preferences, Scotland 1999–2017, percentage
Source: Scottish Social Attitudes Survey.

to a form of 'independence-lite' and the No campaign to devolution-max (see Chapter 4).

There has always been a link between identity and support for independence but the patriot tradition always ensured that Scottishness could also be harnessed for union. For a long time, more independence supporters voted Labour than SNP; although SNP-voting was more associated with support for independence, there were more Labour voters overall. So feeling strongly Scottish, voting SNP and supporting independence overlapped but did not coincide (McCrone and Bechhofer 2008; Bond 2015).

This link also changed as a result of the referendum experience; the relationship between an exclusive or predominant Scottish identity and support for independence became stronger (Bond 2015). McCrone's (2017) analysis of British and Scottish Social Attitude Surveys shows the proportion of exclusive Scots identifiers supporting independence going up from 48 in 1997 to 72 in 2015, with nearly all the change happening between 2011 and 2014. Indeed, identity became a key predictor of a person's referendum vote (Liñeira et al. 2017). This is because, while the proportions of Scots describing themselves as exclusively Scottish had not gone up, it was now more strongly associated with support for independence. British Election Survey data for 2014 and 2017 also show exclusive Scottish identifiers five times as likely to support independence as exclusive British identifiers, although that finding is complicated by a different supply of options.[8]

[8] For that survey, both identities and constitutional options were offered on a scale. Just over half those identifying as only Scottish favoured independence, as against just over 10 per cent of those who

There has been a similar, but less extensive, alignment between supporting independence and voting SNP and between feeling only Scottish and voting SNP but, when these three are put together, the total correlation is far from perfect (McCrone, 2017). Two political events, however, have crystalized attitudes: the independence referendum of 2014 and the European referendum of 2016. These have the potential for a more enduring division among unionists and nationalists, with the removal of the European framework reducing the scope for middle-ground or post-sovereigntist positions.

Although Scotland voted to remain in the (then) EEC in 1975 by a smaller majority than England, opinion did change from the 1990s to be less Eurosceptic. This was not, however, because of nationalist voters adopting the SNP strategy of independence in Europe. Supporters of all parties in Scotland, but particularly of Labour, were less Eurosceptic than in England (Keating 2009). There was some tendency for the strongest unionists and strongest nationalists to be rather more Eurosceptic, with a strong clustering in the middle of support for devolution and critical support for Europe. These findings are confirmed by McCrone's (2019) analysis, which examines both identities and strength of identities, showing surprisingly high levels of European identity in Scotland. While lower than Scottish identity, it is almost as high as British identity, measured on the seven-point scale. It is not, however, the Scottish identifiers who are the most European but the British identifiers and the dual identifiers. Strong Scottish identity has a much weaker effect. All of this suggests that, beyond the simple options for the UK, Scotland and Europe, there may be a division between sovereigntists, who want all the power in one place, whether that is Edinburgh or London, and those who are happy with the idea of multiple levels of authority.

By the time of the 2014 independence referendum, there was a pronounced tendency for opponents of devolution to support leaving the EU, but no appreciable difference on the EU dimension between supporters of devolution and independence.[9] The Brexit referendum of 2016 confirmed the weak connection between the independence and European questions. None of the various combinations of Yes/No to independence and Remain/Leave to Europe commanded anything near to a majority. Table 10.1 is drawn from the British Election Study panel, asking the same electors how they had voted.

felt only British. There was a major gap between those feeling mostly and those feeling exclusively Scottish. Given the devolution-max options, overall support for independence was 35 per cent, as opposed to the mid-40s it was scoring on the simple yes–no question on independence.

[9] This is based on the Scottish Social Attitudes Survey (2014) and the British Election Survey (2017), both of which used scales of support for Europe.

Table 10.1 Vote for EU and independence in Scotland 2014–16, percentage

	Yes independence	No independence	Total
Remain EU	27	34	61
Leave EU	17	21	37
Total	44	55	

Chris Prosser and Ed Fieldhouse, 'A Tale of Two Referendums—The 2017 Election in Scotland', British Election Study, http://www.britishelectionstudy.com/bes-findings/a-tale-of-two-referendums-the-2017-election-in-scotland/#.WeoCaDb9O7M

The decision across the UK as a whole to leave the EU meant that Scots had to choose between the two unions. Initial reactions seemed to suggest that most of them prioritized the UK over the European Union, but by 2019 that seemed to be shifting (Curtice 2019). While voters were still cross-pressured, there was now a majority for independence among those preferring to remain in the EU. While the Scottish Conservatives doubled down on their unionism and switched to Leave on the EU, the SNP made little effort to recover its Leave/Independence supporters, preferring to attract former unionist voters who, after Brexit, were open to persuasion about the merits of independence. Support for independence crept up as Remain and pro-independence support started to coincide (Diffley 2020), with a polarization between nationalists and unionists (McCrone and Keating, 2021).

Wales

Welsh identity has historically been more linked than its Scottish counterpart to cultural markers, including the language and Nonconformist religion. Yet the language has also been divisive, as it is spoken by a minority, too small to demand comprehensive linguistic transformation but large enough to be a political force. Wales shares a densely populated border with England and the proportion of English-born citizens is more than twice as large as in Scotland. The proximity of the most populated areas to England and the density of cross-border transactions often seemed to pose a threat to Welsh identity itself. The creation of the National Assembly and the whole devolution project after the 1980s was intended to overcome these divisions and to promote a broader, civic and institutionally focused conception of Wales (Rawlings 2003).

The Linz/Moreno question on identity has been posed by the Welsh Election Study at intervals since 1999. It shows lower levels of exclusive or mainly Welsh identity (between 17 and 25 per cent) compared with Scottish

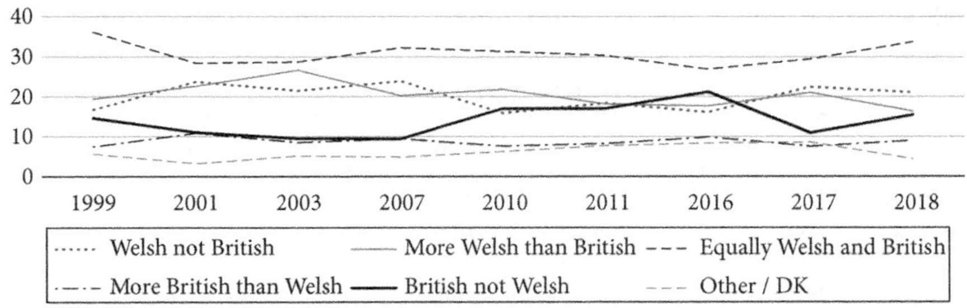

Figure 10.3 National identity, Wales 1999–2018, percentage
Source: Welsh Election Study; British Social Attitudes Survey (2017).

identity in Scotland and higher levels of exclusively British identity (between 10 and 25 per cent). Between half and three-quarters feel both Welsh and British, with a tendency towards the more Welsh side. Devolution was accompanied by a strengthening of Welsh identity, after which it stabilized (Figure 10.3).

When asked about strength of identity, between 37 and 47 per cent feel Welsh on the highest point on the scale and the same proportion score at the highest point on Britishness. This is not a sign of polarization. On the contrary, half of those expressing a strong Welsh identity also express a strong British identity, an even stronger overlap than found in the Scottish case.[10] The Census findings are not directly comparable but the 2011 figures do suggest that Welsh speakers are more likely to opt only for the Welsh identity (77 per cent) than English speakers (53 per cent) (Harries et al. 2014). Welsh identity was also high in the older industrial areas, where a distinct sense of Welshness has long imbued the industrial and working-class culture.[11] In spite of the consolidation of self-government in Wales, these figures show no trend but rather fluctuations around the mean.

By contrast, attitudes to constitutional matters have undergone a dramatic shift since the 1970s. At that time, support for devolution ran around 30 per cent, and fell to 20 per cent in the referendum of 1979 (Wyn Jones and Scully 2012). The few polls conducted in the 1980s showed little support, but interest did pick up again in the 1990s as the Labour Party returned to the question. This was enough to secure a majority in the 1997 devolution referendum but

[10] As for the Scottish case, the scale was collapsed to three points to facilitate analysis. In the 2018 BES survey, 75 per cent of those with a weak Welsh identity had a strong British identity, but so did 62 per cent of those with a strong Welsh identity.

[11] We will not enter into the argument about the geographic divisions among 'three Wales': *Y Fro Gymraeg* (the Welsh speaking areas; Welsh Wales (the industrial areas); and British Wales (the Anglicized areas on the border and in Pembrokeshire) (Balsom 1985). For a criticism, see Scully and Wyn Jones (2012).

Table 10.2 Welsh identity and constitutional preferences 2017, percentage

	Welsh Identity			
	Weak	Moderate	Strong	Total
No Devolution	27.9	20.4	16.5	20.7
Weaker Assembly	13.8	10.9	4.4	8.9
Status Quo	33.7	32	31.1	32.1
Stronger Assembly	21.8	28.9	35.3	29.7
Independence	2.8	7.8	12.7	8.5
Total	100	100	100	100

Source: British Election Study.

by the slimmest of margins, just over 50 per cent on a 50 per cent turnout. Once established, however, the devolved Assembly rapidly gained support and opposition to it fell to around 20 per cent. Around a third of the electorate now leaned towards a stronger form of devolution, rather than the very weak form that was given in 1999, while another third was content with the settlement (calculated from British Election Study, 2014–17; Welsh Election Study 2016).[12] Independence hardly featured as an issue in Wales before the Brexit referendum. In the 1980s, it gained around 8 per cent support and since the 1990s has fluctuated around the low teens.

Support for self-government correlates with identity but far from perfectly (Table 10.2). Support for independence on its own was confined almost entirely to the solely Welsh. In a 2017 survey, while 38 per cent of the most strongly Welsh supported independence or stronger devolution, 16 per cent of them actually wanted no devolution at all (British Election Study 2017). Conversely, 31 per cent of those with no Welsh identity wanted no devolution, but just over 20 per cent wanted stronger devolution or independence. These findings reflect the Scottish ones in showing that identity itself does not drive constitutional preferences unless it is channelled by changes in the political supply and the relationship remains loose. The number of consistent 'nationalists' who feel Welsh and want independence is even lower than in Scotland. The rise in support for self-government is very significant but it does not point directly to the end of union and unionism.

Euroscepticism in Wales appears to run at similar levels to England but, compared with Scotland, there is a marked association between support for self-government and for European integration. In 2017, fully half the supporters

[12] We do not have the same continuous time-series data as in Scotland and so cannot represent this on a graph.

of independence favoured the strongest option on the European scale (fully integrating with Europe), while those opposed to devolution were the most Eurosceptic.[13] This is the context for the strong commitment to Europe of both Plaid Cymru and Welsh Labour. It also appears to have led to a rise in interest in the idea of Welsh independence after the Brexit referendum. Although active support remained small overall, significant numbers appeared to be 'indy curious' (Trystan 2019).

Northern Ireland

Unlike Scotland, Wales and England, Northern Ireland is a divided society, with political divisions based on deep-seated societal cleavages and identities. Unionists, largely Protestant, support remaining within the United Kingdom, while nationalists, overwhelmingly Catholic, favour the reunification of Ireland. Data, available back to the beginning of the most recent conflict, largely sustain this picture. Rose's (1971) survey of 1968 showed that 99 per cent of the vote for unionist parties was from Protestants while 99 per cent of that for nationalist parties came from Catholics; a decade later, nothing had changed (Moxon-Browne 1983).

Yet even in this polarized space, there were qualifications, and the linkage of Catholic-Irish-nationalist-pro Irish unity, and of Protestant-British-unionist-pro-Union sentiments, was not perfect. Around three-quarters of Catholics in 1968 identified as Irish against just a fifth of Protestants (Rose 1971). Yet a minority of Catholics (around 15–25 per cent) identified as British, while a fifth of Protestants identified themselves as Irish (Moxon-Browne 1983, 1991), harking back to the old patriot tradition. From time to time, class politics provided a cross-community space through the Northern Ireland Labour Party, which 27 per cent of Catholics and 11 per cent of Protestants supported in 1968 (Rose 1971). More significantly, an Ulster or Northern Ireland identity has been available. Rose's (1971) survey from 1968 showed a third of Protestants choosing it (but only 5 per cent of Catholics). This Ulster identity was particularly strong in working-class communities and among supporters of the Democratic Unionist Party, and seems to be an expression of Ulster particularism or contractual unionism. The Troubles

[13] These figures are drawn from the British Election Study. The BES 11-point scale of Euroscepticism has been compressed to three points to facilitate the cross-tabulation with a 5-point scale on the self-government dimension.

from the 1960s resulted in a polarization of identities and a shrinking of the middle ground. By the late 1970s, two-thirds of Protestants identified as British, with a sharp fall in those identifying as either Irish or Ulster (Moxon-Browne 1983; McGarry and O'Leary 1995).

There is evidence of change after the Good Friday Agreement. Although the GFA proclaimed the right of people to identify as Irish or British, other possibilities are open, notably a Northern Irish one. While the proportion of the population identifying as Irish remained steady,[14] that identifying as British fell as the Northern Irish alternative came back into play. Northern Ireland is the official name of the province and has less sectarian connotations than Ulster.[15] The new Northern Ireland identity is associated with being neither unionist nor nationalist and with more moderate positions on the main constitutional questions (Garry and McNicholl 2015). Yet the fact that people on both sides see themselves as Northern Irish does not mean that they give it the same meaning. For some, it may be a way of being Irish, while others cling to the old Ulster particularism.

Another question asks respondents whether they see themselves as unionists, nationalists or neither. There is, as one would expect, a relationship with religion and national identity. The proportion of Protestants calling themselves nationalist has rarely exceeded 1 per cent, and the proportion of Catholics self-describing as unionist is even lower. There was, however, a steady increase in those identifying as neither unionist nor nationalist (Figure 10.4) at least until 2019; unionist numbers, in particular, fell. The 'neither' group cuts across the religious divide, although it leans towards Catholics, who were[16] 30 per cent of the group, against 30 per cent who are Protestants and 30 per cent of no religion (Hayward and McManus 2018). This is consistent with a weakening of religious attachment, at least on the Protestant side. The proportion of people without a religious identity doubled in the twenty years after the Good Friday Agreement, from just under a tenth to just under a fifth. While the proportion identifying as Catholics was a constant 40 per cent, the share of Protestants fell, so that the two groups were equal in numbers.[17]

There is still an overlap on the matter of national identity. Half of unionists feel exclusively British but 40 per cent in 2017 recognized some Irish identity.

[14] Demographics played a role here, as the Catholic proportion in the population increased.

[15] Ulster is the name of the nine-county historic province of Ireland, but from the late nineteenth century the term was appropriated by intransigent unionists and was then applied to the six-county unit created by partition.

[16] In the 2018 survey.

[17] Protestants are also more likely to emigrate.

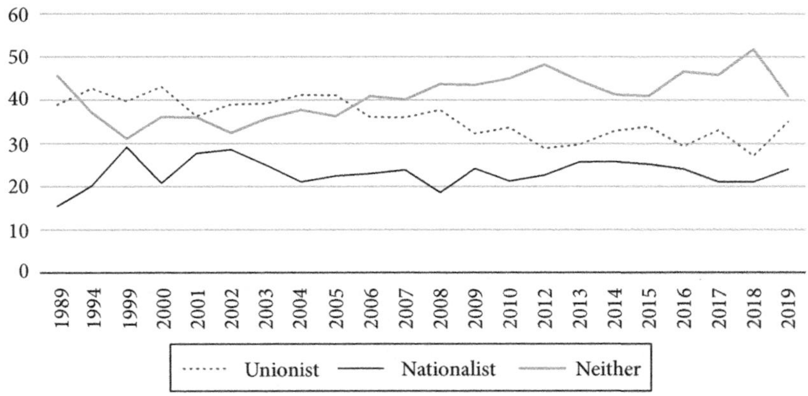

Figure 10.4 Unionist/nationalist identities in Northern Ireland, percentage
Source: Northern Ireland Social Attitudes Survey (1989); Northern Ireland Life and Times Survey.

Nationalists are more homogeneous, as only a quarter claimed some British identity and nearly three-quarters said they were exclusively Irish (Hayward and McManus 2018).

As to constitutional preferences, it remains true that Protestants and British identifiers are more likely to support the Union while Catholics and Irish identifiers will support Irish unification, but there are important qualifications and changes over time depending on the context and the options available. While almost all Protestants have been for the Union, not all Catholics have supported Irish unity. Surveys back to the 1970s showed that around a third of Catholics did not support unification (Moxon-Browne 1983); this is why a putative Catholic majority at some future time would not necessarily have secured majority support for unification. Surveys in the 1970s and 1980s showed that, for many Catholics, Irish unity has been a long-term aspiration, but not their preferred concrete choice at any particular time (Whyte 1990). Given the choice of power-sharing within Northern Ireland, they have usually opted for that (Whyte 1990).

This was supplied by the Good Friday Agreement and was included in the Northern Ireland Life and Times Survey from 2007, immediately becoming the favoured option, with 60 per cent support overall and displacing reunification as the preferred option for Catholics and even those with an Irish identity (Figure 10.5). By 2014 the option of power-sharing within the UK was the most popular option among Catholics, Protestants, those of no religion, Irish identifiers, British identifies and Northern Ireland identifiers. This was in the context of EU membership, an open border and the devolved institutions working.

The role of Europe in sustaining the Northern Ireland settlement has been discussed earlier (Chapter 6). While there was some talk at the time of the

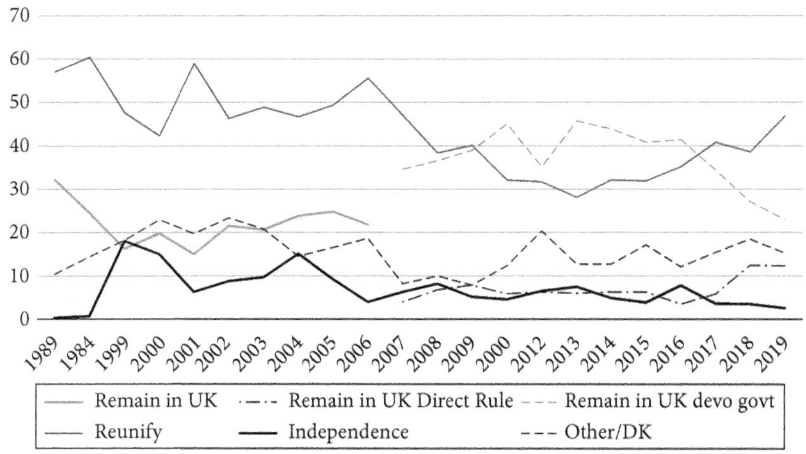

Figure 10.5 Constitutional preferences, Northern Ireland Catholics, 1989–2019, percentage

Source: Northern Ireland Social Attitudes Survey; Northern Ireland Life and Times Survey.

Sunningdale process that the membership of both Ireland and the UK in the (then) EEC might offer new opportunities (Dorr 2017), this was not reflected in popular attitudes. Moxon-Browne's (1983) survey of 1978 showed Catholics a little more favourable to Europe than Protestants (54 to 47 per cent). The main difference was between the moderate and hard-line parties. Sixty per cent of supporters of the moderate nationalist SDLP were pro-Europe and 66 per cent of supporters of the non-aligned Alliance Party, against just 22 per cent of Democratic Unionist Party voters. Hard-line republican nationalists have also historically been Eurosceptic and Sinn Féin opposed every European referendum held in the Irish Republic on sovereigntist grounds. By the time of the 2016 Brexit referendum, Sinn Féin had changed its position and came out for Remain, while the DUP opted for Leave. This is reflected in the voting figures (Table 10.3).

The picture is the same if we use the labels 'Catholic' and 'Protestant' or ask about preferences on the future of Northern Ireland (Garry 2017b). A majority of those identifying as Northern Irish voted Remain, while most of those identifying as Ulster opted for Leave, confirming the meaning of these terms observed earlier. SDLP voters supported Remain by 95 per cent, while 75 per cent of DUP voters went for Leave.[18] Attitudes on the European dimension have thus aligned to those on the national one, especially on the nationalist

[18] As did 91 per cent of supporters of the even harder-line Traditional Unionist Voice (Garry, 2017b).

Table 10.3 Brexit vote, Northern Ireland, percentage

	Nationalist	Unionist	Neither
Remain	88	34	70
Leave	12	66	30
Total	100	100	100

Source: Garry (2017b).

side. More than half of Catholics agreed that Brexit would make them more likely to vote for a united Ireland (Northern Ireland Life and Times Survey 2020). It is this that has put the issue of reunification back on the political agenda. By 2019, with Brexit looming and the institutions out of action, opinion had shifted and Irish reunification was the preference of a majority (56 per cent) of Irish identifiers and a plurality (47 per cent) of Catholics (Table 10.4). As Figure 10.5 shows, opinion among Catholics had been moving slightly back to support for reunification since 2014 but now overtook support for power-sharing devolution. This coincided with a crisis in the devolved settlement, as a result of which the institutions were out of action for three years.[19]

Northern Ireland remains a divided society but the complexities of identity are illustrated in Table 10.4, which shows how identities map onto constitutional preference. Some of the old certainties may be weakening in the face of social change and new opportunities, but this does not presage a convergence on a common identity based on the new territorial institutions (Hayward and McManus 2018; Tonge and Gomez 2015). Indeed, the basis of the settlement was not to engineer such a superordinate identity, with common *demos*, *telos* and *ethos*, but to accommodate the actual aspirations of the populations. So, it allows sections of the community to negotiate their relationship with the political system in diverse ways, allowing institutional cooperation and membership of the various unions in their own manner. It is this which distinguishes the Northern Ireland settlement from other consociational settlements that assume agreement on the boundaries of the unit and focus on power-sharing within it (McGarry and O'Leary 2006). Power-sharing within the United Kingdom, with both UK and all-Ireland dimensions and frameworks, provides such a mode of accommodation, especially when the European framework was available to dilute the sovereignty question and keep

[19] This also explains a rise in support for direct rule among both Catholic/Irish identifiers and Protestant/British identifiers.

Table 10.4 Identities and preferences by religion, Northern Ireland, 2018, percentage

	Catholic	Protestant	Other
National Identity 2018			
Irish	64	4	13
British	5	63	38
N. Irish/Ulster	23	28	35
Constitutional identity 2019			
Nationalist	59	1	9
Unionist	0	67	22
Neither	39	29	62
Constitutional Preference 2019			
Direct rule	12	21	20
Irish reunification	47	3	19
Devolution + Power-sharing	23	73	49
Independent NI	2	1	3
Don't know/other	16	2	15
Would vote in referendum 2019			
Remain in UK	25	85	52
Unify Ireland	49	2	12
Don't know/won't say	26	13	36

Source: Northern Ireland Life and Times Survey.

the border open. Ethnographic evidence further shows how, in everyday life, these questions of identity and political aspirations are constantly negotiated but can become politicized easily at times of tension (Hayward 2017; Todd 2019).

England

England occupies an ambiguous place in the Union, as both the core of the United Kingdom and one of its constituent nations. It is not that people in England, when asked, cannot recognize the difference, more that the two are so closely associated that asking them to choose between them does not seem to make sense as it might elsewhere. Regular surveys since 1999 suggest that devolution to the other nations resulted in a small increase in the proportion defining themselves as more English on the Linz/Moreno scale and in defining themselves as English not British on the forced identity scale (Curtice et al. 2013; Curtice and Heath 2009). Since then, in spite of all the talk about a rising English nationalism,[20] the figures have stabilized, as shown in Figure 10.6.

[20] There was some excitement in 2011 when the Census reported a large number of people offering only an English identity but, as we have seen, this is a poor measure of the relative importance of identities.

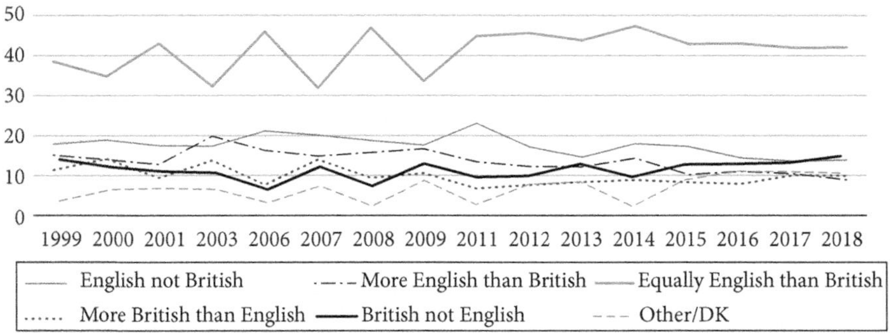

Figure 10.6 National identity, England 1999–2018, percentage
Source: British Social Attitudes Survey.

On the forced identity scale, around 40 per cent consider themselves English rather than British, although this has been lower in some years (Curtice 2018).

There is evidence of diffuse discontent about the place of England (Wyn Jones et al. 2012, Wyn Jones et al. 2013) but, in the absence of a supply of clear and realistic constitutional options for England, it is difficult to show how this links to preferences for change. The concept of English independence is a particularly difficult one, but surveys suggest that support for it has long fluctuated around a fifth of the electorate, and even those are not motivated by a distinct sense of national identity (Figure 10.8). The Future of England Survey (Wyn Jones et al. 2013) suggested that support for independence was identical among those feeling only English and those feeling only British (15 per cent in each case). Nor has the idea of an English Parliament as a way of balancing the constitution or paving the way for a federal settlement, gained much traction, as Figure 10.7 shows. Regional government, seen by some as the counterpart to devolution elsewhere, has not attracted much support either. That is perhaps not surprising, as it would not in fact be the equivalent to the arrangements for Scotland, Wales and Northern Ireland.

There is some consistent evidence that people in England do support the idea of English Votes for English Laws (EVEL), with over 60 per cent agreeing and less than 10 per cent against (Curtice 2018; Wyn Jones et al. 2012). These attitudes may have hardened somewhat, with more people 'strongly' agreeing, but the proposition that English MPs should decide matters that only affect England is hardly evidence of English nationalism, as opposed to a democratic deficit. There is only a modest connection between support for EVEL and strong English identity, which may itself be because so few overall are opposed. There also appears to be a partisan effect, as EVEL is a Conservative policy designed to protect England against governments drawing their majority from the non-English (and less Conservative) parts of the UK.

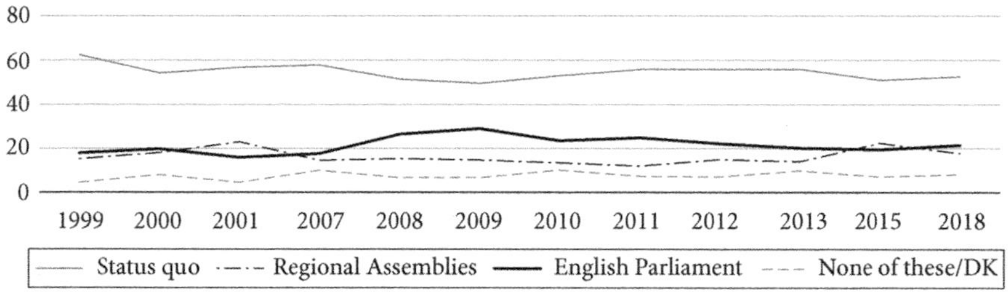

Figure 10.7 Constitutional preferences, England 1999–2018, percentage
Source: British Social Attitudes Survey.

Some of the most interesting attitudes in England concern those towards the future of the UK as a union. While the secession of England is not really a meaningful question, the loss of the peripheral nations would amount to English independence by subtraction. Compared with the majority territories in other plurinational unions like Spain or Canada, there are rather high levels of support for this option. Surveys have long shown that the majority in Great Britain are content to leave Irish unification to the Irish with only around a third preferring that it stay in the UK. A survey in 2019 showed that just half the people in Great Britain cared 'about things that happen in Northern Ireland' while 40 per cent did not.[21] GB voters were equally divided (around 40 per cent to 40 per cent) between those who would be upset if Northern Ireland left the UK and those who would not be bothered either way; 11 per cent would be pleased (rising to 18 per cent in Scotland) (YouGov 2019). Another 2019 survey showed that just 43 per cent and 35 per cent respectively of the English thought that Scotland and Northern Ireland should remain in the UK, with around 40 per cent saying that they did not have a view (Ashcroft 2019). Surveys from 1999 onwards showed support in England for Scottish independence fluctuating around about 20 per cent (British Social Attitudes Survey; Wyn Jones et al. 2012). Support for going back on devolution, with no Scottish Parliament, was around the same level. Devolution within the UK remained the most popular option for Scotland among English voters. English attitudes towards Wales have been equally open minded. Measuring support in England for Welsh independence between 1999 and 2007, the British Social Attitudes Survey showed around 20 per cent in favour, considerably more than in Wales itself. Opposition to Welsh devolution ran at about 15 per cent, rather less than in Wales itself.

[21] Although 57 per cent in Scotland cared.

Brexit provided a test of English attitudes to the United Kingdom as surveys asked respondents how to reconcile their preferences with the Remain preferences in Scotland and Northern Ireland. All surveys, before and after the 2016 referendum have shown a tendency for those defining themselves as English only to favour leaving the EU (Wyn Jones et al. 2013; Heath and Richards 2019). This contrasts with other parts of the United Kingdom. English identifiers are also likely to favour a hard Brexit, prioritizing sovereignty issues more than British identifiers and much more than Scottish and Irish identifiers (Heath and Richards (2018, 2019). This relationship appears to have been forged during the run-up to the referendum of 2016 and reinforced after it (BSA 2019).

According to the Future of England Survey (2019), 80 per cent of English Leave voters thought the failure of the Northern Ireland peace process would be a price worth paying for Brexit, although only a quarter thought that this was likely to happen. Seventy-five per cent said that Scottish independence would be a price worth paying, and half of them thought it likely. Lord Ashcroft's (2019) polling showed very similar findings. This suggests that Brexit has provided a vehicle for a previously inchoate English nationalism, not in favour of secession but which conceivably could lead, by subtraction, to an English state outside the European Union. This combination of Euroscepticism with Englishness would appear to pose one of the strongest challenges to the Union.

This all suggests that English voters are rather relaxed about devolution and even resigned to secession but they will respond to political cues when those are supplied. In spite of the avalanche of literature on the rise of English nationalism, most English voters see the UK constitution as an adequate vehicle for their aspirations. That is hardly surprising then they have 80 per cent of the seats and have had the government of their choice for all but three years since the advent of democracy.

The Sharing Union

A central element in neo-unionist arguments is that the UK is a 'sharing union' in which risks are pooled and each part gets its just allocation of resources (Chapter 8). There is no needs-based allocation formula for public spending in the UK, although the social security system does provide for a degree of equalization by pooling payments to individuals. The Barnett Formula has become a convenient target for English and Welsh complaints about Scotland's advantage in public expenditure although, since Barnett should equalize spending over time, some of these are misplaced. Studies have shown that British citizens, like those in other countries, do recognize a conception of territorial justice and accept redistributive policies, even in the wealthier regions (Henderson et al. 2013). There is some evidence that, since devolution, citizens in England have become more aware of Scotland's advantages in public expenditure and, generally, disapprove (Figure 10.8).

On the Scottish side, however, devolution, or perhaps the debate about the Barnett Formula, assuaged Scottish feelings of unfairness as the number of people complaining dropped up to the 2014 independence referendum (Figure 10.9).

The corresponding figures for Wales show that some 70 per cent think that Wales gets less than its share.[22]

Given the relative gains and losses through the various fiscal settlements, these perceptions are not unreasonable. They are, however, heavily influenced by broader political attitudes. Figures from Ashcroft's (2019) polling suggest half of English voters did not know whether England subsidizes Scotland or Northern Ireland. A third thought that England does subsidize Scotland and Northern Ireland but are happy about it. Resentment towards Scotland and Northern Ireland is highest among Conservative voters and anti-European voters in England. Two-thirds of English Conservative/Leave voters thought that Scotland benefited more from being in the UK, against just one in six Labour/Remain voters. Those thinking that Northern Ireland benefited more

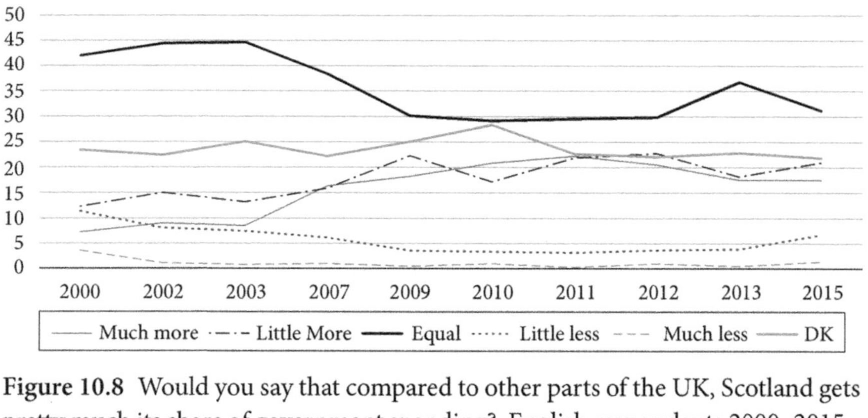

Figure 10.8 Would you say that compared to other parts of the UK, Scotland gets pretty much its share of government spending?, English respondents 2000–2015, percentage

Source: British Social Attitudes Survey.

[22] British Social Attitudes Survey, 2014 and 2015. There is no time series.

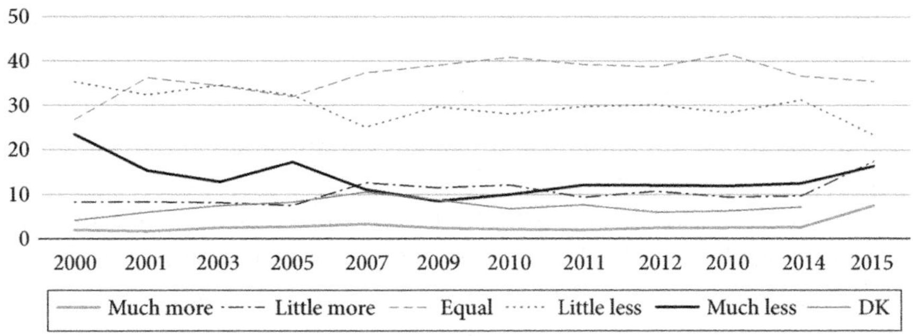

Figure 10.9 Would you say that compared to other parts of the UK, Scotland gets pretty much its share of government spending?, Scottish respondents 2000–2015, percentage

Source: British Social Attitudes Survey. British Election Study (2015).

included half of Conservative/Remain voters and just over a quarter of the Labour/Remain group.

The Foundations of Union

Plurinational unions do not rely on unity of *demos*, *telos* and *ethos*, but neither are they likely to survive if these elements are totally lacking or have been successfully forged and aligned by competing national projects. Unions, rather, rest upon cross-cutting identities and aspirations or what Wittgenstein called 'family resemblances', in which features link individuals together but no one element is common to them all. The data show that there are indeed distinct identities among the nations of the United Kingdom but they are by no means watertight or fixed. Strong national identities in England, Scotland, Wales and Northern Ireland coexist with reserves of British sentiment, with only some citizens regarding these as incompatible. Even in Northern Ireland, where identities and constitutional options are most polarized, large numbers of citizens can take refuge in being neither nationalist nor unionist or in the Northern Ireland identity.

As important as simple figures on identity are the meanings with which these are invested. National identities, long politicized in Northern Ireland have taken on deeper political meanings in the rest of the United Kingdom, reshaping ideas of political community. While it is true, for example, that Scots are not notably to the left of English voters, social democratic values have been linked to a narrative about Scotland (Gall 2005) and, to some extent, Wales.

The context is important, as are the choices on offer at any given time. Once Scottish independence or Brexit were posed as practical possibilities, they reshaped the menu of choice and attracted substantial support. These realignments were not merely transient but appear to reflect substantial political cleavages. Even then, however, they do not determine attitudes completely, as there are different versions of Brexit, Scottish independence and Northern Ireland devolution on offer. When given the choice, many citizens will choose the less radical version of each, one that does not close borders but retains existing relationships, whether as independence-lite, soft Brexit or power-sharing with an Irish dimension for Northern Ireland. As the available options were reduced and polarized by Brexit, so political attitudes seemed to follow.

11
The Future of Union

The argument of this book has been that the United Kingdom should be understood as a union and a contested project—more contested at some times than others. It is not simply a union of nations, each of which has a coherent account of itself, nested into a larger whole. The meaning and implications of nationality themselves differ across, and within, the component parts, and change over time. There have been moments of high unionism, when *demos*, *telos* and *ethos* appeared in alignment, and when political, economic, security and social unions were coterminous within fixed boundaries. In the early twenty-first century, these have become delinked but not entirely separated. The problems inherent in the idea of a unitary UK *demos* are illustrated by the fraught efforts of unionists to reconstruct it. The devolution settlement does not rest upon shared *telos* but is rather one of those constitutional compromises that provide for legitimate government in the absence of consensus on the long-term destiny of the state. This is explicit in the case of Northern Ireland, but the political parties have also recognized that Scotland has a right to secession should its people so resolve. In that case, the argument is about the conditions under which such a right might be exercised. If there is now a shared *ethos*, it is difficult to identify it as specifically British.

Union was never a unified project or ideology but rather a complex structure with numerous strands, which sometimes cohere and sometimes pull apart. To recall the metaphor in our title, it is a bone structure that can survive multiple partial fractures as long as they do not all accumulate in the same place. That happened in Catholic Ireland in the early twentieth century, where a counter-project gained sufficient traction to triumph, but without resolving the national question definitively.

At one level, the union rests upon deep social forces, including economic forces and social structures. It is not difficult to list centrifugal forces in the early twenty-first century. Welfare state restructuring has emptied the concept of social citizenship of much of its meaning. Economic disparities have increased in the absence of state-wide policies aimed at spatial cohesion, although the disparities do not map clearly onto the boundaries of the component nations. Devolution has set in train institutional dynamics which

State and Nation in the United Kingdom: The Fractured Union. Michael Keating, Oxford University Press (2021).
© Michael Keating. DOI: 10.1093/oso/9780198841371.003.0011

critics predicted could lead to the weakening and eventually dissolution of the bonds of union. Scotland and, to an increasing extent, Wales have emerged as distinct political communities with their own political agendas; Northern Ireland has long been a place apart. Until the 1970s, there was a British party system, which even extended partially into Northern Ireland.[1] Now there are distinct systems, and in Scotland as well as Northern Ireland the principal line of division is over the Union itself. Above all, Brexit has removed an external support system which filled some of the abeyances in the devolution settlement and provided important elements of economic union. None of these, on its own, is fatal. The United Kingdom remains a highly integrated economic zone even though the single market was larger, and more strongly institutionalized, within the European Union. Reserved welfare powers do guarantee equity and protection against risk across the Union, if the insistence that the welfare state itself depends on the Union is, at least, exaggerated. There are fiscal transfers to all three devolved territories even they do depend on historic legacies and political bargaining, not on any calculation of need (with the partial exception of the Welsh guarantee). As for shared *ethos* and British values, these are not the property of the British or of unionists but universal values also shared by peripheral nationalists. There is no evidence that fundamental values are diverging significantly or are under any more threat at the periphery than at the centre—unlike during the Stormont regime. There remains a strong substratum of British identities rooted in history, shared experience and values (Bechhofer and McCrone 2014) but this, as always, is a polyvalent phenomenon, negotiated differently across the UK with moments of common endeavour such as the Second World War but also distinct stories and memories.

At another level, the Union rests upon conjectural factors, critical moments and political shifts, which can change matters over short periods. International and historical experience shows that, in these conditions, specific events can result in rapid change. The Easter Rising of 1916 and its aftermath precipitated a shift to radical Irish nationalism. A very different event, the establishment of the National Assembly for Wales, shifted the constitutional ground there very rapidly. Inchoate English discontents was one of a set of elements that crystalized into outright rejection of EU membership by a majority of the population once that option was presented. The Union has come under most intense challenge in recent years from nationalisms in Scotland, Northern Ireland and Wales. Surveys since the Scottish independence referendum have

[1] Given the alliance between the Conservative and Ulster Unionist parties.

provoked some sensationalist headlines but show that substantial numbers of people believe that the union will end within the next twenty years. Yet Brown et al. (1999) found back in 1997 that 60 per cent of Scots thought that Scottish independence was likely in the following twenty years;[2] twenty years later, the expectation was much the same.[3] Irish unification is also viewed differently depending on whether it is presented as a long-term prospect or an imminent proposition. The reason is that, in the absence of an external shock, it has hitherto been possible to accommodate nationalist pressures by conceding autonomy and ingenious arrangements such as the Northern Ireland settlement. It was the failure to concede Home Rule that provided the opportunity for Irish separatism in the early twentieth century.

Between the deeper forces and historical conjunctures is statecraft, in which leaders read long and short-term change and respond more or less skilfully. The Millennium settlement was an effort to restabilize union at a different point from the old territorial management formulas, providing a new balance between centre and periphery. It is, as we have seen, subject to different interpretations, themselves rooted in contrasting historical perspectives. Two features stand out: the failure to change constitutional understandings and practices at the centre; and the continued position of England as the dominant partner, but constitutionally unrecognized as such. The settlement as a whole, while described as a constitutional reform, was very weakly constitutionalized. Not only was the principle of Westminster sovereignty and supremacy conspicuously asserted as a legal principle. The settlement was not scaffolded with wider and deeper understandings of constitutionalism as theory and practice. Conventions were invoked as the way of squaring the sovereignty circle but then reduced to mere 'politics', meaning in practice, power. English constitutional assumptions continue to govern the Union while much of the UK Government continues as if there were still a unitary state with devolution tacked on. In spite of the reams that have been written about constitutionalism since the nineteenth century, matters seem always to return to the 'Dicey of English constitutional orthodoxy' (McCrudden 2015: 214). It used to be thought that all this was mere constitutional formalism since political prudence would ensure that the centre would not overstep itself (essentially the position of Dicey[4]) or that, were devolution introduced, the new bodies would become weighty political actors so that sovereignty would de

[2] Nineteen per cent very likely and 41 per cent quite likely.

[3] Twenty-five per cent thought it likely within five years http://whatscotlandthinks.org/questions/how-soon-do-you-think-scotland-will-be-independent#line/, accessed 1 November 2020.

[4] Although, as we have seen, Dicey was scarcely consistent (McLean 2010).

facto be divided (Bogdanor 1999). Events, particularly since the Brexit referendum, have shown otherwise. A new 'muscular' strain of unionism emerged within the Conservative Party (Kenny and Sheldon 2020). The UK Government's (2020) Internal Market White Paper described the union as a 'unitary state' and the measures in the Internal Market Bill (Chapter 8) undermined the regulatory autonomy of the devolved authorities. It contained a new power for UK ministers to spend money in devolved fields, with or without the agreement of the devolved governments. This built on the extension of city and regional deals beyond England. UK Government 'hubs' were established in Scotland, Wales, Northern Ireland and the English regions to provide greater presence and capacity. During the Covid crisis, the UK Government established 'paid for partnerships', which allowed it to place self-congratulatory articles in newspapers. All of this was part of a conscious effort to raise its profile and take credit for spending by 'flying the unionist flag' (Keating, 2020).

There have been proposals to refound the United Kingdom on the basis of popular sovereignty and a written constitution, usually based on deliberation within a citizens' assembly or constitutional convention. The assumption is that there is a unitary *demos*, which can agree on a *telos* or constitutional future. That clashes with the basis for the devolution settlements, which are efforts to accommodate different teleological visions of the constitution. It is not merely that substantial numbers of citizens in Scotland and Northern Ireland favour secession from the state. There are also very different conceptions of devolution. In Wales, there is a strong demand for a cooperative federalist model, in which there would be common policy-making but with a strong territorial input. In Scotland, the emphasis is more on autonomous policy-making. The Northern Ireland agenda is different again, with the emphasis on power-sharing internally and on cross-border relations. In England, there is an inchoate discontent focused on the loss of voice, but with no obvious territorial solution.

In many ways, the problem of the Union is one of the centre as much as the periphery. Historically, England has provided an anchor for union and a dominating presence. The confounding of England, Britain and the United Kingdom both in the minds of many English people and in institutions, has prevented the UK from becoming a federation. Yet that has also permitted concessions of self-government to the other nations, without England feeling threatened. Whatever concessions were made to the smaller nations, Britain/England could carry on as normal. It is an extraordinary historical amnesia that allows the UK to present itself as a model of stability and territorial integrity in spite of being one of only two western European nations to experience a secession in the twentieth century. It could equally survive the secession of Northern Ireland and, if Scotland were to secede, the successor state might look much the same, only a bit smaller. The weight of England has even been recognized by secessionists. Irish citizens continued to enjoy rights in the UK after the declaration of the Republic in 1949; in return, Great Britain gained much-needed Irish labour. The pro-independence side in the Scottish referendum of 2014 proposed to use the pound sterling, although the UK Government strongly refuted the idea.

The secession of England is an unlikely prospect. What is more realistic is an increasing divergence between English and other conceptions of union. The Brexit project is about re-establishing a bounded nation-state whose founding assumptions are far from the common premises underlying both the European and UK unions. The heartland of this project is in England, and surveys have shown that supporters of Brexit would prioritize that over the maintenance of the plurinational union; whatever its substantive merits. this may well be a logical conclusion. Analysis of coverage of legal rulings on Brexit across the UK has shown an absence of appreciation within England of the territorial dimension (Davies and Wincott 2020). Similarly, government announcements and press coverage of the four nations during the Covid crisis in 2020 continued to confuse what were British with English measures. It is as though UK ministers would feel diminished to be described as the *English* Secretary of State for Health or whatever. The idea of England by subtraction may have to give way to a positive conception of what is England and English.

There is no shortage of suggestions as to what to do about England. There is no real demand for an English Parliament to sit alongside Westminster. An English committee of Westminster, extending the English Votes for English Laws principle, may assuage discontent but would not amount to English self-government as long as there was no separate English executive. An English Parliament would rival Westminster in its scope and financial capacity and so would not achieve the aim of separating out England from the UK. As critics have regularly argued, this is a way of solving successive Irish and Scottish demands for self-government by giving England something that it does not want.

It has been said that the British gifted federalism to many countries of the former Empire but could never see its relevance for themselves. The idea regularly returns as the solution or 'wonder drug' (Jackson 2018) to the national conundrum of the United Kingdom, often favoured by unionists as a coherent system. It has many attractions, especially if we abandon American-inspired assumptions that it can only work in mononational states. Yet it has never been specified adequately. For some, it is a means of allowing greater divergence across the union; for others it is about constraining divergence (Kettle, Payne). Some versions would leave sovereignty intact, while others would entrench it in a written constitution. Federalism, in itself, no more resolves the questions of *demos* and *telos* and sovereignty than does devolution, but merely allows it to be rehearsed over again.

While federation for the UK may be a pipedream, there is no shortage of proposals for a middle way between the devolution settlement and the break-up of the Union, although a lot of semantic confusion has been sown in the process. The old term 'Home Rule' has been revived, since it sounds more muscular than devolution but, historically, it has shared the same central ambiguity: is it based on the inherent rights of the nations, or is it a mere gift from the centre? Here, the federal *principle* is of more relevance and might be introduced in the absence of comprehensive constitutional reform. This could address the Diceyean incubus by curtailing Westminster supremacy. Removing the word 'normally' from the statutory expression of the Sewel Convention would be a start. If England did not want a parliament, it could at least be constituted as a distinct place within the Union and so subject to whatever constraints might be put on Scotland, Wales and Northern Ireland. The argument that this is impossible because by definition the Monarch-in-Parliament cannot abridge its own sovereignty is no more than a tautological ploy dependent on the prior acceptance of its own premise. The logical response is that, if Westminster is omnicompetent, it can curtail its own sovereignty. This having been done, the constitution, non-codified as it is, could start to be understood in a deeper and wider sense than the Monarch-in-Parliament, and to encompass statute law, convention, historic understanding and epistemic reasoning grounded in the principles of democracy and union rather than unitarism. This requires a further decentring of Westminster, which would then become one, albeit important, element in the constitution.

The Bingham Centre (2015) proposals eschew grand designs for a more limited reform of the territorial constitution but evade this central issue of parliamentary sovereignty and supremacy itself. Its proposal for a Charter of the Union would provide that the Scotland, Wales and Northern Ireland Acts 'shall be construed and have effect' subject to it (Bingham Centre 2015: 21). It would not bind Westminster in respect either of the UK or of England. The Constitution Reform Group (2018) also seek to build on existing institutions and introduce the radical idea of a voluntary union of self-determining nations, but then vitiate the concept by insisting that the principle of central parliamentary sovereignty will still prevail; this is perhaps why it attracted such broad, if shallow, support.

Statecraft in the United Kingdom has historically been slow to catch up with social and political change. Extension of the franchise was late, piecemeal and incremental. Even the enfranchisement of women after the First World War was not done in a single step but took ten years to complete. Reform of the House of Lords has stretched over a hundred years and has never been completed. Home Rule for Ireland was delayed until it no longer met the needs of the times, and with it was lost the prospect of a federal-type United Kingdom. Scottish devolution was delayed for decades in spite of being favoured by every poll ever taken on it. The devolution reforms at the end of the twentieth century were an opportunity to break decisively with the model of the unitary state imposed on a plurinational union, but instead tried to bolt devolution onto that unitary state. Statecraft is once again behind the times.

Unionism and nationalism, as we have seen, are broad fields rather than precise doctrines and overlap in many ways. Nationalism runs from an ontological claim that the nation exists, to a teleological and normative argument that it should become an independent state. Unionism ranges from an integral and centralizing British nationalism to a manner of accommodating multiple local patriotisms, each on its own terms. The evidence shows that the public, far from seeking simplicity and certainty, recognizes itself in this complexity. Yet electoral dynamics have served increasingly to define political competition on nationalist–unionist lines, both Scotland and in Northern Ireland, while England is caught up in the Brexit pipe-dream of national sovereignty.

Relations among the peoples of 'these islands' are too complex to fit into such constitutional straitjackets. Experience has shown that the union can be pulled and stretched in a way that other compound states, constrained by written constitutions or unitarist doctrines, have found impossible. Many ties between the United Kingdom and Ireland survived Irish independence, which was itself a rather drawn-out process. Proposals for secession have been informed by ideas of union, whether as Dominion status, an 'islands' framework inspired by Nordic cooperation, the British-Irish Common Travel area and mutual citizen rights, or the European Union. It is true that proposals for new political ties do not usually survive secession but commonalities do persist. Were unionists to become a minority in Scotland or Northern Ireland, the social ties would remain, and they would retain legitimate expectations of recognition. Union and unionism, which always carried a historical burden in Northern Ireland, may now be too associated with anti-nationalism to serve as a theme to link together even Great Britain. To put it differently, unionism has tried to take on the guise of nationalism, with its claims to a higher *demos*, *telos* and *ethos*. It could never be the theme to address the 'totality of relationships' embracing the islands as a whole. The challenge must be to find renewed practices and institutions to manage the common problems, and complex, economic, social, cultural and historical interdependencies within the archipelago without resorting to domination.

References

Advocate General and Attorney General (2018), *Case for Her Majesty's Attorney General and Her Majesty's Advocate General in the Supreme Court of the United Kingdom*, Case No. UKSC 2018/0080.

Alesina, Alberto and Enrico Spoloare (2003), *The Size of Nations* (Cambridge, Mass: MIT Press).

Alexander, Wendy (2003), *Chasing the Tartan Tiger: Lessons from a Celtic Cousin?* (London: The Smith Institute).

Anderson, James (2018), 'Ireland's Borders, Brexit Centre-Stage: A Commentary', *Space and Polity*, 22/2: 255–69.

Ansari, Ali (2018), *These Islands: A Letter to Britain* (London: Haus).

Ansari, Ali (2020), 'Scotland, Britain and the Union', in Michael Keating, ed., *The Oxford Handbook of Scottish Politics* (Oxford: Oxford University Press).

Anthony, Gordon (2015), 'Devolution Issues, Legislative Power, and Legal Sovereignty', in Aurêlien Antoine, ed., *Le Droit public britannique: État des lieux et perspectives* (Paris: Société de Législation Comparée/Lextenso).

Applegate Celia (1999), 'A Europe of Regions: Reflections on the Historiography of Sub-National Places in Modern Times', *American Historical Review*, 104/4: 1157–82.

Arden, Mary (2015), *Common Law and Modern Society* (Oxford: Oxford University Press).

Armstrong, Kenneth (2003), 'United Kingdom: Divided on Sovereignty', in Neil Walker, ed., *Sovereignty in Transition* (Oxford: Hart).

Armstrong, Kenneth (2017), *Brexit Time. Leaving the EU. Why, How and When*? (Cambridge: Cambridge University Press).

Artola, Miguel (1999), *La Monarquía de España* (Madrid: Alianza).

Ascherson, Neal (2020), 'The State of Scotland', in Michael Keating, ed., *The Oxford Handbook of Scottish Politics* (Oxford: Oxford University Press).

Ashcroft, Brian and James H. Love (1993), *Takeovers, Mergers and the Regional Economy* (Edinburgh: Edinburgh University Press).

Ashcroft, Lord (2019), 'England and the Union', Lord Ashcroft Polls, https://lordashcroftpolls.com/2019/10/england-and-the-union/, accessed 31 October 2020.

Ask About Ireland (nd), 'Irish Export Patterns', http://www.askaboutireland.ie/reading-room/life-society/ireland-and-the-eu/irish-export-patterns/. accessed 31 October 2020.

Aughey, Arthur (2001a), *Nationalism, Devolution and the Constitutional Challenge to the United Kingdom State* (London: Pluto).

Aughey, Arthur (2001b), 'Unionism, Conservativism and the Anglo-Irish Agreement', in D. George Boyce and Alan O'Day, eds, *Defenders of the Union: A Survey of British and Irish Unionism since 1801* (London: Routledge).

Aughey, Arthur (2007), *The Politics of Englishness* (Manchester: Manchester University Press).

Aughey, Arthur (2018), *The State of the Union: Lessons for a Shared, Prosperous Future* (London: Policy Exchange).

Aughey, Arthur and Christine Berberich (2011), 'Introduction: These Englands–A Conversation on National Identity', in Arthur Aughey and Christine Berberich, eds, *These Englands: A Conversation on National Identity* (Manchester: Manchester University Press).

Baird, Sandy, John Foster and Richard Leonard (2007), 'Scottish Capital: Still in Control in the 21st Century', *Scottish Affairs*, 58: 1–35.

Baldersheim, Harald and Michael Keating (eds) (2015), *Small States in the Modern World: Vulnerabilities and Opportunities* (Cheltenham: Edward Elgar).

Balsom, Denis (1985), ' The Three-Wales Model', in John Osmond, ed., *The National Question* (Llandysul: Gomer).

Barkey, Karen (2008), *Empire of Difference: The Ottomans in Comparative Perspective* (Cambridge: Cambridge University Press).

Barnett, Joel (2011), *House of Lords Debates*, 15-06-2011.

Barry, Brian (2000), *Culture and Equality* (Oxford: Oxford University Press).

Bartlett, Thomas (2004), 'Ireland, Empire and Union, 1690-1801', in Kevin Kenny, ed., *Ireland and the British* Empire (Oxford: Oxford University Press).

Bartolini, Stefano (2005), *Restructuring Europe. Centre Formation, System Building, and Political Structuring between the Nation State and the European Union* (Oxford: Oxford University Press).

Bauböck, Rainer (2017), 'Political Membership and Democratic Boundaries', in Ayelet Shacharlk, Rainer Bauböck, Irene Bloemraad and Maarten Vink, eds., *The Oxford Handbook of Citizenship* (Oxford: Oxford University Press).

Bauböck, Rainer (2018), *Democratic Inclusion* (Manchester: Manchester University Press).

Bechhofer, Frank and David McCrone (2007), 'Being British: A Crisis of Identity?', *The Political Quarterly*, 78.2: 251–60.

Bechhofer, Frank and David McCrone (2009), 'Being Scottish', in Frank Bechhofer and David McCrone, eds, *National Identity, Nationalism and Constitutional Change* (Basingstoke: Palgrave).

Bechhofer, Frank and David McCrone (2014), 'The End of Being British?', *Scottish Affairs*, 23/3: 309–22.

Bechhofer, Frank and David McCrone (2015), *Understanding National Identity* (Cambridge: Cambridge University Press).

Berger, Stefan and Alexei Miller (eds) (2015), *Nationalizing Empires* (Budapest: Central European University Press).

Bew, John (2009), *The Glory of being Britons: Civic Unionism in Nineteenth-Century Belfast* (Dublin: Irish Academic Press).

Bew, Paul (1994), *Ideology and the Irish Question. Ulster Unionism and Irish Nationalism 1912–1916* (Oxford: Oxford University Press).

Bew, Paul, Peter Gibbon and Henry Patterson (1996), *Northern Ireland, 1921–1996* (London: Serif).

Bew, Paul (2007), *Ireland. The Politics of Enmity, 1789–2006* (Oxford: Oxford University Press).

Billig, Michael (1995), *Banal Nationalism* (Los Angeles: Sage).

Bingham Centre for the Rule of Law (2015), *A Constitutional Crossroads: Ways Forward for the United Kingdom* (London: Bingham Centre).

Blewett, Neal (1965), 'The Franchise in the United Kingdom, 1885-1918', *Past & Present*, 32/1.1: 27–56.

Blondel, Jean (1974), *Voters, Parties, and Leaders. The Social Fabric of British Politics*, revised edition (Harmondsworth: Penguin).

Bodin, Jean (1992), *On Sovereignty: Four Chapters from the Six Books of the Commonwealth* (Cambridge: Cambridge University Press).

Bogdanor, Vernon (1984), *What is Proportional Representation*? (Oxford: Martin Robertson).
Bogdanor, Vernon (1999), *Devolution in the United Kingdom* (Oxford: Oxford University Press).
Bogdanor, Vernon (2007), 'Tory plans for an "English Parliament" will wreck the Union', *The Observer,* 4 November.
Bond, Ross (2003), 'Identity Matters: The Personal and Political Significance of Feeling Scottish', in Catherine Bromley, John Curtice, Kerstin Hinds and Alison Parks, eds, *Devolution—Scottish Answers to Scottish Questions* (Edinburgh: Edinburgh University Press).
Bond, Ross (2015), 'National Identities and the 201 Independence Referendum in Scotland', *Sociological Research Online,* 20/4: 11, http://www.socresonline.org.uk/20/4/11.html/, accessed 31 October 2020.
Boyce, D. George (2006), 'A Place Apart? Ulster, Britain and Devolution, 1886-1939', in Duncan Tanner, Chris Williams, Wil Griffith and Andrew Edwards, eds, *Debating Nationhood and Governance in Britain, 1884–1945* (Manchester: Manchester University Press).
Boyce, Rab (2018), 'Scotland and the Twentieth Century', ScotFact, https://www.scotfact.com/article_scotland20thCentury/, accessed 31 October 2020.
Boyle, Stephen (2018), 'Economic Policy Performance', in Kenneth Gibb, Duncan Maclennan, Des MacNulty and Michael Comerford, eds, *The Scottish Economy* (London: Routledge).
Bradley, John (1999), 'The History of Economic Development in Ireland, North and South', *Proceedings of the British Academy*, 88: 25–68.
Brand, Jack (1978), *The National Movement in Scotland* (London: Routledge).
Braudel, Fernand (1986), *L'identité de la France. Espace et Histoire* (Paris: Arthaud-Flammarion).
Breuilly, John (1982), *Nationalism and the State* (Manchester: Manchester University Press).
Bristow, Gillian (2005), 'Everyone's a "Winner": Problematising the Discourse of Regional Competitiveness', *Journal of Economic Geography*, 5/3: 285–304.
Bristow, Gillian (2008), 'The Barnett Formula and its Consequences for Wales', *Economic Affairs*, 21/3: 44–7.
Bristow, Gillian (2010), *Critical Reflections on Regional Competitiveness* (London: Routledge).
Brogan, Steve (1997), 'Blair Has Trouble with his Kilt', *The Independent*, 05-04-97.
Brouillet, Eugénie and Tom Mullen (2018), 'Constitutional Jurisprudence on Federalism and Devolution in the UK and Canada', in Michael Keating and Guy Laforest, eds, *Constitutional Politics and the Territorial Question in Canada and the United Kingdom. Federalism and Devolution Compared* (London: Palgrave).
Brown, Alice, David McCrone, Lindsay Paterson and Paula Surridge (1999), *The Scottish Electorate: The 1997 General Election and Beyond* (Basingstoke: Macmillan).
Brown, Gordon (2006), 'The Future of Britishness', Lecture to the Fabian Society, 14 January, www.fabians.org.uk/, accessed 31 October 2020.
Brown, Gordon (2012), Speech at Edinburgh Book Festival, https://www.theguardian.com/uk/video/2012/aug/13/gordon-brown-scotland-independence-edinburgh-video/, accessed 31 October 2020.
Brown, Gordon (2014), *My Scotland, Our Britain: A Future Worth Sharing* (London: Simon and Schuster).
Brown, Gordon (2019), Speech to Fabian Society, 25 June, https://fabians.org.uk/fabian-society-speech-gordon-brown-on-combatting-the-far-right/, accessed 31 October 2020.
Bruce, Steve, Tony Gledinning, Iain Paterson and Michael Rosie (2004), *Sectarianism in Scotland* (Edinburgh: Edinburgh University Press).
Bryant, Christopher (2006), *The Nations of Britain* (Oxford: Oxford University Press).

Bryce, James (1887), 'How We Became Home Rulers', in James Bryce, ed., *Handbook of Home Rule* (London: Kegan Paul).

Bryce, James (1901), *Studies in History and Jurisprudence*, vol.1 (New York: Oxford University Press), https://oll.libertyfund.org/titles/2003/, accessed 31 October 2020.

Brzinski, Joanny Bay, Thomas D, Lancaster, and Christian Tuschoff (1999), 'Federalism and Compounded Representation: Key Concepts and Project Overview', *Publius: The Journal of Federalism*, 29/1: 1–17.

Bulpitt, James (1983), *Territory and Power in the United Kingdom: An Interpretation* (Manchester: Manchester University Press).

Burgess, Michael (2006), *Comparative Federalism. Theory and Practices* (London: Routledge).

Burgess, Michael (2009), 'Federalism', in Antje Wiener and Thomas Diez, eds, *European Integration Theory* (Oxford: Oxford University Press).

Burgess, Michael (2012), *In Search of the Federal Spirit. New Theoretical and Empirical Perspectives in Comparative Federalism* (Oxford: Oxford University Press).

Butt Philip, Alan (1975), *The Welsh Question: Nationalism in Welsh Politics* (Cardiff: University of Wales Press).

Butt, Isaac (1870), *Home Government for Ireland: Irish Federalism, its Meaning, its Objects and its Hopes* (Dublin: Irish Home Rule League).

Butt, Isaac (1874), *Hansard*, 30-06-1874.

Butterfield, Herbert (1944), *The Englishman and his History* (Cambridge: Cambridge University Press).

Butterfield, Herbert (1968), *The Whig Interpretation of History* (Harmondsworth, Penguin) (first published Bell, 1931).

Byrne, Liam (2011), Speech at Labour Party Conference, https://www.theguardian.com/politics/blog/2011/sep/26/labour-conference-2011-live-coverage

Campbell, A. D. (1955), 'Changes in Scottish Incomes 1922–1949', *Economic Journal*, 65/258: 225–40.

Carl, Noah (2017), 'National Identity and Support for Leave versus Remain', *CSI Brexit 3* (Oxford: Centre for Social Investigation).

Casanas Adam, Elisenda (2017), 'An Unanswered or Unanswerable Question? The Scottish Parliament's Competence to Legislate for an Independence Referendum for Scotland', *Revista Catalana de Dret Públic*, 54: 81–99.

Chamberlain, Joseph (1887), *Home Rule and the Irish Question* (London: Swan, Sonnenschein, Lowery and Co).

Chen, Wen, Bart Los, Philip McCann, Raquel Ortega-Argilés, Mark Thissen and Franc van Oort (2017), 'The Continental Divide? Economic Exposure to Brexit in Regions and Countries on Both Sides of The Channel', *Papers in Regional Science*, 97/1: 25–54.

Claim of Right (1988), *The Crown and the Unicorn*, https://thecrownandtheunicorn.wordpress.com/the-claim-of-right-1989/, accessed 31 October 2020.

Clarke, Harold D., Matthew Goodwin, and Paul Whitely (2017), *Brexit: Why Britain Voted to Leave the European Union* (Cambridge: Cambridge University Press).

Clyde Valley Regional Planning Committee (1946), *The Clyde Valley Regional Plan 1946* (Edinburgh: HMSO).

Coakley, John and Jennifer Todd (2020), *Negotiating a Settlement in Northern Ireland, 1969–2019* (Oxford: Oxford University Press).

Colley, Linda (1992, 2003), *Britons: Forging the Nation 1707–1837* (London: Pimlico. 1st edition, 2nd edition).

Colley, Linda (1999), 'Britishness in the 21st Century', Downing Street Millennium Lecture, https://webarchive.nationalarchives.gov.uk/20040809182858/http://www.pm.gov.uk/output/Page3049.asp

Colls, Robert (2002), *Identity of England* (Oxford: Oxford University Press).
Colomer, Josep (2006), *Grandes imperios, pequeñas naciones* (Barcelona: Anagrama).
Commission on Scottish Devolution (Calman Commission) (2008), The Future of Scottish Devolution within the Union: A First Report, presented to the Presiding Officer of the Scottish Parliament and to the Secretary of State for Scotland, on behalf of Her Majesty's Government.
Connelly, Tony (2017), *Brexit & Ireland: The Dangers, the Opportunities, and the Inside Story of the Irish Response* (Dublin: Penguin Ireland).
Connelly, Tony (2018), 'Brexit: A Brief History of the Backstop', RTE, 20 Oct. 2018, https://www.rte.ie/news/brexit/2018/1019/1005373-backstop-tony-connelly/ accessed 31 October 2020.
Connolly, Sean (2014), 'Patriotism and Nationalism', in Alvin Jackson, ed., *The Oxford Handbook of Modern Irish History* (Oxford: Oxford University Press).
Constitution Reform Group (2015), *Towards a New Act of Union Towards a New Act of Union*, https://www.constitutionreformgroup.co.uk/download/towards-a-new-act-of-union-pdf/
Constitution Reform Group (2018), *Act of Union Bill*, https://www.constitutionreformgroup.co.uk/the-herald-new-act-of-union-bill-published/
Convery, Alan (2015), *The Territorial Conservative Party: Devolution and Party Change in Scotland and Wales* (Manchester: Manchester University Press).
Cooper, Lord (1953), *MacCormick v. Lord Advocate (1953) SC 396*. Court of Session (on appeal).
Corthorn, Paul (2012), 'Enoch Powell, Ulster Unionism and the British Nation', *Journal of British Studies*, 51/4: 967–97.
Coupland, Reginald (1954), *Welsh and Scottish Nationalism. A Study* (London: Collins).
Court of Session (2013), *Opinion of Lord Docherty in the Petition on Judicial Review of the Alcohol (Minimum Pricing) (Scotland) Act 2012 and of Related Decisions*, CSOH 70.
Crafts, Nicolas (2005a), 'Market Potential in British Regions, 1871–1931', *Regional Studies*, 39: 1159–66.
Crafts, Nicolas (2005b), 'Regional GDP in Britain, 1871-1911', *Scottish Journal of Political Economy*, 52/1: 54–64.
Craig, Cairns (2018), *The Wealth of the Nation: Scotland, Culture and Independence* (Edinburgh: Edinburgh University Press).
Crammond, Edgar (1912), 'The Economic Position of Scotland and Her Financial Relations with England and Ireland', *Journal of the Royal Statistical Society*, LCCV.II: 157–82.
Crewe, Ivor (1989), 'Values: The Crusade that Failed', in Dennis Kavanagh and Anthony Seldon, eds., *The Thatcher Effect: A Decade of Change* (Oxford: Blackwell).
Crowther-Hunt Lord and A.T. Peacock (1973), *Memorandum of Dissent. Royal Commission on the Constitution, 1969–1973* (London: Stationery Office).
Curtice, John (2018), 'How Do People in England Want to Be Governed?', in Michael Kenny, Iain McLean and Akash Paun, eds, *Governing England. English Identity and Institutions in a Changing United Kingdom* (Oxford: Oxford University Press).
Curtice, John (2019), 'Could Brexit Yet Undermine the Future of the British State?', *What Scotland Thinks*, http://blog.whatscotlandthinks.org/2019/07/could-brexit-yet-undermine-the-future-of-the-british-state/, accessed 31 October 2020.
Curtice, John and Anthony Heath (2009), 'England Awakes? Trends in National Identity in England', in Frank Bechhofer and David McCrone, eds, *National Identity, Nationalism and Constitutional Change* (Houndmills: Palgrave).
Curtice, John and Ian Montagu (2018), 'Do Scotland and England & Wales Have Different Views About Immigration?', NatCen, http://natcen.ac.uk/our-research/research/

do-scotland-and-england-wales-have-different-views-about-immigration/, accessed 31 October 2020.

Curtice, J. and Ormston, R. (2011), 'Is Scotland More Left-Wing Than England?', *British Social Attitudes*, 28.42, http://www.scotcen.org.uk/media/176048/2011-is-scotland-more-left-wing-than-england.pdf/, accessed 31 October 2020.

Curtice, John and Rachel Ormson (2013), *Attitudes towards Scotland's Constitutional Future* (Edinburgh: Scottish Centre on Social Research).

Curtice, John, Paula Devine and Rachel Ormson (2013), 'Trends in National Identity', *British Social Attitudes*, 30 (London: National Centre for Social Research).

Curtice, John and Rachel Ormson (2013), *Attitudes towards Scotland's Constitutional Future* (Edinburgh: Scottish Centre on Social Research).

Dahrendorf (2000), 'La sconfitta della vecchia democrazia', *La Repubblicca*, 12 January.

Dalyell, Tam (1977), *Devolution: The End of Britain?* (London: Jonathan Cape).

Davies, Gregory and Daniel Wincott (2020), 'Brexit, the Press and the Territorial Constitution', *Social and Legal Studies*, doi: 10.1177/0964663920921922 2–21.

Davies, Norman (1999), *The Isles. A History* (London: Macmillan).

Davies, Nye (2017), 'The Difference Between Sheep: Bevan and the "Welsh Day" Debate', Thinking Wales, http://blogs.cardiff.ac.uk/thinking-wales/2017/04/26/the-difference-between-sheep-bevan-and-the-welsh-day-debate/, accessed 31 October 2020.

De Montpensier, Roy Stone (1966), 'The British Doctrine of Parliamentary Sovereignty. A Critical Inquiry', *Louisiana Law Review*, 26/4: 753–87.

Delors, Jacques (1985), Speech in Luxembourg, *Bulletin of the European Communities.* September 1985, No 9 (Luxembourg: Office for Official Publications of the European Communities).

Denham, John (2018), *A Nation Divided? The Identities, Politics and Governance of England*, Open Democracy, https://www.opendemocracy.net/en/opendemocracyuk/nation-divided-identities-politics-and-governance-of-england/, accessed 31 October 2020.

Deutsch, Karl W. (1972) *Nationalism and Social Communication: An Inquiry into the Foundations of Nationality* (Cambridge, Mass: MIT Press).

Devine, T. M. (ed.) (2000), *Scotland's Shame? Bigotry and Sectarianism in Modern Scotland* (Edinburgh: Mainstream).

Devine, T. M. (2004), *Scotland's Empire, 1600–1815* (Harmondsworth: Penguin).

Devine, T. M. (2008), 'Three Hundred Years of the Anglo-Scottish Union', in T. M. Devine, ed., *Scotland and the Union 1707–2007* (Edinburgh: Edinburgh University Press.

Devine, T. M. (ed.) (2015), *Recovering Scotland's Slavery Past. The Caribbean Connection* (Edinburgh: Edinburgh University Press).

Dicey, A. V. (1912), *A Leap in the Dark. A Criticism of the Principles of Home Rule as Illustrated by the Bill of 1893*, 3rd edition (London: John Murray).

Dicey, A. V. (1913), *A Fool's Paradise. Being a Constitutionalist's Criticism on the Home Rule Bill of 1912* (London: John Murray).

Dicey, A. V. (1959), *Introduction to the Study of the Law of the Constitution* (Basingstoke: Macmillan).

Dicey, A. V. (1973), *England's Case Against Irish Home Rule* (Richmond: Richmond Publishing Co).

Dicey, Albert V. and Robert Rait (1920), *Thoughts on the Union Between England and Scotland* (London: Macmillan).

Diener, Alexander C. (2017), 'Rescaling the Geography of Citizenship', in Ayelet Shachar, Rainer Bauböck, Irene Bloemraad and Maarten Vink, eds., *The Oxford Handbook of Citizenship* (Oxford: Oxford University Press).

Diffley Mark (2020), 'Tory Revival in Scotland? Recent Evidence, Future Prospects', in David Torrance, ed., *Ruth Davidson's Conservatives* (Edinburgh: Edinburgh University Press).

Dorr, Noel (2017), *The Search for Peace in Northern Ireland. Sunningdale* (Dublin: Royal Irish Academy).

Dorsett, Richard (2013), 'The Effect of the Troubles on GDP in Northern Ireland', *European Journal of Political Economy*, 29: 119–33.

Douglas Home, Alec (1970), *Scotland's Government. The Report of the Scottish Constitutional Committee* (Edinburgh: Scottish Constitutional Committee).

Douglas-Scott, Sionaidh (2017), 'Popular Sovereignty v Parliamentary Sovereignty', in Denis Galligan, ed., *Constitution in Crisis. The New Putney Debates* (London: Tauris).

Douglas-Scott, Sionaidh (2018), 'A Brexit Case of Great Complexity and Greater Importance', *Prospect*, July.

Douglas-Scott, Sionaidh (2019), 'The Constitutional Implications of the EU (Withdrawal) Act 2018: A Critical Appraisal', *Queen Mary School of Law Legal Studies Research Paper No. 299/2019.* Available at SSRNhttps://ssrn.com/abstract=3316710/, accessed 31 October 2020.

Dudley Edwards, Owen (ed.) (1988), *A Claim of Right for Scotland* (Edinburgh: Polygon).

Durkheim, Emile (1964), *The Division of Labour in Society* (New York: Free Press).

Edgerton David (2018), *The Rise and Fall of the British Nation* (Harmondsworth: Penguin).

Ekins, Richard and Graham Gee (eds) (2017), *Judicial Power and the Left. Notes on a Sceptical Tradition* (London: Policy Exchange).

Elazar, Daniel (1987), *Exploring Federalism* (Tuscaloosa: University of Alabama Press).

Elliott, J. H. (1992), 'A Europe of Composite Monarchies', *Past & Present*, 137: 48–71.

Elliot, J. H. (2018), *Scots and Catalans. Union and Disunion* (London: Yale University Press).

Elliot, Mark (2015), 'Parliamentary Sovereignty', in Jeffery Jowell, Dawn Oliver and Colm O'Cinneide, eds, *The Changing Constitution*, 8th edn. (Oxford: Oxford University Press).

English Labour Network (2017), 'Submission to the Labour Party Democracy Review 2017–18', https://englishlabournetwork.org.uk/briefings-and-key-speeches/english-manifesto-democracy-review-submission/, accessed 31 October 2020.

English, Richard (1996), 'The Same People with Different Relatives? Modern Scholarship, Unionists and the Irish Nation', in Richard English and Graham Walker (eds), *Unionism in Modern Ireland. New Perspectives on Politics and Culture*, Basingstoke: Macmillan.

English, Richard and Graham Walker (1996), 'Introduction', in Richard English and Graham Walker, eds, *Unionism in Modern Ireland. New Perspectives on Politics and Culture* (Basingstoke: Macmillan).

Fabbrini, Sergio (2007), *Compound Democracies: Why the United States and Europe Are Becoming Similar* (Oxford: Oxford University Press).

Farrington, Christopher (2006), *Ulster Unionism and the Peace Process in Northern Ireland* (Basingstoke: Palgrave).

Ferguson, Yale, H. and Richard W. Mansbach (1996), *Polities: Authority, Identities, and Change* (Columbia: University of South Carolina Press).

Field, William (1997), *Regional Dynamics: The Basis of Electoral Support in Britain* (London: Routledge).

Finer, Samuel (1974), *Comparative Government* (Harmondsworth: Penguin).

Finlay, Richard (1998), 'Caledonia or North Britain? Scottish Identity in the Eighteenth Century', in Dauvit Broun, R. J. Finlay and Michael Lynch, eds, *Image and Identity. The Making and Remaking of Scotland through the Ages* (Edinburgh: John Donald).

Foley, Michael (2012), *The Silence of Constitutions. Gaps, 'Abeyances' and Political Temperament in the Maintenance of Government* (London: Routledge Revivals).

Ford, J. D. (2007), 'The Legal Provisions in the Acts of Union', *Cambridge Law Journal*, 66/1: 106–141.

Forsyth, Murray (1981), *Unions of States* (Leicester: Leicester University Press).

Foster, Arlene (2018), 'Awkward Relationship. Ulster Unionism and the Rest of the UK', Speech at Policy Exchange, 21 May 2018, https://policyexchange.org.uk/wp-content/uploads/2018/05/An-Awkward-Relationship.pdf/, accessed 31 October 2020.

Freeden, Michael (1998), 'Is Nationalism a Distinct Ideology?', *Political Studies*, VLVI: 748–65.

Frost, Robert (2013), 'The Polish-Lithuanian Union, 1386-1795', *British Academy Review*, 21: 7–10.

Frost, Robert (2015a), 'Parcelling up the Rogues: On Writing the History of Political Unions, in J. Hezde, K. Holste, D. Hüchtker, Y. Kleinmann and K. Steffen, eds, *Dekonstruieren und doch erzählen. Polnische und andere Geschichten: Polnische und andere Geschichten*, 1st edn, Polen: Kultur–Geschichte–Gesellschaft, no. 2, vol. 2 (Wallstein Verlag, Göttingen), 225–31.

Frost, Robert (2015b), *The Making of the Polish-Lithuanian Union 1385–1569*: vol. I (Oxford: Oxford University Press).

Fry, Michael (1987), *Patronage and Principle: A Political History of Modern Scotland* (Aberdeen: Aberdeen University Press).

Fry, Michael (2002), *The Scottish Empire* (Edinburgh: Birlinn).

Fry, Michael (2006), *The Union. England, Scotland and the Treaty of 1707* (Edinburgh: Birlinn).

Fus, Juan Pablo (2000), *España. La evolución de la identidad nacional* (Madrid: Temas de Hoy).

Future of England Survey (2019), https://www.cardiff.ac.uk/__data/assets/pdf_file/0010/1708624/Copy-of-Wales-16-Oct-AH.pdf/, accessed 31 October 2020.

Gagnon, Alain-G., and Michel Seymour (eds) (2012), *Multinational Federalism. Problems and Prospects* (Basingstoke: Palgrave).

Gagnon Alain-G and James Tully (eds) (2000), *Struggles for Recognition in Multinational Societies. In Search of Justice and Stability in the European Union, the United Kingdom, Canada, Spain and Belgium* (Cambridge: Cambridge University Press).

Gailey, Andrew (2001), 'The Destructiveness of Constructive Unionism. Theories and Practice, 1890s-1960s', in D. George Boyce and Alan O'Day, eds, *Defenders of the Union. A Survey of British and Irish Unionism since 1801* (London: Routledge).

Gaitskell, Hugh (1962), Speech to Labour Party Conference, https://www.independent.co.uk/arts-entertainment/classic-podium-the-end-of-1000-years-of-history-1190761.html/, accessed 1 November 2020.

Gall, Gregor (2005), *The Political Economy of Scotland. Red Scotland? Radical Scotland?* (Cardiff: University of Wales Press).

Gallagher, Jim (2018), 'The Ghost in the Machine? The Government of England', in Kenny, Michael, Iain McLean and Akash Paun, eds, *Governing England, English identity and institutions in a changing United Kingdom* (London: British Academy).

Gallagher, Jim (2020), *Jim Gallagher's Reflections on These Islands*, Newcastle Conference, These Islands, https://www.these-islands.co.uk/publications/d6/q/psearch-type/v2%7c1/, accessed 1 November 2020.

Gallagher, Jim and Daniel Hinze (2005), 'Financing Options for Devolved Government in the UK', Working Papers 2005_24 (Glasgow: University of Glasgow Business School).

Galligan, Brian and Scott Brenton (2015), *Constitutional Conventions in Westminster Systems: Controversies, Changes and Challenges* (Cambridge: Cambridge University Press).

Garry, John (2017a), Opinion Poll Results: Is There Support for a Border in the Irish Sea?, http://ukandeu.ac.uk/opinion-poll-results-is-there-support-for-a-border-in-the-irish-sea/, accessed 1 November 2020.

Garry John (2017b), 'The EU Referendum Vote in Northern Ireland: Implications for Our Understanding of Citizens' Political Views and Behaviour', https://www.qub.ac.uk/brexit/Brexitfilestore/Filetoupload,728121,en.pdf/, accessed 1 November 2020.

Garry, John and Kevin McNicholl (2015), 'Understanding the "Northern Irish" Identity', Briefing Paper, Knowledge Exchange Seminar Series, Belfast: Northern Ireland Assembly.

Geary, F. and T. Stark (2002), 'Examining Ireland's Post-Famine Economic Growth Performance', *Economic Journal*, 112: 919–35.

Gellner, Ernest (1983), *Nations and Nationalism* (Ithaca: Cornell University Press).

Girvin, Brian (1989), *Between Two World:. Politics and Economy in Independent Ireland* (Dublin: Gill and Macmillan).

Girvin, Brian (2002), *From Union to Union. Nationalism, Democracy and Religion in Ireland—Act of Union to EU* (Dublin: Gill and Macmillan).

Gladstone, William Ewart (1886), Speech on Second Reading Government of Ireland Bill, *Hansard*, 07-06-1886.

Glover, Daniel and Michael Kenny (2018a), 'Interpreting EVEL: Latest Station in the Conservative Party's English Journey', in Kenny, Michael, Iain McLean and Aksh Paun, eds, *Governing England: English Identity and Institutions in a Changing United Kingdom* (London: British Academy).

Glover, Daniel and Michael Kenny (2018b), 'Answering the West Lothian Question? A Critical Assessment of "English Votes for English Laws" in the UK Parliament', *Parliamentary Affairs*, 71/4: 760–82.

Goldsmith, Lord (2008), *Our Common Bond. Report of Citizenship Review* (London: Ministry of Justice).

Gordon, Michael (2015), *Parliamentary Sovereignty in the UK Constitution: Process, Politics and Democracy* (Oxford: Hart).

Gove, Michael (2018), 'A New National Consensus: Building a Union Which Endures', Speech at Policy Exchange, 18 May, https://policyexchange.org.uk/wp-content/uploads/2018/05/A-New-National-Consensus.pdf/, accessed 1 November 2020.

Grammond, Sébastien (2016), 'Compact is Back: The Supreme Court of Canada's Revival of the Compact Theory of Confederation', *Osgoode Hall Law Journal*, 53/3: 798–823.

Gray, Ann Marie, Goretti Horgan and Paula Devine (2018), 'Do Social Attitudes to Abortion Suggest Political Parties in Northern Ireland are out of Step with their Supporters?', Ark, https://www.ark.ac.uk/ARK/sites/default/files/2018-06/Feature7.pdf/, accessed 1 November 2020.

Greenfeld, Liah (1992), *Nationalism. Five Roads to Modernity* (Cambridge Mass: Harvard University Press).

Grégoire, Graham and C. N. Webber (2010), 'What Is a Political Constitution?', *Oxford Journal of Legal Studies*, 30/2: 273–99.

Gribbon, H. D. (1989), 'Economic and Social History, 1850-1921', in W. E. Vaughan, ed., *Ireland under the Union, 1870–1921* (Oxford: Oxford University Press).

Griffith, Wil (2006), 'Devolutionist Tendencies in Wales, 1885-1914', in Duncan Tanner, Chris Williams, Wil Griffith and Andrew Edwards, eds, *Debating Nationhood and Governance in Britain, 1884–1945* (Manchester: Manchester University Press).

Gros-Fitzgibbon, Benjamin (2016), *Continental Drift: Britain and Europe from the End of Empire to the Rise of Euroscepticism* (Cambridge: Cambridge University Press).

Guardian (2016), 'Theresa May Calls for "Red, White and Blue Brexit"', *Guardian*, 6 December.

Habermas, Jürgen (1998), 'Die postnationale Konstellation und die Zukunft der Demokratie', in *Die postnationale Konstellation. Politische Essays* (Frankfurt: Suhrkamp).

Hague, Kevin (2017), 'Barnett Formula: Keep it Simple', Chokka Blog, http://chokkablog.blogspot.com/2017/08/barnett-formula-keeping-it-simple.html/, accessed 1 November 2020.

Halkier, Henrik (2006), *Institutions, Discourse and Regional Development. The Scottish Development Agency and the Politics of Regional Policy* (Brussels: Presses interuniversitaire européennes).

Harries, Bethan, Bridget Byrne and Kitty Lymperopolou (2014), *The Dynamics of Diversity: Evidence from the 2011 Census* (London: Joseph Rowntree Foundation).

Hassan, Gerry and Eric Shaw (2019), *The People's Flag and the Union Jack. An Alternative History of Britain and the Labour Party* (London: Biteback).

Hastings, Adrian (1997), *The Construction of Nationhood. Ethnicity, Religion and Nationalism* (Cambridge: Cambridge University Press).

Hayward, Katy (2017), *Bordering on Brexit. Views from Local Communities in the Central Border Region or Ireland/Northern Ireland* (Belfast: Irish Central Border Area, Queen's University).

Hayward, Katy (2018), 'The Pivotal Position of the Irish Border in the UK's Withdrawal from the European Union', *Space and Polity*, 22/2: 238–54.

Hayward, Katy and Cathal McManus (2018), 'Neither/Nor: The Rejection of Unionist and Nationalist Identities in Post-Agreement Northern Ireland', *Capital and Class*, 43/1: 1–17.

Hazell, Robert (2008), 'Hokey cokey votes on English laws', *Guardian*, 3 July.

Heath, Anthony and Linday Richards (2018), 'Sovereignty and Cooperation: Different Dimensions of Brexit', UK in a Changing Europe, https://ukandeu.ac.uk/, accessed 1 November 2020.

Heath, Anthony and Linday Richards (2019), 'National Identity and Brexit Preferences', in Anand Menon, ed., *Brexit and Public Opinion*, https://ukandeu.ac.uk/brexit-and-public-opinion-national-identity-and-brexit-preferences/, accessed 1 November 2020.

Hechter, Michael (1975), *Internal Colonialism. The Celtic Fringe in British National Development, 1536–1966* (London: Routledge and Kegan Paul).

Henderson, Ailsa, Charlie Jeffery and Daniel Wincott (2013), *Citizenship after the Nation-State* (Basingstoke: Macmillan).

Herrero de Miñon, Miguel (1998), *Derechos Históricos y Constitución* (Madrid: Tecnos).

Herrero de Miñon, Miguel and Ernest Lluch (eds) (2001), *Foralismo, Derechos Históricos y Democracia* (Bilbao: Fundación BBV).

Himsworth, Chris and Christine O'Neill (2015), *Scotland's Constitution: Law and Practice*, 3rd edition (Hayward's Heath: Bloomsbury).

HM Treasury (2016), *Public Expenditure Statistical Analysis* (London: Treasury).

Hobolt, Sarah (2016), 'The Brexit Vote: A Divided Nation, a Divided Continent', *Journal of European Public Policy*, 23: 1259–77.

Hobsbawm, Eric (1992), 'Nationalism: Whose Fault-Line is it Anyway?', *Anthropology Today*, February.

Holtham Commission (Independent Commission on Funding and Finance for Wales) (2009), First Report (Cardiff: Commission).

Holtham Commission (Independent Commission on Funding and Finance for Wales) (2010), Final Report (Cardiff: Commission).

Honohan, Iseult (2017), 'Liberal and Republican Conceptions of Citizenship', in Ayelet Shachar, Rainer Bauböck, Irene Bloemraad and Maarten Vink, eds., *The Oxford Handbook of Citizenship* (Oxford: Oxford University Press).

Hope, Lord (2011), in *AXA General Insurance Limited and others (Appellants) v The Lord Advocate and others (Scotland)* UKSC 46.
Hope, Lord (2012a), in *Imperial Tobacco Limited (Appellant) v The Lord Advocate (Scotland)* UKSC 61.
Hope, Lord (2012b), in *BH (AP and Another) v Lord Advocate (Scotland)* UKSC 24.
Hoppit, Julian (2018), 'Scotland, Ireland and the Taxing Unions of 1707 and 1801', UCL Working Papers, https://www.ucl.ac.uk/debt-politics/sites/debt-politics/files/12_Hoppit.pdf/, accessed 1 November 2020.
Hoppit, Julian (2019), 'Scotland and the Taxing Union of 1707', *Scottish Historical Review*, 98/1: 45–70.
House of Commons Public Administration and Constitution Committee (2018), *Devolution and Exiting the EU: Reconciling Differences and Building Strong Relationships* HC 1485.
House of Lords (2002), *Judgments—Robinson v Secretary of State for Northern Ireland and Others*, UKHL 32.
House of Lords and House of Commons Joint Committee on Human Rights (2008), *A Bill of Rights for the UK? Twenty-ninth Report of Session 2007–08*, HL Paper 165-I, HC 150-I.
House of Lords Select Committee on the Constitution (2020), *6th Report of Session 2019–21*, HL Paper 71.
Howe, Stephen (2000), *Ireland and Empire: Colonial Legacies in Irish History and Culture* (Oxford: Oxford University Press).
Hroch, Miroslav (1985), *Social Preconditions of National Revival in Europe: A Comparative Analysis of the Social Composition of Patriotic Groups Among the Smaller European Nations* (Cambridge: Cambridge University Press).
Hueglin, Thomas (2013), 'Federalism and Democracy: A Critical Reassessment', in Grace Skogstad, David Cameron, Martin Papillon and Keith Banting, eds, *The Global Promise of Federalism* (Toronto: University of Toronto Press).
Jackson, Alvin (2004), *Home Rule. An Irish History 1800–2000* (London: Phoenix).
Jackson, Alvin (2012), *The Two Unions. Ireland, Scotland and the Survival of the United Kingdom, 1707–2007* (Oxford: Oxford University Press).
Jackson, Alvin (2014a), 'Irish History in the Twentieth and Twenty-First Centuries', in Alvin Jackson, ed., *The Oxford Handbook of Modern Irish History* (Oxford: Oxford University Press).
Jackson, Alvin (2014b), 'Loyalists and Unionists', in Alvin Jackson, ed., *The Oxford Handbook of Modern Irish History* (Oxford: Oxford University Press).
Jackson, Alvin (2018), 'The Failure of British and Irish Federalism, circa 1800–1950', in Robert Schütze and Stephen Tierney, eds, *The United Kingdom and the Federal Idea* (Oxford: Hart).
Jay, Douglas (1976), Speech on Second Reading of Scotland and Wales Bill, *Hansard online*, https://hansard.parliament.uk/Commons/1976-12-15/debates/ce96ec85-146c-46e8-98b7-555d103c7e54/ScotlandAndWalesBill
Jellinek, Georg (1981), *Fragmentos de Estado*, translation by Miguel Herrero de Miñon of *Uber Staatsfragmente* (Madrid: Civitas).
Johnes, Martin (2012), *Wales since 1939* (Manchester: Manchester University Press).
Johnes, Martin (2019), *Wales: England's Colony?*, (Cardigan: Parthian).
Jones, Barry and Michael Keating (1985), *Labour and the British State* (Oxford: Oxford University Press).
Jones, Carwyn (2014), A Keynote Speech by the Rt Hon Carwyn Jones AM, Minister of Wales: Our Future Union—A Perspective from Wales, Institute for Government https://

www.instituteforgovernment.org.uk/events/keynote-speech-rt-hon-carwyn-jones-am-minister-wales-our-future-union---perspective-wales/, accessed 1 November 2020.

Judson, Pieter (2016), *The Habsburg Empire: A New History* (Cambridge, Mass: Harvard University Press).

JUSTICE (2007), *A British Bill of Rights: Informing the Debate* (London: JUSTICE).

Kane, Nathan (2015), 'A Study of the Debate on Scottish Home Rule, 1886–1914', PhD thesis, University of Edinburgh.

Kanter, Douglas (2009), *The Making of British Unionism, 1740–1848* (Dublin: Four Courts Press).

Katwala, Sunder (2005), *Fabian Review*, 117/4.

Kearney, Richard (1997), *Postnationalist Ireland. Politics, Culture, Philosophy* (London: Routledge).

Keating, Michael (1975), 'The Role of the Scottish MP', PhD thesis, CNAA and Glasgow College of Technology (now Glasgow Caledonian University).

Keating, Michael (1982), 'The Debate on Regional Reform', in Brian Hogwood and Michael Keating, eds, *Regional Government in England* (Oxford: Oxford University Press).

Keating, Michael (1988a), Labour in Scotland, 1951-65', in I. Donnachie, C. Harvie and I.S. Wood, eds, *Forward! Labour Politics in Scotland, 1888–1988* (Edinburgh University Press), 84–98.

Keating, Michael (1988b), *State and Regional Nationalism: Territorial Politics and the European State* (Brighton: Wheatsheaf).

Keating, Michael (1998), *The New Regionalism in Western Europe. Territorial Restructuring and Political Change* (Aldershot: Edward Elgar).

Keating, Michael (2001), *Plurinational Democracy. Stateless Nations in a Post-Sovereignty Era* (Oxford: Oxford University Press).

Keating, Michael (2009), *The Independence of Scotland: Self-Government and the Shifting Politics of Union* (Oxford: Oxford University Press).

Keating, Michael (2013), *Rescaling the European State. The Making of Territory and the Rise of the Meso* (Oxford: Oxford University Press).

Keating, Michael (2017a), 'Europe as a Multilevel Federation', *Journal of European Public Policy*, 24/4: 615–32.

Keating, Michael (2017b), 'Plurinational Democracy', in Denis Galligan, ed., *Constitution in Crisis: The New Putney Debates* (London: Tauris).

Keating, Michael (2020), 'Flying the Unionist Flag', https://sceptical.scot/author/michael-keating/

Keating, Michael and David Bleiman (1979), *Labour and Scottish Nationalism* (Basingstoke: Macmillan).

Keating, Michael and Malcolm Harvey (2014), *Small Nations in A Big World: What Scotland Can Learn* (Edinburgh: Luath).

Keating, Michael and Barry Jones (eds) (1985), *Regions in the European Community* (Oxford: Oxford University Press).

Keating, Michael and Peter Lindley (1981), 'Devolution. The Scotland and Wales Bills', *Public Administration Bulletin*, 37: 37–54.

Keating, Michael and Nicola McEwen (2017), 'The Scottish Independence Debate', in Michael Keating, ed., *Debating Scotland: Issues of Independence and Union in the 2014 Referendum* (Oxford: Oxford University Press).

Keating, Michael and Alex Wilson (2014), 'Regions with Regionalism? The Rescaling of Interest Groups in Six European States', *European Journal of Political Research* 53/4: 840–57.

Keen, Lord (2018), *House of Lords Debates*, 26-03-2018.
Keep, Matthew (2018), 'The Barnett Formula, Briefing Paper 7386' (London: House of Commons Library).
Keep, Matthew (2019), 'Country and Regional Public Sector Finances', Briefing Paper 8027 (London: House of Commons Library).
Kelly, James (2014), 'Patriot Politics, 1750-91', in Alvin Jackson, ed., *The Oxford Handbook of Modern Irish History* (Oxford: Oxford University Press).
Kendle, John (1997), *Federal Britain: A History* (London: Routledge).
Kenny, Kevin (2004), 'The Irish in the Empire', in Kevin Kenny, ed., *Ireland and the British Empire* (Oxford: Oxford University Press).
Kenny, Michael (2014), *The Politics of English Nationhood* (Oxford: Oxford University Press).
Kenny, Michael (2018), 'English Nationalism in Historical Perspective', in Michael Kenny, Iain McLean and Aksh Paun, eds, *Governing England, English Identity and Institutions in a Changing United Kingdom* (London: British Academy).
Kenny, Michael and Jack Sheldon (2020), 'When Planets Collide: The British Conservative Party and the Discordant Goals of Delivering Brexit and Preserving the Domestic Union, 2016–2019', *Political Studies*, https://doi.org/10.1177/0032321720930986
Keogh, Dermot (1997), 'The Diplomacy of "Dignified Calm": An Analysis of Ireland's Application for Membership of the EEC, 1961-63', *Chronicon*, 14: 1–68.
Kerr, Lord (2018), *House of Lords Debates*, 26-03-2018.
Kidd, Colin (1993), *Subverting Scotland's Past: Scottish Whig Historians and the Creation of an Anglo-British Identity, 1689–1830* (Cambridge: Cambridge University Press).
Kidd, Colin (2008), *Union and Unionisms: Political Thought in Scotland, 1500–2000* (Cambridge: Cambridge University Press).
Kidd, Colin (2018), 'Union and the Ironies of Displacement', in Gerard Carruthers and Colin Kidd, eds, *Literature and Union. Scottish Texts, British Contexts* (Oxford: Oxford University Press).
Kilbrandon, Lord (1973), Royal Commission on the Constitution, Report of the Commission, Cmnd 5460 (London: Her Majesty's Stationery Office).
Kinnock, Neil (1975), Speech on Scotland and Wales Bill, *Hansard*, 925, 01-02-1977.
Knudsen, Line (2016), *Do Scots Hold More Conservative Views on Abortion?*, Edinburgh: ScotCen, http://www.scotcen.org.uk/blog/do-scots-hold-more-conservative-views-on-abortion/, accessed 1 November 2020.
Kumar, Krishan (2003), *The Making of English National Identity* (Cambridge: Cambridge University Press).
Kumar, Krishan (2010), 'Nation-States as Empires, Empires as Nation-States: Two Principles, on Practice?', *Theory and Society*, 39/2: 119–43.
Kymlicka, Will (1995), *Multicultural Citizenship* (Oxford: Oxford University Press).
Kymlicka, Will (2007), *Multicultural Odysseys: Navigating the New International Politics of Diversity* (Oxford: Oxford University Press).
Lafont, Robert (1967), *La révolution régionaliste* (Paris: Gallimard).
Lakin, Stuart (2018), 'The Manner and Form Theory of Parliamentary Sovereignty: A Nelson's Eye View of the UK Constitution?', *Oxford Journal of Legal Studies*, 38/1:168–89.
Lee, C. H. (1995), *Scotland and the United Kingdom. The Economy and the Union in the Twentieth Century* (Manchester: Manchester University Press).
Lee, Simon (2011), 'Gordon Brown and the Negation of England', in Arthur Aughey and Christine Berberich, eds, *These Englands. A Conversation on National Identity* (Manchester: Manchester University Press).

Lenman, Bruce (1977), *An Economic History of Modern Scotland* (London: Batsford).
Lennard, Jason and Fredrik Andersson (2016), 'Irish GDP between the Famine and the First World War: Estimates Based on a Dynamic Factor Model', Working Papers, 2016, 13 (Lund: Department of Economics, Lund University).
Levitt, Ian (ed.) (2014), *Treasury Expenditure Control and Public Expenditure in Scotland 1885–1979* (London: British Academy/Oxford University Press).
Liñeira, Robert, Ailsa Henderson and Liam Delaney (2017), 'Voters' Response to the Campaign', in Michael Keating, ed., *Debating Scotland. Issues of Independence and Union in the 2014 Referendum* (Oxford: Oxford University Press).
Lipset, Seymour Martin (1985), 'The Revolt against Modernity', in *Consensus and Conflict: Essays in Political Sociology* (New Brunswick: Transaction).
Llobera, Josep (2003), *De Catalunya a Europa: Fonaments de la identitat nacional* (Barcelona: Ampúries/Anagrama).
Lloyd, John (2020), *Should Auld Acquaintance Be Forgot: The Great Mistake of Scottish Independence* (Cambridge: Polity).
Lord Advocate (2016), *Written Case of Lord Advocate, in the Supreme Court of the United Kingdom, the Queen on the Application of Gina Miller and Deir Tozetti dos Santos*, UKSC 2016/0196.
Loughlin, Martin (2003), 'Ten Tenets of Sovereignty', in Neil Walker, ed., *Sovereignty in Transition* (Oxford: Hart).
Loughlin, Martin (2017), 'The Political Constitution Revisited', LSE Law, Society and, Economy Working Papers 18/2017, London School of Economics and Political Science Law Department.
Loughlin, Martin and Stephen Tierney (2018), 'The Shibboleth of Sovereignty', *Modern Law Review* 81/6: 989–1016.
Lynch, Peter (2002), *SNP. The History of the Scottish National Party* (Cardiff: Welsh Academic Press).
McAlister, Siobhán, Nicola Carr and Gail Neill (2014), 'Queering the Family: Attitudes towards Lesbian and Gay Relationships and Families in Northern Ireland', Research Report, https://pureadmin.qub.ac.uk/ws/portalfiles/portal/11457791/research_update.pdf/, accessed 1 November 2020.
Macartney, Allan (1980). 'Summary of Opinion Polls Relating to Voting Intention and Constitutional Change', in Henry Drucker and Nancy Drucker, eds, *Scottish Government Yearbook* (Edinburgh: Paul Harris).
Macartney, C. A. (1969), *The Habsburg Empire, 1790–1918* (London: Weidenfeld and Nicolson).
McCann, Philip (2016), *The UK Regional-National Economic Problem: Geography, Globalisation and Governance* (London: Routledge).
McCann, Philip (2019), 'Perception Of Regional Inequality and the Geography of Discontent: Insights from the UK', *Regional Studies*, 43/2: 256–67.
McCorkindale, Christopher, Aileen McHarg and Paul D. Scott (2017), 'The Courts, Devolution, and Constitutional Review', *University of Queensland Law Journal*, 36/3: 289–310.
MacCormick, Neil (1999), *Questioning Sovereignty: Law, State and Nation in the European Commonwealth* (Oxford: Oxford University Press).
McCrone, David (2019), 'What Makes a European in Scotland?', *Scottish Affairs*, 28/2: 228–43.
McCrone, David (2017), *The Sociology of Scotland* (London: Sage).
McCrone, David and Frank Bechhofer (2008), 'National Identity and Social Inclusion', *Ethnic and Racial Studies*, 31/7: 1245–66.

McCrone, David and Frank Bechhofer (2015), *Understanding National Identity* (Cambridge: Cambridge University Press).

McCrone, David and Michael Keating (2021), 'Questions of Sovereignty: Redefining Politics in Scotland?', *The Political Quarterly*, in press.

McCrudden, Christopher (2015), 'State Architecture: Subsidiarity, Devolution, Federalism and Independence', in Mark Elliot and David Feldman, eds, *The Cambridge Companion to Public Law* (Cambridge: Cambridge University Press).

McCrudden, Christopher and Daniel Halberstam (2018), 'Miller and Northern Ireland: A Critical Constitutional Response', *The UK Supreme Court Yearbook*, 8.

MacDonagh, Oliver (1989), 'The Economy and Society, 1830-45', in W. E. Vaughan (ed.), *Ireland under the Union, 1801–70* (Oxford: Oxford University Press).

McEwen, Nicola (2006), *Nationalism and the State: Welfare and Identity in Scotland and Quebec* (Brussels: Peter Lang).

McGarry, John and Brendan O'Leary (1995), *Explaining Northern Ireland: Broken Images* (Oxford and Cambridge, Mass: Blackwell Press).

McGarry, John and Brendan O'Leary (2006), 'Consociational Theory, Northern Ireland's Conflict, and its Agreement: What Consociationalists can Learn from Northern Ireland', *Government and Opposition*, 41/1: 43–63.

McGarry, John and Brendan O'Leary (2007), 'Federations and Managing Nations', in Michael Burgess and John Pinter, eds., *Multinational Federations* (London: Routledge).

McGarry John and Brendan O'Leary (2016), 'Power-Sharing Executives: Consociational and Centripetal Formulae and the Case of Northern Ireland', *Ethnopolitics*, 15/5: 497–515.

McHarg, Aileen (2018), 'Navigating Without Maps: Constitutional Silence and the Management of the Brexit Crisis', *International Journal of Constitutional Law*, 16/3: 952–68.

Mackintosh, John (1968), *The Devolution of Power* (Harmondsworth: Penguin).

McLean, Iain (2010), *What's Wrong with the British Constitution?* (Oxford: Oxford University Press).

McLean, Iain and Alastair McMillan (2003), *State of the Union: Unionism and the Alternatives in the United Kingdom Since 1707* (Oxford: Oxford University Press).

McLean, Iain, Jim Gallagher and Guy Lodge (2013), *Scotland's Choices: The Referendum and What Happens Afterwards* (Edinburgh: Edinburgh University Press).

McLeish, Henry (2004), *Scotland First. Truth and Consequences* (Edinburgh: Mainstream).

McLoughlin, Eoin (2017), 'The Irish Revolution and its Aftermath: The Economic Revolution', in John Crowey, Donal Ó Driscoeoil and Mike Murphy, eds, *Atlas of the Irish Revolution* (Cork: Cork University Press).

McRoberts, Kenneth (2019), *Misconceiving Canada: The Struggle for National Unity*, 2nd edn (Toronto: Oxford University Press).

Major, John (1993) 'Foreword by the Prime Minister', in Secretary of State for Scotland, *Scotland in the Union: A Partnership for Good* (Edinburgh: HMSO).

Mann, Michael (1993), *The Sources of Social Power, volume II. The Rise of Classes and Nation-States, 1760–1914* (Cambridge: Cambridge University Press).

Marko, Joseph (2020), 'Law and Sociology', in Joseph Marko, ed., *Human and Minority Rights Protection by Multiple Diversity Governance* (London: Routledge).

Mansergh, Danny (2005), *Grattan's Failure: Parliamentary Opposition and the People in Ireland 1779–1800* (Dublin: Irish Academic Press).

Marshall, T. H. (1992), *Citizenship and Social Class*, ed. T. Bottomore (London: Pluto).

May, Theresa (2019a), Full text of Theresa May's Speech Introducing her 'New Brexit deal', Brexit Central, https://brexitcentral.com/full-text-of-theresa-mays-speech-introducing-her-new-brexit-deal/, accessed 1 November 2020.

May, Theresa (2019b), PM Speech on the Union, Stirling, 4 July, https://www.gov.uk/government/speeches/pm-speech-on-the-union-4-july-2019/, accessed 1 November 2020.

Mill, John Stuart (1972), *Utilitarianism, On Liberty and Considerations on Representative Government* (London: Dent).

Miller, David (1995), *On Nationality* (Oxford: Oxford University Press).

Miller, David (2000), *Citizenship and National Identity* (Cambridge: Polity).

Milward, Alan S. (2000), *The European Rescue of the Nation-State*, 2nd edn. (London: Routledge).

Mitchell, J. D. B (1968), *Constitutional Law*, 2nd ed. (Edinburgh: W. Green).

Mitchell, James (1990), *Conservatives and the Union: A Study of Conservative Attitudes to Scotland* (Edinburgh: Edinburgh University Press).

Mitchell, James (1996), *Strategies for Self-Government: The Campaigns for a Scottish Parliament* (Edinburgh: Polygon).

Mitchell, James (2010), 'The Westminster Model and the State of Unions', *Parliamentary Affairs*, 63/1: 85–8.

Mitchell, James (2014), *The Scottish Question* (Oxford: Oxford University Press).

Mitchell, James, Lynn Bennie and Rob Johns (2012), *The Scottish National Party. Transition to Power* (Oxford: Oxford University Press).

Monopolies and Mergers Commission (1982), The Hongkong and Shanghai Banking Corporation, Standard Chartered Bank Limited, the Royal Bank of Scotland Group Limited: A Report on the Proposed Mergers, Cmd 8472 (London: HMSO).

Montolio, Daniel and Gilberto Turati (2017), 'Constitutions as Incomplete Social Contracts', *Politica economica*, 33/3: 259–68.

Moore, Cormac (2019), *Birth of The Border: The Impact of Partition in Ireland* (Dublin: Irish Academic Press).

Moral, Félix (1998), 'Identidad regional y nacionalismo en el Estado de las autonomías', in *Opiniones y Actitudes*, 18 (Madrid: Centro de Investigaciones Sociológicas).

Moran, Mick, John Tomaney and Karel Williams (2018), 'The Political Economy of Manchester and Beyond', in Michael Kenny, Iain McLean and Akash Paun, eds, *Governing England: English Identity and Institutions in a Changing United Kingdom* (Oxford: Oxford University Press).

Moreno, Luis (1986), 'Scotland, Catalonia, Europeanization and the "Moreno Question"', *Scottish Affairs*, 54: 1–21.

Morgan, Kenneth (1981), *Wales: Rebirth of a Nation* (Oxford: Oxford University Press).

Morton, Graeme (1999), *Unionist Nationalism: Governing Urban Scotland, 1830–60* (East Linton: Tuckwell).

Moxon-Browne, Edward (1983), *Nation, Class and Creed in Northern Ireland* (Aldershot: Gower).

Moxon-Browne, Edward (1991), 'National Identity in Northern Ireland', in Peter Stringer and Gillian Robinson, eds, *Social Attitudes in Northern Ireland* (Belfast: Blackstaff).

Murphy, Mary (2018), *Europe and Northern Ireland's Future: Negotiating Brexit's Unique Case* (Newcastle: Agenda).

N-VA (2019), 'The N-VA's Ideology and Purpose', https://english.n-va.be/frequently-asked-questions#ideology, accessed 1 November 2020.

Nairn, Tom (1977), *The Break-Up of Britain: Crisis and Neo-Nationalism* (London: New Left Books).

Nairn, Tom (1994), *The Enchanted Glass: Britain and its Monarchy* (London: Vintage).

NatCen (2017), 'Charting Changing Attitudes—Same-Sex Relationships', https://natcen.ac.uk/blog/charting-changing-attitudes-%E2%80%93-same-sex-relationships

Nguyen, David (2019), 'Regional Economic Disparities and Development in the UK', NIESR Policy Paper 010 (London: National Institute of Economic and Social Research).

Nicolaidis, Kalypso (2012), 'The Idea of European Demoicracy', in Julie Dickson and Pavlos Eleftheriadis, eds, *Philosophical Foundations of European Union Law* (Oxford: Oxford University Press).

Nicolaïdis, Kalypso (2013), 'European Democracy and Its Crisis', *Journal of Common Market Studies*, 51/2: 351–69.

Noël, Alain (2013), 'Ideology, Identity, Majoritarianism: On the Politics of Federalism', in Grace Skogstad, David Cameron, Martin Papillon and Keith Banting, eds, *The Global Promise of Federalism* (Toronto: University of Toronto Press).

Nora, Pierre (1984), 'Entre mémoire et histoire', in Pierre Nora, ed., *Lieux de Mémoire, 1. La République* (Paris: Gallimard).

Northern Ireland Assembly (2011), 'Parity and Social Security in Northern Ireland. Research and Information', Briefing Paper, 99/11 (Belfast, Northern Ireland Assembly).

Núñez Seixas, Xose-Manuel (2001), 'The Region as Essence of the Fatherland: Regionalist Variants of Spanish Nationalism (1849-1936)', *European History Quarterly*, 31/4: 486–518.

O'Brien, R. Barry (1887), 'The "Unionist" Case for Home Rule', in James Bryce, ed., *Handbook of Home Rule* (London: Kegan Paul).

O'Day, Alan (2001), 'Defending the Union: Parliamentary Opinions 1869 and 1886', in D. George Boyce and Alan O'Day, eds, *Defenders of the Union. A Survey of British and Irish Unionism since 1801* (London: Routledge).

O'Leary, Brendan (2004), 'Federations and the Management of Nations: Agreements and Arguments with Walker Connor and Ernest Gellner', in Daniele Conversi, ed., *Ethnonationalism in the Contemporary World. Walker Connor and the Study of Nationalism* (London: Routledge).

O'Leary, Brendan (2016), 'The Dalriata Document. Towards a Multinational Compromise that Respects Diversity in the United Kingdom' (Belfast: Queen's University), https://www.qub.ac.uk/Research/GRI/mitchell-institute/FileStore/Filetoupload,756968,en.pdf/, accessed 1 November 2020.

O'Leary, Brendan (2019a), *A Treatise on Northern Ireland, vol. I: Colonialism* (Oxford: Oxford University Press).

O'Leary, Brendan (2019b), *A Treatise on Northern Ireland, vol. II: Control* (Oxford: Oxford University Press).

O'Leary, Brendan (2019c), *A Treatise on Northern Ireland, vol. III: Consociation* (Oxford: Oxford University Press).

O'Neill, Aidan (2011), 'We Need to Talk about the Referendum', *Guardian*, 8 November.

O'Neill, Aidan (2017), 'Miller, BrEXIT and BreUK-up', *Counsel*, March.

O'Rourke, Kevin (2016), 'Independent Ireland in Comparative Perspective', WP 16/20, UCD Centre for Economic Research (Dublin: University College Dublin).

OECD (2018), *Regions and Cities at a Glance 2018—United Kingdom* (Paris: OECD).

Office for National Statistics (2017), *Regional Gross Value Added (Balanced), UK: 1998 to 2016* (London: ONS).

Ofsted (2014), 'Strengthened Guidance on Improving the Spiritual, Moral, Social and Cultural Development of Pupils', https://www.gov.uk/government/news/guidance-on-promoting-british-values-in-schools-published/, accessed 1 November 2020.

Orwell, George (2018 [1914]), *The Lion and the Unicorn. Socialism and the English Genius* (Harmondsworth: Penguin Classics).

Osborne, George (2012), 'George Osborne's Speech to the Conservative Conference: Full Text', *New Statesman*, 8 October 2012.

Osiander, Anders (2001), 'Sovereignty, International Relations and the Westphalian Myth', *International Organization*, 55: 251–87.

Owen, David (2015), 'Variations in National Identity, Diversity and Integration within the UK', https://www.ukdataservice.ac.uk/media/455488/owen.pdf/, accessed 1 November 2020.

Pacificus (Frederick Scott Oliver) (1910), *Federalism and Home Rule* (London: John Murray).

Parkes, Susan (1989), 'Higher Education, 1793-1908', in W. E. Vaughan, ed., *Ireland under the Union, 1870–1921*, vol. VI, *A New History of Ireland* (Oxford; Oxford University Press).

Parnell, Charles Stewart (1886), Speech on Second Reading Government of Ireland Bill.

Paterson, Lindsay (1994), *The Autonomy of Modern Scotland* (Edinburgh: Edinburgh University Press).

Paterson, Lindsay, Alice Brown, John Curtice, Kerstin Hinds, David McCrone, Alison Park, Kerry Sproston and Paula Surridge (2001), *New Scotland, New Politics* (Edinburgh: Polygon).

Patterson, Henry (2006), *Ireland Since 1939* (London: Penguin).

Patterson, Henry (2013), 'Unionism, 1921–72', in Alvin Jackson, ed., *The Oxford Handbook of Modern Irish History* (Oxford: Oxford University Press).

Pocock, J. G. A. (1975), 'British History: A Plea for a New Subject', *Journal of Modern History*, 47/4: 601–28.

Peden, G. C. (2005), 'The Managed Econom: Scotland, 1919–2000', in T. M. Devine, C. H. Lee and G. C. Peden, ed., *The Transformation of Scotland. The Economy Since 1700* (Edinburgh: Edinburgh University Press).

Poole, Ed, Guto Ifan and David Phillips (2016), 'Options for a Funding Floor after Tax Devolution. Second Report on the Fiscal Framework Negotiations for Wales' (Cardiff: Wales Governance Centre and Institute for Fiscal Studies).

Powell, Jonathan (2008), *Great Hatred, Little Room: Making Peace in Northern Ireland* (London: Bodley Head).

Price, Adam (2019), *Wales: The First and Final Colony* (Talybont: Y Lolfa Cyr).

Prosser, Chris and Ed Fieldhouse (2017), 'A Tale of Two Referendums—the 2017 Election in Scotland', British Election Study, http://www.britishelectionstudy.com/bes-findings/a-tale-of-two-referendums-the-2017-election-in-scotland/#.WeoCaDb9O7M/, accessed 1 November 2020.

Publius (1787), 'Federalist Papers', Library of Congress Research Guide, https://www.congress.gov/resources/display/content/The+Federalist+Papers, accessed 1 November 2020.

Randerson, James (2018), 'Michael Barnier: EU Won't Break Single Market for Brexit UK', *Politico*. https://www.politico.eu/article/michel-barnier-brexit-customs-eu-wont-break-the-single-market-for-brexit-uk/

Rawlings, Richard (2003), *Delineating Wales: Constitutional, Legal and Administrative Aspects of National Devolution* (Cardiff: University of Wales Press).

Rawlings, Richard (2017), *Brexit and the Territorial Constitution; Devolution, Reregulation and Intergovernmental Relations* (London: Constitution Society).

Redwood, John (2017), 'The EU Now Threatens the Republic of Ireland with a Hard Border', https://johnredwoodsdiary.com/2017/11/10/the-eu-now-threatens-the-republic-of-ireland-with-a-hard-border/, accessed 11 November 2020.

Reicher, Stephen, Nick Hopkins and Kate Harrison (2009), 'Identity Matters: On the Importance of Scottish Identity for Scottish Society', in Frank Bechhofer and David McCrone, eds, *National Identity, Nationalism and Constitutional Change* (Basingstoke: Palgrave).

Reid, Colin W. (2014), 'An Experiment in Constructive Unionism: Isaac Butt, Home Rule and Federalist Political Thought during the 1870s', *The English Historical Review*, 129/537: 332–61.

Renan, Ernest (1882), 'Qu'est-ce qu'une nation?' (Conférence prononcée le 11 mars 1882 à la Sorbonne), http://www.iheal.univ-paris3.fr/sites/www.iheal.univ-paris3.fr/files/Renan_-_Qu_est-ce_qu_une_Nation.pdf/, accessed 1 November 2020.

Requejo, Ferran (1999), 'Cultural Pluralism, Nationalism and Federalism: A Revision of Democratic Citizenship in Plurinational States', *European Journal of Political Research*, 35: 255–86.

Rokkan, Stein and Derek Urwin (1983), *Economy, Territory, Identity. Politics of West European Peripheries* (London: Sage).

Romney, Paul (1999), *Getting it Wrong. How Canadians Forgot Their Past and Imperilled Confederation* (Toronto: University of Toronto Press).

Rose, Richard (1971), *Governing Without Consensus. An Irish Perspective* (Boston: Beacon Press).

Rose, Richard (1982), *Understanding the United Kingdom: The Territorial Dimension in Government* (London: Longman).

Rosie, Michael and Ross Bond (2007), 'Social Democratic Scotland?', in Michael Keating, ed., *Scottish Social Democracy* (Brussels: Presses interuniversitaires européennes/Peter Lang).

Roshwale, Aviel (2001), *Ethnicr Nationalism and the Fall of Empires. Central Europe, Russia & The Middle East, 1914–1923* (London: Routledge).

Royal Commission on the Constitution (Kilbrandon) (1973), Report, Cmnd 5460 (London: Her Majesty's Stationery Office).

Royal Commission on the Financial Relations Between Great Britain and Ireland (1896), Final Report (London: Commission on the Financial Relations Between Great Britain and Ireland).

Royal Commission on the Reform of the House of Lords (2000), A House for the Future, Cm. 4534 (London: Cabinet Office).

Royal Society of Edinburgh (2018), Response to Scottish Affairs Committee on Intergovernmental Relations, Advice Paper 18–21 (Edinburgh: Royal Society of Edinburgh).

RTE 20-01-17, 'Govts Want "Seamless, Frictionless Border" after Brexit, says May'.

Russell, Meg and Guy Lodge (2006), 'The Government of England by Westminster', in Robert Hazell, ed., *The English Question* (Manchester: University Press).

Russell, Meg and Jack Sheldon (2018), 'An English Parliament: An Idea Whose Time has Come?', in Michael Kenny, Iain McLean and Akash Paun, eds, *Governing England: English Identity and Institutions in a Changing United Kingdom* (Oxford: Oxford University Press).

Russell, Michael (2017), Letter from Michael Russell (Scottish Minister for Brexit negotiations) to Joan McAlpine (Convenor of Scottish Parliament European Committee, 4 May (Edinburgh: Scottish Parliament).

Russell, Peter, Robert Décary, William Lederman, Noel Lyon and Dan Soberman (1982), *Comments on the Supreme Court Reference on Constitutional Amendment*, (Kingston Ont: Institute of Intergovernmental Relations).

Salmond, Alex (2012), *Hugo Young Lecture*, https://www.theguardian.com/politics/2012/jan/25/alex-salmond-hugo-young-lecture

Schertzer, Robert (2017), *The Judicial Role in a Diverse Federation. Lessons from the Supreme Court of Canada* (Toronto: University of Toronto Press).

Scott, John and Michael Hughes (1980), *The Anatomy of Scottish Capital* (London: Croom Helm).

Scottish Government (2016), *Scotland's Place in Europe* (Edinburgh: Scottish Government).

Scottish National Party (2015), 'Do the SNP Support English Votes for English Laws (EVEL)?', https://www.snp.org/policies/pb-do-the-snp-support-english-votes-for-english-laws-evel/, accessed 1 November 2020.

Scully Roger and Richard Wyn Jones (2012), 'Still Three Wales? Social Location and Electoral Behaviour in Contemporary Wales', *Electoral Studies*, 31: 656–67.

SDLP (Social Democratic and Labour Party) (2017), 'Securing Our Future in Europe', https://newry.ie/attachments/article/4720/eustatus.pdf./ accessed 1 November 2020.

Seeley, J. R. (1883), *The Expansion of England* (London: Macmillan).

Select Committee on Scottish Affairs (1969), Minutes of Evidence, 19 May.

Sinn Féin (2017), 'The Case for the North to Achieve Special Status Within the EU', http://www.sinnfein.ie/files/2016/The_Case_For_The_North_To_Achieve_Special_Designated_Status_Within_The_EU.pdf/, accessed 1 November 2020.

Smith, Anthony (1998), *Myths and Memories of the Nation* (Oxford: Oxford University Press).

Smith, Mark (2020), 'The Declaration of Arbroath – 700 years of Myths, Misunderstandings and Contested Meanings', *The Herald*, 04-04-20.

Smith, T. B. (1961), *British Justice: The Scottish Contribution* (London: Stevens).

Smyth, Jim (2001), *The Making of the United Kingdom, 1660–1800* (Edinburgh: Pearson).

Stapleton, Julia (2009), 'England', in Matthew Flinders, Andrew Gamble, Colin Hay and Michael Kenny, eds, *The Oxford Handbook of British Politics* (Oxford: Oxford University Press).

Stevenson, Garth (2006), *Parallel Paths. The Development of Nationalism in Ireland and Quebec* (Montreal: McGill/Queens University Press).

Stewart, John (2003), 'The National Health Service in Scotland 1947–74: Scottish or British?', *Historical Research*, 76/193: 389–410.

Steyn, Lord (2005), *House of Lords Judgments—Jackson and Others (Appellants) v Her Majesty's Attorney General (respondent),* UKHL 56.

Storm, Eric (2018), 'A New Dawn in Nationalism Studies? Some Fresh Incentives to Overcome Historiographical Nationalism', *European History Quarterly*, 48/1: 113–129.

Straw, Jack (2008), 'Modernising the Magna Carta', Speech at George Washington University, Washington, DC, 13 February.

Tanner, Duncan (2006), 'How Devolution Died: The Labour Party's Constitutional Agenda, 1900–45, in Duncan Tanner, Chris Williams, Will Griffith and Andrew Edwards, eds, *Debating Nationhood and Governance in Britain, 1884–1945* (Manchester: Manchester University Press).

Tarlton, Charles (1965), 'Symmetry and Asymmetry as Elements of Federalism: A Theoretical Speculation', *Journal of Politics*, 27/4: 861–74.

Taylor, Sam (2019), 'What is the UK Single Market?', These Islands, https://www.these-islands.co.uk/publications/i336/what_is_the_uk_single_market.aspx/, accessed 1 November 2020.

Thatcher, Margaret (1984), Speech to 1922 Committee ('the enemy within'), Margaret Thatcher Foundation, https://www.margaretthatcher.org/document/105563/, accessed 1 November 2020.

Thatcher, Margaret (1993), *The Downing Street Years* (London: HarperCollins).

Tierney, Stephen (2004), *Constitutional Law and National Pluralism* (Oxford: Oxford University Press).

Tierney, Stephen (2009), *Constitutional Referendums: The Theory and Practice of Republican Deliberation* (Oxford: Oxford University Press).

Tierney, Stephen (2018), 'Drifting Towards Federalism? Appraising the Constitution in Light of the Scotland Act 2016 and Wales Act 2017', in Robert Schütze and Stephen Tierney, eds, *The United Kingdom and the Federal Idea* (Oxford: Hart).

Todd, Jennifer (1987), 'Two Traditions in Unionist Political Culture', *Irish Political Studies*, 2/1: 1–26.

Todd, Jennifer (2018), *Identity Change after Conflict. Ethnicity, Boundaries and Belonging in the Two Irelands* (Basingstoke: Palgrave).

Todd, Jennifer (2019), 'Unionisms and the Challenges of Change', SIPRe Working Paper WP 17 (Dublin: UCD).

Tomkins, Adam (2013), 'What's Left of the Political Constitution?', *German Law Journal*, 14/12: 2275–92.

Tomkins, Adam (2015), *Confusion and Retreat: The Supreme Court on Devolution*, UK Constitutional Law Association.

Tomkins, Adam (2018), 'Scottish Unionists Shun a Tailored Northern Ireland Brexit Deal', *Financial Times*, 17 October.

Tonge, Jonathan and Raul Gomez (2015), 'Shared Identity and the End of Conflict? How Far Has a Common Sense of "Northern Irishness" Replaced British or Irish Allegiances since the 1998 Good Friday Agreement?', *Irish Political Studies*, 30/2: 276–98.

Tonge, Jonathan, Máire Braniff, Thomas Hennessey, James W. McAuley and Sophie A. Whiting (2014), *The Democratic Unionist Party: From Protest to Power* (Oxford: Oxford University Press.

Troper, Michel (2012), 'Sovereignty', in Michel Rosenfeld and András Sajó, eds, *The Oxford Handbook of Comparative Constitutional Law* (Oxford: Oxford University Press).

Torrance, David (2009), *We in Scotland: Thatcherism in a Cold Climate* (Edinburgh: Birlinn).

Torrance, David (2014), *Britain Rebooted: Scotland in a Federal UK* (Edinburgh: Luath).

Torrance, David (2017), '"Standing up for Scotland": The Scottish Unionist Party and "Nationalist Unionism", 1912–1968', PhD thesis, University of the West of Scotland.

Torrance, David (2020a), *'Standing up for Scotland'. Nationalist Unionism and Scottish Party Politics, 1884–2014* (Edinburgh: Edinburgh University Press).

Torrance, David (2020b), '"Ruth Davidson's Conservatives", 2011–2019', in David Torrance, ed., *Ruth Davidson's Conservatives* (Edinburgh: Edinburgh University Press).

Townend, Paul A. (2016), *The Road to Home Rule: Anti-Imperialism and the Irish National Movement* (Madison: Wisconsin University Press).

Trench, Alan (2010), 'Intergovernmental Relations and Social Citizenship: Opportunities Labour Missed', in Guy Lodge and Katie Schmueker, eds, *Devolution in Practice 2010* (London: IPPR).

Trevelyan, George Macaulay (1926), *History of England* (London: Longmans, Green).

Trevor Roper, Hugh (2008), *The Invention of Scotland: Myth and History* (London: Yale University Press).

Trystan, Dafydd (2019), 'Indycurious and Curiouser: New Poll Shows Support for Welsh Independence on the Rise', *Nation Cymru*, https://nation.cymru/opinion/indycurious-and-curiouser-new-poll-shows-support-for-welsh-independence-on-the-rise/, accessed 1 November 2020.

UK Government (2017a), The United Kingdom's Exit from and New Partnership with the European Union, Cm 9417 (London: UK Government).

UK Government (2017b), Legislating for the United Kingdom's Withdrawal from the European Union, Cm 9446 (London: UK Government).

UK Government (2020), *Policy paper. UK internal market*, https://www.gov.uk/government/publications/uk-internal-market

UK Supreme Court (2017), Judgment (on the application of Miller and another) (Respondents) v Secretary of State for Exiting the European Union (Appellant). Reference by the Attorney General for Northern Ireland in the Matter of an Application by Agnew and Others for Judicial Review. Reference by the Court of Appeal (Northern Ireland)—in the Matter of an Application by Raymond McCord for Judicial Review, UKSC 5 (2017).

UK Supreme Court (2018), Judgment: The European Union (Legal Continuity) Scotland Bill, UKSC 64 (2018).

UK Supreme Court (2019), Judgment (on the Application of Miller) (Appellant) v The Prime Minister (Respondent). Cherry and others (Respondents) v Advocate General for Scotland (Appellant) (Scotland), UKSC 41 (2019).

Vaughan, W. E. (1989), 'Ireland c. 1870', in W. E. Vaughan, ed., *A New History of Ireland, V. Ireland under the Union 1801–70* (Oxford: Oxford University Press).

Viroli, Maurizio (1995), *For Love of Country: An Essay on Patriotism and Nationalism* (Oxford: Oxford University Press).

Wade, E. C. S. (1959), 'Introduction', in A. V. Dicey, ed., *Introduction to the Study of the Law of the Constitution* (Basingstoke: Macmillan).

Walker, Graham (2004), *A History of the Ulster Unionist Party: Protest, Pragmatism and Pessimism* (Manchester: Manchester University Press).

Walker, Graham (2010), 'Scotland, Northern Ireland, and Devolution, 1945-1979', *Journal of British Studies*, 49/1: 117–42.

Walker, Neil (2003), 'Late Sovereignty in the European Union', in Neil Walker, ed., *Sovereignty in Transition* (Oxford: Hart).

Walker, Neil (2019), 'Teleological and Reflexive Nationalism in the New Europe', in Jacint Jordana, Michael Keating, Alex Marx and Jan Wouters, eds, *Changing Borders in Europe. Exploring the Dynamics of Integration, Differentiation and Self-Determination in the European Union* (Abingdon: Routledge).

Walters, Mark D (2012), 'Dicey on Writing the Law of the Constitution', *Oxford Journal of Legal Studies*, 32/1.1: 21–49.

Ward, Matthew (2018), UK Trade, 1948–2018, Briefing Paper CBP 8261 (London: House of Commons Library).

Ward, Matthew (2020), Statistics on UK-EU Trade, Briefing Paper 7851 (London: House of Commons Library).

Ward, Paul (2005), *Unionism in the United Kingdom, 1918–1974* (Basingstoke: Macmillan).

Weatherill, Stephen (2017), *The Internal Market as Legal Concept* (Oxford: Oxford University Press).

Weight, Richard (2002), *Patriots: National Identity in Britain, 1940–2000* (London: Macmillan).

Wellings, Ben (2011), *English Nationalism and Euroscepticism. Losing the Peace* (Oxford: Peter Lang).

Welsh Government (2017a), Transition from the European Union to a new relationship with Europe, https://gov.wales/sites/default/files/2017-01/30683%20Securing%20Wales%C2%B9%20Future_ENGLISH_WEB.pdf/, accessed 1 November 2020.

Welsh Government (2017b), *Brexit and Devolution* (Cardiff: Welsh Government).

Weinstock, Daniel (2017), 'Compromise, Pluralism, and Deliberation', *Critical Review of International Social and Political Philosophy*, 20/5: 636–55.

Whatley, Christopher (2006), *The Scots and the Union* (Edinburgh: Edinburgh University Press).

Whatley, Christopher (2012), 'Scotland: A Truer Picture', *History Today*, 62/7.

Whyte, John (1990), *Interpreting Northern Ireland* (Oxford: Clarendon).

Wilford, Rick and Robin Wilson (2006), *The Trouble with Northern Ireland. The Belfast Agreement and Democratic Governance* (Dublin: Tasc).

Williams, Gwyn A. (1979), *When Was Wales?* (London: BBC).

Wilson, Charles (1970), 'Note of Dissent', Scotland's Government. Report of the Scottish Constitutional Committee (Edinburgh: Scottish Constitutional Committee).

Wimmer, Andreas and Nina Glick Schiller (2002), 'Methodological Nationalism and Beyond: Nation-State Building, Migration and the Social Sciences', *Global Networks*, 2/4: 301–34.

WITS (2017), 'World Integrated Trade Solutions', https://wits.worldbank.org/CountryProfile/en/Country/IRL/Year/2017/TradeFlow/EXPIMP/Partner/by-country/, accessed 1 November 2020.

Wood, Peter (1994), 'The Transformation of Spatial Planning in the UK', *Espace Géographique*, 23/1: 65–73.

Wren, Colin (2005), 'Regional Grants: Are They Worth It?', *Fiscal Studies*, 26/2: 245–75.

Wyn Jones, Richard and Roger Scully (2012), *Wales Says Yes. Devolution and the 2011 Welsh Referendum* (Cardiff: University of Wales Press).

Wyn Jones, Richard, Guy Lodge, Ailsa Henderson and Daniel Wincott (2012), *The Dog That Finally Barked: England as an Emerging Political Community* (London: Institute for Public Policy Research).

Wyn Jones, Richard, Guy Lodge, Charlie Jeffery, Glenn Gottfried, Roger Scullt, Ailsa Henderson and Daniel Wincott (2013), *England and Its Two Unions: The Anatomy of a Nation and Its Discontents* (London: Institute for Public Policy Research).

YouGov 2019, Opinion Poll, https://d25d2506sfb94s.cloudfront.net/cumulus_uploads/document/1ed2x72rmn/YouGov%20-%20Northern%20Ireland%20sentiment.pdf/, accessed 1 November 2020.

Ziblatt, Daniel (2006), *Structuring the State: The Formation of Italy and Germany and the Puzzle of Federalism* (Princeton: Princeton University Press).

Zielonka, Jan (2006), *Europe as Empire: The Nature of the Enlarged European Union* (Oxford: Oxford University Press).

Index

Note: Figures and tables are indicated by an italic '*f*', '*t*' and notes are indicated by 'n' following the page numbers.

For the benefit of digital users, indexed terms that span two pages (e.g., 52–53) may, on occasion, appear on only one of those pages.